Surviving Debt

Gerald Thomas

Surviving Debt

A GUIDE FOR CONSUMERS

Second Edition

From
THE NATIONAL CONSUMER LAW CENTER,
America's Consumer Law Experts

Principal Authors
Jonathan Sheldon
Gary Klein

For reprint permissions or ordering information, contact
Publications, NCLC, 18 Tremont St., Boston MA 02108,
(617) 523-8089, Fax (617) 523-7398.

Library of Congress Catalog No. 96-92323
ISBN 1-881793-40-0

This project was supported by AT&T Universal Card Services Partners in
Credit Education, the Public Welfare Foundation, the National Consumer
Law Center, the AFL-CIO, the United Auto Workers, and others.

Printed in the United States of America

10 9 8 7 6 5 4 3 2

This book is intended to provide accurate and authoritative information in
regard to the subject matter covered. This book cannot substitute for the independent judgment and skills of a competent attorney or other professional.
Non-attorneys are cautioned against using these materials in conducting litigation without advice or assistance from an attorney or other professional.
Non-attorneys are also cautioned against engaging in conduct which might be
considered the unauthorized practice of law.

Cover design and illustration by Lightbourne Images, copyright ©1996.

ABOUT THE AUTHORS

The National Consumer Law Center (NCLC) is the nation's expert on the rights of consumer borrowers. Since 1969, NCLC has been at the forefront in representing low income consumers before the courts, government agencies, Congress, and state legislatures.

NCLC has appeared before the United States Supreme Court and numerous federal and state courts and has successfully presented many of the most important cases affecting consumer borrowers. NCLC provides consultation and assistance to legal services, private, and government attorneys in all fifty states. It authored an influential model statute in 1974 to protect the rights of consumer debtors.

NCLC publishes a nationally acclaimed series of manuals on all major aspects of consumer credit, collections, and sales. NCLC also conducts state and national training sessions on the rights of consumer borrowers for attorneys, paralegals, and other counselors.

This book draws on the expertise of fourteen present and former NCLC attorneys, each averaging about twenty years of consumer law specialization. Two of these attorneys, Jonathan Sheldon and Gary Klein, were the principal authors of this edition.

Jonathan Sheldon has been an NCLC staff attorney since 1976 specializing in repossessions, leasing, student loans, credit reporting, and deceptive practices. His many publications include *Repossessions and Foreclosures* (3d ed. 1995), *Fair Credit Reporting Act* (3d ed. 1994), *Unfair and Deceptive Acts and Practices* (3d ed.1991), *Credit Discrimination* (1993) and *Sales of Goods and Services* (2d ed. 1989). He formerly was a staff attorney with the Federal Trade Commission.

Gary Klein is an NCLC staff attorney specializing in consumer bankruptcy, mortgage secured credit, and foreclosure law. He is the co-author of the Third and Fourth Editions of *Consumer Bankruptcy Law and Practice* and *Truth in Lending* (3d ed. 1995), and is the author of the foreclosure chapters in *Repossessions and Foreclosures* (3d ed. 1995). He has over ten years experience litigating bankruptcy, foreclosure, and other consumer issues in Pennsylvania, New Hampshire, and Massachusetts.

ACKNOWLEDGMENTS

Surviving Debt is the culmination of years of work and numerous contributions from experts in the field. Along the way, we have received generous support from the AFL-CIO, the United Auto Workers, the Public Welfare Foundation, various church groups, and particularly AT&T Universal Card Services Partners in Credit Education. The AT&T Universal Card Services grant not only allowed completion of this project, but an exceptionally wide distribution of the final product.

The views in this book are NCLC's and should not be construed as those of the AT&T Universal Card Services Partners in Education, the Public Welfare Foundation, or any other entity contributing to the development of *Surviving Debt.*

Numerous individuals contributed to the writing and final production of this volume and also the prior edition. Jonathan Sheldon and Gary Klein were the principal authors of this edition. Other NCLC staff contributing to this book include Margot Saunders (particularly the chapter on utility terminations), Chris Norris (particularly the chapters on home foreclosures), Robert Hobbs, Kathleen Keest, Willard Ogburn, Elizabeth Ryan, Judy O'Donnell, and Nancy Brockway. We would like to thank former NCLC attorneys and consumer law experts in the field for their assistance in this project, including Carolyn Carter, Mark Budnitz, Elizabeth Imholz, Robert Sable, Ernest Sarason, Yvonne Rosmarin, Roger Colton, Robert Rowe, Michael Eakin, Neil Fogarty, Dan Haller, Joanna George Allison, Jesse Toca, Robert Jackson, Jr., Mark Kaufman, Patricia Baker, Deborah Harris, Timothy Casey, and Henry Sommer. Thanks also to Mary Kingsley and Chuck Jackson for research.

Ani Tashjian designed and typeset this edition, Donna Wong provided advice on style, Mary Ellen Hassan and Laurie Silverman provided administrative assistance, and Lightbourne Images designed the cover.

CONTENTS

— Introduction —

How to Use This Book

YOU HAVE MANY IMPORTANT CONSUMER RIGHTS

When struggling with financial hardship, you may feel overwhelmed and powerless. You may not have the resources to pay pressing debts, to meet family needs, and to get necessary legal help. You may feel helpless to fight debt collectors pressing you for payment or threatening to seize your home, car, or other possessions.

In writing this book, we hope to help you even the playing field, and to make the best choices possible despite difficult financial circumstances. We will explain which debts you can ignore for a time while you get back on your feet. When you cannot ignore a particular debt without serious consequences, like foreclosure or repossession, this book sets out helpful options to deal with these problems, both in the short term and the long run.

This book also sets out your rights as a consumer. You are not powerless. Many federal and state laws are designed to help people facing financial problems. These include protection against abusive debt collectors, relief from unfair business practices, limits on wage garnishment and seizures of property, and the right to eliminate many obligations in bankruptcy. In most cases, however, you need to know your rights in order to exercise them. This book attempts both to explain these rights and tell you when and how to use them.

HOW THIS BOOK
IS ORGANIZED

This book is organized into five parts, each one dealing with different types of choices you may face. The process of dealing with financial problems is mostly about making good choices. Each part of the book is further divided into chapters which cover more specific issues.

Part I (Making the Right Choices, Chapters 1 - 4) covers the different choices you will face when you cannot keep current on your debts. Part I helps you reevaluate your budget and correctly prioritize your debts. The goal is to enable you to deal with your most pressing problems first and to have as much money as possible available to meet those needs. This book is not intended to second guess your choices about small issues like what groceries to buy, but rather to point out some larger areas in which you can increase your income or where savings may be possible, so that you can use that money to pay for pressing needs, including your home and car.

Similarly, people can easily make poor choices about which debts to pay. It is common for consumers to pay debts, like credit card bills, which do not urgently have to be paid, just because that creditor is employing the most obnoxious collection techniques. If you are having financial problems, you should instead be paying those creditors who can do the most to actually hurt you — especially those who can take your home or car.

Part I also warns about a number of unwise choices you may be tempted to make to resolve financial problems. Getting your financial house in order is as much about avoiding the wrong choices as it is about picking the right ones. If you cannot repay your debts, you may also be tempted to refinance them, meaning that you replace old debt with new debt. Part I provides advice as to when to and when *not* to refinance existing debt, including potential difficulties involved in refinancing, and ways to avoid the worst pitfalls.

Part II (Debt Collection, Your Credit Rating, and Collection Lawsuits, Chapters 5 - 8) focuses on problems when you are delinquent on "unsecured debt," that is debt where you have not put up your home, car or other property as collateral for the debt. Common examples are credit card, doctor and hospital bills, and charges with retailers.

Creditors' major techniques for collecting on such debt are debt collection contacts, threats about your credit record, and, less frequently, collection lawsuits. Part II provides strategies for dealing with all of these collection techniques.

Part III (Home Foreclosures, Chapters 9 - 12) deals in depth with one of the most severe consequences of financial distress — the potential loss of your home. If you have put up your home as collateral on a loan, that lender can seize the home if you fall behind on payments. Part III explains the foreclosure process, tells you what steps to take to avoid it, and what you should do if the lender has actually started the foreclosure process.

Part IV (Evictions, Shutoffs, Repossessions, and Other Seizures, Chapters 13 - 17) covers your best choices, both in the short and the long term, to deal with other debts that can threaten your property. In Part IV, we attempt to explain:

- •how to determine whether or not a particular debt can be temporarily ignored;
- •options you may have for negotiating with that creditor;
- •special rights you may have to repay the debt over time;
- •strategies to create delay and to gain time to get back on your feet;
- •legal protections and rights you have in the debt collection process;
- •how to go about enforcing your rights; and
- •situations in which it makes sense to get help.

Each chapter covers a different type of debt problem that may lead to the immediate loss of property, such as evictions, utility terminations, or car repossessions. The basic lesson of each chapter is that there are many things you can do for almost every common consumer debt. Giving up is almost always the wrong choice.

Part V (Your Bankruptcy Rights, Chapter 18) provides a basic discussion of your bankruptcy option, which may make particular sense for dealing with your long term financial difficulties. Bankruptcy is your most basic protection against unmanageable debt. The information in Part V is intended to help you make the right choices about when bankruptcy relief makes sense.

Business and Tax Debts. This book does not address business-related debts. Although some of the issues related to enforcement of business debts are the same as those discussed here, major business-related debts may create problems of special complexity. These can include the extent of your liability for debts of corporations and partnerships with which you have been affiliated, enforcement of personal guarantees, and special liabilities associated with employment relationships. We recommend that, if you have significant business-related debts, that you consult a lawyer.

Income tax issues can also be very complicated. In this book, we do little more than alert you to the need to deal with those debts and to some issues in dealing with IRS income tax collection activity. We recommend that you consult a tax lawyer or an accountant if you have significant potential debts to the IRS or state taxing authorities.

WHAT YOU NEED TO READ

We recommend that everyone facing financial difficulties read this book's first three chapters. You cannot make good choices about specific debts until you understand the priorities about which debts to pay, as set out in Chapter One. You will also need to set up an appropriate budget so that you have a good idea of how much money you have to pay your debts, as explained in Chapter Two. Chapter Two also advises how to increase your income, decrease your expenses, deal with medical care, and consider if you should dip into your savings. Chapter Three warns against certain options you might be tempted to try to get yourself out of financial trouble, but which could just make matters worse.

After you read these three chapters, you can then pick and choose chapters from the rest of the book which covers specific situations. For example, if you are a homeowner, you should read the chapters on foreclosure rather than on your rights as a tenant and vice versa. Read Chapter Four if you are considering refinancing your debt, Chapter Five if you are concerned with debt collectors, and Chapter Six if you are worried about your credit rating. Other chapters discuss collection lawsuits, utility terminations, repossessions, and government collection of student loans and taxes.

Chapter Eighteen on bankruptcy may be applicable to almost any consumer in financial trouble, and should at least be skimmed by all readers. This will help you decide whether to consider the bankruptcy option. Read the chapter in full if you want the complete picture of whether, when and how you should file for bankruptcy.

OBTAINING PROFESSIONAL ASSISTANCE

This book outlines your rights and gives you basic information about enforcing them. In many cases, exercising your rights is difficult because the applicable law and court procedures are complicated. You may need a lawyer or a non-profit counselor to help you with enforcing many of your legal rights. You may also need help to apply material in this book to your particular situation.

An additional factor is that state instead of federal law governs many of your rights. These laws can vary substantially from state to state. You may need to get more information on the laws in your state. We have tried to point this out whenever possible.

Hiring a Lawyer. It can be difficult to get legal help when you do not have much money. In most communities (or close by if you live in a rural area), there are organizations that provide free help with legal problems to people whose income fall below certain amounts. Although Congress has cut back on funding for these organizations, they still exist and should be sought out if you need help.

These organizations vary widely on the type of cases they handle. They also have strict income limits so that they are forced to turn away many cases. However, it can't hurt to ask. If they can't help you, they generally will make a referral to the appropriate legal organization (often called "bar association"), sometimes for free help from a private lawyer. They also may have special pamphlets or other helpful information on your state's laws.

If you need to pay for a lawyer, it is important to get competent help. All lawyers, like all doctors and all accountants, are not the same. You should try to find someone you feel comfortable with who has expertise in consumer rights. A first step is to try to get a referral from a friend or relative to a lawyer who has done good work in the past. If you cannot get a referral, try calling your state or county bar association. Most such organizations maintain a referral service that will give you names of lawyers who specialize in consumer credit problems.

You should always have an opportunity to talk to a lawyer before you agree to pay for that lawyer's services. Make sure you have a clear idea of what the lawyer will do for you and what you will be charged. You should know whether you are paying an hourly rate or if you are paying a flat fee for a particular service. If you pay a flat fee, you should be sure to get a written statement of what the fee covers.

Even after you have signed a retainer, if you are dissatisfied with the service you are getting, you can always cancel. You will only have to pay for services already received. If you are entitled to a refund which you do not receive, consider making a complaint to the local disciplinary agency for attorneys.

Unfortunately, the cheapest lawyer will not necessarily be the best. Cost should not be the only consideration when hiring a lawyer — although it is always a factor. Be sure to get someone who you feel comfortable will help you with the specifics of your problem. Most lawyers should be willing to provide a free initial consultation and they should be willing to explain the consequences of your doing nothing about your delinquent debt. You do not want to pay a lawyer if there are no negative consequences for you if you just ignore your debts.

Finally, lawyer advertising has become a problem in our society. Some lawyers review court lists to find out who is being sued or read published foreclosure notices, and then solicit these individuals. Some lawyers make outrageous claims in their advertisements. Although not all lawyers who advertise are bad, you should not take an advertisement at face value. Make sure you know what the lawyer will do for you and whether the advertised services meet your needs. An eye-catching advertisement alone is not a good reason to hire a particular lawyer.

Getting Help From a Counselor. If you cannot afford a lawyer or if you feel you don't want one, another place to get help is from a non-profit counselor. Many communities have both non-profit "debt" counselors and non-profit "housing" counselors. If you have a housing related problem, a housing counselor is probably preferable.

Counselors cannot offer the full range of services which a good lawyer can provide, but they can often help with some specific issues. Counselors, like lawyers, may focus on some options rather than others. You should understand what the counselor can do for you and make sure you feel the options offered include the right choices for your circumstances.

Some non-profit counselors charge a fee to cover their costs. Others are free. Make sure you know from the beginning if there is a charge for counseling and how much it will be. If the fee seems unreasonable, seek other help.

Finding a non-profit counselor can be difficult. Try calling city officials, legal services, a consumer help line, or a friend or relative who has had similar problems. Sometimes a helpful creditor will make a recommendation. No matter where the recommendation comes from, make sure you are dealing with a legitimate *non-profit* counselor from a reputable organization with expertise in the area in which you need help.

Always avoid "for profit" debt counseling. This has become a significant consumer rip off. The charge for such counseling will almost always exceed the value of the counseling. Additionally, many such counselors are geared to funneling business to hard money lenders and other disreputable businesses which take advantage of people with financial problems. These businesses will only make your problems worse.

NOTE TO COUNSELORS USING THIS BOOK

This book is a revision of an earlier publication which was addressed directly to debt counselors. Although the book is now written to consumers directly, it is still very valuable to counselors. Most of your clients will need your help to exercise the basic rights and options discussed in this book. Although we have tried to write simply, many clients will need help to understand the discussion here. We have not shied away from discussing complicated issues when they are necessary to a complete understanding of rights and options.

Because you see clients with financial problems on a repeated basis, you will almost always have more expertise in addressing these problems than the particular individual who seeks your help. Although we encourage you to recommend this book to your clients, you can also use it to advise clients on specific issues. Your explanations and background as a counselor will frequently reinforce the discussion that this book provides.

We recognize that many of the strategies discussed in this book go beyond what you are accustomed to doing in the counseling process. Each counselor must make his or her own decision about how far to go in actively intervening in a client's debt problems. At a minimum, however, we ask that you make every effort to give financially stressed consumers their full range of choices by counseling them on the availability of options which go beyond the scope of what your organization would be able to do.

For example, if you work for an organization which helps consumers make payment agreements with their creditors, you should nevertheless explain that bankruptcy is an alternative to some payment agreements, and cover the circumstances in which bankruptcy may make sense. Similarly, if you are accustomed to dealing with credit card issues, we ask that you be sure that you do not recommend a strategy for dealing with credit cards which undermines a consumer's ability to deal with a mortgage, car or utility payment. Whenever possible, problems should be dealt with in the context of all of the consumer's problems, rather than in isolation.

NOTE TO LAWYERS USING THIS BOOK

For lawyers who do not specialize in consumer rights, this book is intended to be a useful introduction to strategies for dealing with debts. Although we have deleted statutory references due to their inaccessibility to consumers, we have tried to include references to treatises containing more detailed legal information.

The best source of information for lawyers on consumer claims related to credit and utility issues is the National Consumer Law Center's series of consumer law manuals. For more details, see the bibliography, call NCLC Publications at (617) 523-8089, FAX (617) 523-7398, or write: National Consumer Law Center, Publications Department, 18 Tremont Street, Suite 400, Boston, MA 02108.

Lawyers who do specialize in consumer credit problems may already own other NCLC publications. You should consider using *Surviving Debt* to educate your clients, paralegals, law students or others in your office. Bulk publication orders can be arranged at substantial discounts by contacting NCLC Publications at the phone number or address above.

SOME FINAL THOUGHTS

This book is not intended to be a treatise on the law related to consumer credit. Readers who want more information should refer to the bibliography and the sources mentioned in each chapter. As stated in an earlier disclaimer, the book is also not intended to substitute for the independent judgment and skills of a competent attorney or other professional. Please read the disclaimer on the reverse of the title page for related information.

Finally, we are always eager to have feedback on your use of this book. If you have other suggestions about how to deal with debts, experiences which are contrary to the advice given here, or other comments, please feel free to write the authors.

— 1 —

Choosing Which Debts To Pay

- *Sixteen Rules to Help Choose Which Debts to Pay First*
- *The Consequences of Not Paying Different Types of Debt*
- *What If You Cannot Pay All Your High Priority Debts?*

SIXTEEN RULES ABOUT CHOOSING WHICH DEBTS TO PAY FIRST

If you are having serious financial problems, you probably are having trouble keeping current on all of your debts. You can only cut expenses so much, and your income cannot be stretched to cover all of your obligations. This leaves you with no choice but to delay or eliminate payment on certain of your debts.

One of the most important choices you will have to make is which debts to pay first. Your home or apartment, your utility service, your car, and even your household possessions may be at stake. Following the rules in this chapter may make the difference between keeping or losing this property.

Instead of delaying or eliminating certain debt repayments, you may be tempted to take out more debt to repay old debts. This is generally a bad idea. When you should refinance, consolidate, or take out new loans is discussed in Chapter Four. Chapter Two describes ways to increase your income or decrease your expenses to help you to make ends meet.

Nevertheless, your main strategy in dealing with too much debt is deciding which debts to pay first, which you can refuse to pay, and which you can put off until later. The most important creditor to pay is not necessarily the creditor that screams the loudest or the most often. Creditors who yell the loudest often do so only because they have no better way to get their money than to pressure you to pay. Of more concern are creditors who not only threaten, but actually *can* take quick action against your residence, utility service, car, or other important assets.

You should direct your limited resources to what is most necessary for your family — typically food, clothing, shelter and utility service. Unfortunately, there is no universally applicable list of the order in which debts should be paid. Everyone's situation will be different. Instead what follows are sixteen rules about how to set priorities, followed by a more detailed sketch of the consequences of not paying certain types of debts.

Pay off creditors who can take the quickest action to hurt you, *not* those who are calling you the most often. Pay your mortgage or rent first; worry about credit card or doctor bills later.

---

1. Always Pay Family Necessities First. Usually this means food and essential medical expenses. You may want to look at ways to keep these expenses to a minimum as discussed in Chapter Two.

2. Next Pay Your Housing-Related Bills. Keep up your mortgage or rent payments if at all possible. If you own your home, real estate taxes and insurance must also be paid unless they are included in the monthly mortgage payment. Similarly, any condo fees or mobile home lot payments should be considered a high priority. Failure to pay these debts can lead to loss of your home.

If you are having very serious unresolvable financial problems which will require you to move to a cheaper residence, you might choose to stop paying the mortgage or rent on your existing residence. When you do so, you should not use that money to pay other debts, but rather save it as a fund to use for moving. Dealing with mortgage debts is discussed in more detail in Chapters Nine through Twelve. Rent payments and dealing with land-lords are discussed in Chapter Thirteen.

3. Pay What You Must to Keep Essential Utility Service. While this may not always require full payment (such as during a winter moratorium on disconnections), whatever payments are necessary should be made if at all possible. Working hard to keep your house or apartment makes little sense if it is not liveable because you have no utilities. Options for dealing with utility payments are discussed in Chapter Fourteen.

4. Pay Car Loans or Leases Next If You Really Need Your Car. If you need your car to get to work or for other essential transportation, you will usually make your car loan or lease payments next after food, housing costs, new medical expenses, utilities, and clothing. You may even want to pay your car loan first if the car is essential to holding onto your job.

If you do keep the car, stay current on your insurance payments as well. Otherwise the creditor may buy at *your* expense even more costly collision and theft insurance that gives you much less protection. In most states it is also illegal not to have automobile liability coverage. If you can do without your car or one of your cars, you not only save on car payments, but also on gasoline, repairs, insurance, and the like. Car loan debts are discussed in Chapter Fifteen.

5. You Must Pay Child Support Debts. These debts will not go away and can result in very serious remedies — including prison for nonpayment.

6. Income Tax Debts Are Also High Priority. You must pay any income taxes you owe that are not automatically deducted from your wages, and you certainly must file your federal income tax return even if you can-not afford to pay any balance due. The government has many collection rights, particularly if you do not file your tax return, that are not available to other creditors. Remember, though, if you have lost income due to a change of circumstances, your tax obligations will also be reduced. Pay only what is necessary.

7. Loans Without Collateral Are Low Priority. Most credit card debts, attorney, doctor and hospital bills, and other debts to professionals, open accounts with merchants, and similar debts are low priority. You have not pledged any collateral for these loans, and there is rarely anything that these creditors can do to hurt you in the short term. Many won't bother to try to collect in the long term.

8. Loans With Only Household Goods Collateral Are Also Low Priority. Sometimes a creditor requires you to put some of your household goods up as collateral on a loan. You should generally treat this loan the same as an unsecured debt, that is as a low priority. Creditors rarely seize household goods because they have little market value, it is hard to seize them without court process, and it is time consuming and expensive to use a court process to seize them. See Chapter Sixteen.

9. Do *Not* Move a Debt Up in Priority Because the Creditor Threatens Suit. Many threats to sue are not carried out. Even if the creditor does sue, it will take a while for the collector to be able to reach your property, and much of your property may be exempt from seizure. On the other hand, non-payment of rent, mortgage and car debts may result in immediate loss of your home or car. Debt collection lawsuits and threats to sue are discussed in Chapters Five and Seven.

10. Do Not Pay When You Have Good Legal Defenses to Repayment. Some examples of legal defenses are that goods purchased were defective, or that the creditor is asking for more money than it is entitled to. If you have a legal defense, you should obtain legal advice to determine whether your defense will succeed. In evaluating these options, remember that it is especially dangerous to withhold mortgage or rent payments without legal advice. However, for all debts you should consider fighting back when you have a valid defense as discussed in Chapter Eight.

11. Court Judgments Against You Move Debt Up in Priority, But Often Less Than You Think. After a collector obtains a court judgment, that debt often should move up in priority, because the creditor can enforce that judgment by asking the court to seize certain of your property, wages, and bank accounts. Nevertheless, how serious a threat this really is will depend on your state's law, the value of your property, and your income. It may be that all your property and wages are protected under state law. Then you should pay this debt only after more pressing obligations. For more detail, see Chapter Seven. This is also a good time to obtain professional advice if you have not done so already.

12. Student Loans Are Medium Priority Debts. They should generally be paid ahead of low priority debts, but after top priority debts. Most student loans are backed by the United States and federal law provides special collection remedies against you, such as seizure of your tax refunds and denying you new student loans and grants that are not available for other types of loans. These issues are discussed in Chapter Seventeen.

13. Debt Collection Efforts Should *Never* Move Up a Debt's Priority. Be polite to the collector, but make your own choices about which debts to pay based on what is best for your family. Debt collectors are unlikely to give you good advice. Debt collectors may be most aggressive to get you to pay debts which you should actually pay last. You can easily stop debt collection contacts and you have legal remedies to deal with collection harassment. See Chapter Five.

14. Threats to Ruin Your Credit Record Should *Never* Move Up a Debt's Priority. In many cases, when a collector threatens to report your delinquency to a credit bureau, the creditor has already provided the credit bureau with the exact status of the deliquency. And, if the creditor has not done so, a collector hired by the creditor is very unlikely to do so. In fact, your mortgage lender, your car creditor, and other big creditors are *much* more likely to report your delinquency (without any threat) than is a debt collector that threatens you about your credit record. See Chapter Six.

15. Cosigned Debts Should Be Treated Like Your Other Debts. If you have put up your home or car as collateral on a loan you have cosigned, that is a high priority debt for you if the other co-signers are not keeping the debt current. If you have not put up such collateral, treat cosigned debts as a lower priority. If others have cosigned for you and you are unable to pay the debt, you should tell your cosigner about your financial problems so that he or she can decide what to do about that debt.

16. Refinancing Is Rarely the Answer. You should always be careful about refinancing. It can be very expensive and it can give creditors more opportunities to seize your important assets. A short term fix can lead to long term problems. Some simple refinancing rules and techniques to avoid scams are discussed in Chapter Four.

WHAT HAPPENS TO YOU
IF YOU DO NOT PAY
DIFFERENT TYPES OF DEBTS

To better understand the basis for these sixteen rules and how to apply them in particular cases, you should learn the potential consequences of not paying different types of debt. This section is a brief overview. More on specific types of debt is found in the rest of this book.

Unsecured vs. Secured Debt. The most important principle in setting your priorities is understanding the concept of "collateral." Collateral is property which a creditor has the right to seize if you do not pay a particular debt. The most common forms of collateral are your home in the case of a mortgage (or deed of trust) and your car in the case of most car loans.

A creditor may also have collateral in your household goods, business property, bank account, or even wages. Collateral can take many forms. When a creditor has taken collateral for your loan, it has a "lien" on your property.

Determine which of your
debts are "secured" and which
are "unsecured." You should almost
always pay secured debts first.

Creditors who have collateral are usually referred to as "secured" creditors. They have the security of knowing that they can take the collateral and sell it to get their money. Creditors without collateral are often referred to as "unsecured." It is usually hard for unsecured creditors to collect what they are owed unless you pay voluntarily.

Home Foreclosure. If you own a home and do not pay the mortgage, deed of trust, or land contract (we will refer to all of these as "mortgages"), the creditor can foreclose on your home. This means the lender can sell the home and you will have to move. You will also typically lose all your equity in the house. This is because foreclosure sales rarely are for full market value.

It is sometimes difficult to stop a foreclosure once you have fallen behind. Even filing for bankruptcy may not help you permanently prevent a foreclosure. It is thus critical to prioritize your bills and make your home mortgage payments first.

Real estate taxes and property insurance are also high priorities if they are not paid with the mortgage, because failure to pay these obligations can result in defaults on your mortgage and loss of your home. Additionally, you can lose your home to fire or other catastrophe if your insurance is canceled.

If you own a condo, condo association fees need to be paid as well, although they will usually be a slightly lower priority than the mortgage. In some states condo associations can enforce a lien against your property for condo fees by foreclosure or another similar process.

If you own a mobile home, and you rent your lot, you will need to treat your lot rent as a priority. Failure to pay lot rent can result in eviction. In some states seizure of the home can also result. If you are evicted, even if you do not lose the mobile home, you are likely to have difficulties finding a new lot.

There are two important exceptions to the rule of always paying a mortgage and related debts first. Sometimes a fraudulent home improvement contractor, shady finance company, or other questionable company will obtain a second mortgage or lien on your home. In that case, you may have legal reasons why you do not have to repay the loan — e.g., the aluminum siding was never installed or the replacement windows are shoddy and overpriced. Before making a final decision about whether to pay a loan of this type, make sure to obtain legal representation.

The other exception arises when you know that you will not be able to afford the home for the long term. Further payments after that point will generally go to waste. Consider selling the home in that situation or using one or more of the other options discussed in Chapter Ten.

Apartment Eviction. If you do not pay rent, your landlord can evict you. If you are jointly responsible on a lease with others, their failure to pay can also result in your eviction. You cannot be evicted for failing to pay your other bills (except that under some leases a utility termination may lead to eviction). While a bankruptcy may offer short term relief from an eviction, the only way to stay in an apartment is to keep current on future rent payments, and, in most cases, to pay any arrears in rent.

Utility Termination. Every household is hooked up to a series of utilities — telephone, water, gas, and/or electric service. Nonpayment of the utility bill may result in disconnection of service, although in many instances this can be delayed or avoided even though the bulk of the bill is outstanding. If service is turned off, you will usually be required to pay some or all of the back bill plus a reconnection fee to get the service turned back on. The essential nature of utility service means that these debts usually should be given very high priority.

Each utility bill must be dealt with independently. Failure to pay a telephone bill will have no impact on the continuation of your electric service and vice versa. In fact, the only bill that can lead to utility termination is the bill for that particular utility. A bankruptcy can wipeout old utility bills, and can allow service to be reconnected as long as you stay current on new bills and pay any required deposit.

Car Repossession. When you take out a loan to purchase a car, typically you put up the car as collateral for the loan. You may have also put up your car as collateral on other loans. Alternatively, you may be leasing your car. Whenever a car is collateral on a loan, the lender can seize the car if you get behind on that loan. The same can happen if you get behind on lease payments. In almost all states, no court procedure is required; the creditor just drives away with the car, unless you are present and object. This is called "repossession."

Not only will you lose the car, but the creditor will usually sell the car for less than it is worth and then seek a "deficiency" — the amount owed on the debt less the amount for which the car is sold.

As a consequence, whenever a car is essential transportation, auto loan and lease payments should be treated as high priority debts. Related insurance payments must be made as well.

Seizure of Household Goods. Sometimes creditors who have taken your household goods as collateral threaten to repossess those goods, but this repossession is much more difficult and less profitable than the seizure of an automobile. Creditors cannot enter your home to seize property without your permission. You have no legal obligation to grant permission and you should not do so. Unless you choose to grant permission, the creditor will have to go to court to gain possession of the items.

Goods the creditor does seize rarely have any market value. From a purely financial point of view, it is generally not worth it for creditors to seize household goods. Additionally, goods taken as collateral for a loan unrelated to the purchase of the household goods are generally protected from seizure if you file for bankruptcy. Typically, a creditor's threat to seize household goods is just that — an empty threat.

For these reasons debts which involve household goods as collateral should usually be a relatively low priority. Nevertheless, you should probably pay them if you can, before debts with no collateral at all.

Lawsuits to Collect a Debt. You may be worried by a threat that a particular creditor will go to court to collect a debt. These threats almost always occur when the creditor has little or no collateral for the loan. Many such threats are never carried out.

You should also understand that a creditor's filing a lawsuit does not immediately harm you. First of all, you may win the lawsuit. Second, your decision to contest the lawsuit may be enough to convince the creditor to drop the case.

If the court eventually rules in the creditor's favor, then the court will order you to pay the debt. Even this court order to pay should not be viewed as especially threatening — failure to pay does not place you in contempt of court. Instead, the judgment triggers the creditor's ability to take certain actions to garnish wages, seize property, or examine you about your assets. It is these actions, and not the filing of a lawsuit by itself, which can cause special concern.

This is not to say that you should ignore lawsuits entirely — only that lawsuits and threats of lawsuits should not by themselves change your financial priorities. If you are sued, you should try to obtain immediate assistance from a lawyer or counselor to understand your risks, to determine whether you have defenses, and to evaluate the consequences of inaction.

Wage Garnishment and Seizure of Bank Accounts. In most cases, creditors can only seize wages or bank accounts *after* they go to court and convince a judge that you owe them money. Before the creditor can take action, you have a right to a trial to determine whether you owe the money. Only after the court orders you to pay can the creditor get an order to garnish, i.e., seize your wages or bank account.

The probability of wage garnishment or seizure of a bank account varies a great deal depending on which state you are in. In some states garnishment is not possible, while in others garnishment is rarely, or never, used because the procedure is difficult. However, in a few states garnishment is very common. Depending on state procedure, a garnishment order can come from the court, a court clerk, or a sheriff. The order for garnishment is presented to your employer or bank, but even then state and federal law limit what can be taken.

Under federal law, the first $127.50 a week of take home pay is exempt from garnishment. ($127.50 is 30 times the minimum wage of $4.25. If the minimum wage goes up to $5, $150 a week would be protected instead.) After that, only 25% of your wages can be seized (with the exception of certain child support obligations). State law may give you even greater protections. In some states, wage garnishment is not allowed at all, while in others the amount that can be garnished is less than the federal standard.

Wage garnishments, bank account seizures, and judgment liens are not nearly as imminent or dangerous to you as home foreclosures, car repossessions, or evictions.

Additionally, many forms of government benefits, such as social security payments, veterans benefits, AFDC payments, and similar income cannot be garnished. If this government benefit is placed in a bank account, particularly if no other funds are in the same account, the account may also be exempt from garnishment. Filing bankruptcy is another method of dealing with garnishments. A bankruptcy filing generally eliminates garnishment as a threat.

Judgment Liens. Creditors' rights to seize your property are limited when you have not put up property as collateral for a loan. Where property is not collateral, lenders must first obtain a court order that you owe them money before they can seize your property. You can contest the debt in court. Court permission or a final decision on the debt is required before the creditor can put a "judgment lien" on your home or other property. Once the lien is in place, a further request to the court or a sheriff is required to sell or seize your property.

In many cases creditors with judgment liens will not ask for permission to seize your property, or will not do so for many years. This is because seizing and forcing the sale of property may be expensive and once seized, the property may not have enough value to satisfy the creditor's claim after a sale. Instead of forcing a sale, some creditors may be willing to wait until you voluntarily sell the property and then collect from the proceeds of the sale.

If a creditor does seek to seize and sell your property, state law protects certain family possessions from seizure. Household goods of little economic value are generally exempt from seizure. This usually includes most of your furniture and appliances. Even a home or a car may be exempt from seizure, particularly if your equity in the property is not very much. In some states, there are additional protections against seizure of property (including homes) which are owned jointly by husband and wife, if only one of the spouses is responsible for the underlying debt.

Filing bankruptcy will postpone the threat of seizure of real estate and personal property, at least for a period of time, and sometimes permanently. In bankruptcy many judgment liens can be eliminated entirely.

Creditors may be willing to work out payment schedules even shortly before a threatened seizure. They often prefer to receive cash rather than deal with the costs of seizing and selling property.

Debt Collection. Debt collectors are companies or individuals who are hired by creditors to collect money. Debt collectors cannot take steps against your property other than those discussed in this book. Most debt collectors are not even allowed by the creditor who employs them to take those steps themselves. Usually, debt collection agencies can only recommend that the creditor take those steps.

It is usually not difficult to stop a debt collector from contacting you or others with respect to a debt. The federal debt collection law, for example, gives you the right to stop all collection contacts simply by requesting the collection agency to stop. (A written request is best.) The creditor or the collector then may use only other means to collect, including lawsuits and attempts to seize collateral if they have any.

Many creditors and collectors, however, will go away entirely when told to stop making collection calls. This is because they have no real remedies other than to bother you for payment on the telephone. For these and other reasons, a particular collection agency's aggressiveness in collecting a debt should have no bearing on whether you pay that debt.

Credit Record. If you are having financial problems, you are likely to have negative information listed on your credit record. There is no way to avoid this. Deciding to pay one creditor instead of another usually will not help your credit record. Just because one creditor says it will report the default to a credit bureau does not mean it will. On the other hand, creditors who do not make threats may in fact report you to credit bureaus — without notice to you. Sadly, even if you make an effort to work with a particular creditor, a negative report may already have been made or it may still be made in the future despite your efforts.

Always focus your resources on dealing with your highest priority debts. Sensible choices about which debts to pay have nothing to do with your credit record. It is often better to try to improve your credit in the long term by rehabilitating it, rather than to worry about one more negative reference today.

One exception is that if you have a credit source with a small balance or no balance, you may choose to keep up with payments to that creditor only. Although this does not really improve your long term prospect for new credit, it is unlikely that your credit with that one creditor will be canceled as long as you are up to date on that obligation. Of course, this does not mean that you should make heroic efforts to pay one debt when thousands of dollars are due. If you do so, you may jeopardize more important priorities and lose your credit anyway.

Taxes, Student Loans, and Other Debts Owed to the Government. The government has special powers not available to other creditors to collect tax obligations, student loans and other debts owed to a government agency. The I.R.S., after a series of warning letters that take a number of months, will send a final 90 day warning. At that point the I.R.S. will start putting liens on your property and may begin to seize your property. While certain minimal possessions are exempt from seizure, most of a family's property can be seized. A court procedure is not required.

The consequences of nonpayment of student loans and other obligations to government agencies are not so serious. But be prepared for the government to intercept income tax refunds and earned income tax credits. The government will also utilize debt collection agencies and may seek large collection costs. Up to ten percent of your wages can be garnished to pay student loan claims if you have been working continuously for a year, but you can avoid this, after receiving the garnishment notice, by agreeing to a payment plan. Student loan defaults will definitely be reported to credit reporting agencies. Student loan defaulters may also be ineligible for future student loans and grants.

Cosigned Debts. You have to be very careful of not only your own debts, but those you incur as a cosigner. If your property serves as collateral, you can lose the property if the debt is not paid, even if you are not responsible for the failure to pay. You can also be sued. In that case, your liability is the same as if you had incurred the debt alone. If you have cosigned any debts, it is a good idea to make sure that the debt is being paid.

If others have cosigned for you on your debts, you should let your cosigners know that you are not able to pay, so that they can get independent advice and decide what to do to protect themselves.

IF YOU CAN'T PAY ALL
YOUR HIGH PRIORITY DEBTS

Although everyone has slightly different priorities, most people will want to pay debts required to maintain essential shelter and transportation before worrying about other debts. In some cases, you may find that your financial situation is so bad that you cannot even maintain required payments on those high priority debts. Your income, for example, may not be enough to pay the mortgage and the car loan.

One serious mistake that some people make in this situation is to pay smaller, low priority debts if they cannot keep up with their high priority debts — "If I can't pay my mortgage, at least I will keep up with my credit cards."

This is a bad idea. Almost any long term plan for saving your home and your car will require that you start making payments again at some point. In the short term, if you don't have enough to make full payments, you can try to negotiate with the creditor to accept partial payments. If you are unsuccessful, save the money. You can use it later to make a lump sum down payment as part of a process of getting caught up or to cover the costs of moving to a new residence or buying a new car.

Another pitfall to avoid is making desperate choices. Although it is hard to accept that you will lose a home or a car or other valuable property, the alternatives can sometimes be worse. For example, refinancing a low rate mortgage with a high rate mortgage may buy you a few months, but in the long term the situation is likely to be hopeless. You have a better chance of working out a solution with the existing lender than you do of avoiding foreclosure with an aggressive finance company making high rate loans.

There are many strategies for dealing with debt problems discussed throughout this book. Occasionally, though, it is best to step back and accept the inevitable change which money problems sometimes require. You may be living in a home you can't afford or you may need to substitute a cheaper auto to fit a new lifestyle.

Once that point is reached, you can do things which make it easier to address the transition. These may include selling the property at a good retail price to avoid a low foreclosure sale price or giving up the property in exchange for a promise that the creditor will let you off the hook for a deficiency.

These choices are difficult and have to be made based on your individual evaluation of your long term prospects. Once the choice is made however, it is a good idea to stop making payments on that debt in favor of other pressing items. Continuing to pay a debt on property which you will lose in the long term anyway is expensive. You do not want to "throw good money after bad."

USING BANKRUPTCY TO GET A FRESH START

When you file for bankruptcy, most of your *unsecured* debts will be "discharged." This means that your legal obligation to pay those debts will be ended even if you can't pay. On the other hand, despite your bankruptcy, a creditor usually will eventually be able to seize its collateral unless you make a plan to pay that debt.

This difference in bankruptcy between unsecured and secured debts is another reason to make unsecured debts a lower priority. In oversimplified terms, you don't want to pay debts which bankruptcy can eliminate, in preference to debts for which the creditor has collateral. (This is also a good reason not to give a creditor collateral in a refinancing deal.)

Bankruptcy can also be used to get a creditor to back off of aggressive collection efforts. If a creditor refuses to give you some time to get things together, or if a creditor refuses to accept small but affordable payments, filing bankruptcy can take care of the problem. Sometimes just telling a creditor that you are considering bankruptcy will make that creditor more reasonable.

Even if you do not plan on filing bankruptcy, you should understand how your bankruptcy would affect your debts and your creditors.

Making a choice about whether to file bankruptcy can be difficult. Complicated issues are involved for which legal help is usually necessary. Necessary background for making a good choice about bankruptcy is provided in Chapter Eighteen. Since there are situations in which rights in bankruptcy can be lost by delay, you should consider bankruptcy as an option from the start of your planning process for surviving your financial problems.

FEELINGS OF MORAL OBLIGATION
TO PARTICULAR CREDITORS

In deciding your priorities, you may feel that some creditors are more entitled to repayment than others. You may have good feelings toward some creditors, but bad feelings toward others. These feelings should rarely be a factor in deciding which debts to pay first. Giving up the family home to pay off a creditor for whom you have good feelings is too big a sacrifice. If a creditor is sympathetic or has done you favors in the past, they are more likely to be patient as you work out your financial problems.

A related issue comes up in small communities where there may only be one store or one doctor or one pharmacist with whom you can do business. You may not want to lose your ability to obtain services from that particular creditor and you may feel you have no choice other than to pay that debt first. This may be right, but only in limited situations.

You should not assume that a business or a doctor will cut you off from future service right away if you don't pay. Explain the situation and ask for tolerance, if necessary. Similarly, before assuming that you need to use a particular creditor, look around. There may be others in or near your community who are available in a pinch.

Everyone has financial problems at one time or another. It is nothing to be embarrassed about. Ask for help from creditors with whom you have a good relationship if you need it, and explain that you will make every effort to pay when you get back on your feet.

— 2 —

Establishing a Budget and Making Ends Meet

• The Income and Expense Budget
• Increasing Your Income and Lowering Your Expenses
• Making Choices About Your Savings and Your Assets
• Dealing With Pressures Caused By a Tight Budget

THE INCOME AND EXPENSE BUDGET

It Is Essential That You Set Up (and Try to Stay on) an Income and Expense Budget. The first step in deciding your best strategy for dealing with your financial problems is to set up a budget based on your expected income and expenses. This budget will help you decide your best options. Most importantly, your budget will tell you what you can and cannot afford to pay.

There are three primary reasons to set up a budget as soon as you recognize that you are likely to be facing financial problems. These are:

1. The budget will help you determine how much money you have to cover your necessities and how much is left over to pay back your debts. This will give you a sense of the range of choices you are facing to deal with your debts.
2. The budget will help guide your spending habits. Your budget is likely to be based on your best planning about what you need. If

you can live within the budget, you can be assured that you are not overspending and making your problems worse.

3. In some cases you will want to work with creditors that offer options for payment plans and modification of debts. These options will be particularly important if you wish to save your home and your car. Your ability to qualify for these programs will be based on your budget. If you have already done the work to develop a budget, you will have a sense of what you can afford to offer your creditors and you will be able to provide basic information which will make the process move more smoothly.

How to Set Up a Budget. Your budget is nothing more than a list of your anticipated income and a list of your expected expenses. Setting up a budget for the future involves making predictions based on your best information about what your income and expenses are likely to be.

A good place to start is with your existing income and expenses, without trying to adjust for future changes. Usually this is easiest to do on a monthly basis, using the most recent calendar month. What were your sources of income? How did you spend your money? You will then need to subtract your expenses from your income. In doing so, you should not be surprised if you find out that your expenses exceed your income. This is why you are having financial problems.

Once you have your current income and expenses on paper, you will need to begin the difficult work of evaluating what you expect for the future. Is your income likely to go up or down over the next few months? Can you change your spending patterns to reduce your expenses? Do you anticipate new expenses which were not included in the current budget?

Throughout the budgeting process, your goal should be to minimize any shortfall between your income and expenses. This means on one side, that you should be evaluating whether you have ways to increase your income. On the other side, you should look at whether there are ways to reduce expenses to make things more manageable.

In making these choices, it is essential to be realistic about what is possible. For example, you may feel that you can reduce your family food expenses by cutting out restaurant meals, but it is unrealistic to say that you can cut your food expenses to zero. Everyone has to eat. Unrealistic budgeting will lead to wrong choices about which debts to pay and potentially to a sense of hopelessness when your chosen strategies do not work out.

After completing the process of setting up a realistic budget for the future, subtract your expenses from your income again. Can you afford the future budget you have set out? If not, don't despair. Much of the rest of this book is about options for reducing or eliminating your obligations on various debts. You can come up with a combination of strategies which will address your shortfall.

Once you have a budget in place, try to live with it for a month to get a sense of whether it works. At the end of the month, go back and put in your actual income and expenses. Afterwards you can make adjustments based on your experience to make your budget more realistic for future months.

Try photocopying the budget forms at the back of this book. They come with instructions to help you along.

To help you write up a budget, we have included, as an appendix at the back of this book, sample budget forms with some notes about how to use them. The forms include many potential sources of income and common expenses. However, don't assume we have thought of everything. Your budget should be based on your personal experience.

Income Budget. Your income budget should include all your present sources of income. Employment income is a good place to start. If you are not working on salary, you should try to use the best realistic estimate of what you will earn. Overtime should be included if it is guaranteed, but it is a bad idea to budget based on hopes for extra work.

Your income budget should also include any other money that you receive on a regular basis, including child support and alimony, trust payments, dividends, royalties, insurance, pensions and public benefits.

One problem which sometimes occurs is how to deal with expected future increases or decreases in your income. If you know of an expected change and that change is certain, you can use it in planning your budget. If you then share your budget forms with a creditor from whom you are seeking a modification of loan terms, the expected change should be fully explained. Most creditors will want documentation.

When you prepare your income budget, you should carefully evaluate whether you are maximizing your income. Do you have opportunities for overtime? Can you begin drawing on your pension? Is there a manageable part-time job which will help you get through a tough period? Can you permanently or temporarily cancel wage deductions which you have been making voluntarily?

Does it make sense to draw down money you have been saving for the future and then to rebuild your savings plan after your financial problems are resolved? There are no easy answers to these questions, and you will have to make a decision which is right for you.

A later section in this chapter provides some ideas for increasing your income, including availability of the earned income tax credit and a variety of public benefit and entitlement programs. Many people overlook these options for increasing their income. You have a right to use these income sources to help you manage your financial problems, and you should not hesitate to do so.

Expense Budget. Your expense budget should include all of your expected monthly expenses, including food, shelter costs, utilities, clothing, transportation and medical expenses. It is often difficult to figure out exactly where all of your money goes. A review of your checkbook and your credit card bills may serve as a reminder.

Computing the true cost of various expense categories can also be difficult. Food expenses, for example, consist of your costs at the grocery store, plus (most likely) a few trips to the convenience store for special needs each week, plus the costs of occasionally dining out. If you look at your grocery store bills alone, you may underestimate your food expenses. You should do your best to estimate the real total. Then, think about ways you can minimize unnecessary food expenses, by, for example, regularly taking your lunch to work.

On the other hand, you need to be realistic about the real costs of feeding your family. For example, if the kids aren't going to drink powdered milk, it makes little sense to budget as if they will.

Other expenses can be more tightly controlled. New clothing purchases, for example, can usually be minimized until you get back on your feet. Later in this chapter, we list a dozen ways to reduce your expenses which you might not think of on your own. A family discussion and the understanding of all concerned may be necessary to get through a tough period.

Finally, you need to exercise care to budget enough to deal with the real costs of essentials. Home maintenance, for example, can be minimized but not eliminated. If you need your car, auto insurance and repairs are essential related costs. It may also be a good idea to reserve a small percentage of your budget for inevitable but unknown emergency needs.

How to Treat Credit Card Bills and Other Unsecured Debts in Your Expense Budget. Unless you can afford to meet all of your obligations, you should generally not include credit card and other unsecured debts in your expense budget. If you do not have enough income in your budget to pay all of your debts, Chapter One discusses the best ways to prioritize among your various bills. Credit card and other unsecured debts are low priorities.

You should always budget to pay for necessities, including shelter costs and necessary transportation costs, before paying anything on your credit cards and other debts for which the creditor has no collateral. This means you should not even budget to make minimum payments on your credit cards, if the result will be that you cannot pay for your home and car. For reasons discussed throughout this book, you should always protect important property by making plans to prevent foreclosure or repossession before you worry about your credit rating and your ability to borrow again in the future.

How to Include Your Savings and Other Assets in Your Budget. You will have to decide how to treat your savings and other assets in your budget plan. Are you better off spending your retirement money now, or toughing it out now so you have money when you retire? Should you take a little money out of your savings account each month to help balance your budget or should you take all your savings and pay it in one lump sum toward getting your mortgage current? Should you sell off stocks or other property to make ends meet? Later in this chapter, there are tips about how to deal with your savings and other assets. Read that section carefully, make smart choices, and then reflect your decision in your budget plan.

How to Budget Lump Sums You Are Expecting But Have Not Received. Many people have money which they expect in the future, but which is not yet in hand. Sometimes the expectation is no more than a possibility, while in other cases it is guaranteed. Examples include:

- money or property which has been left to you by a deceased relative, but which is tied up in probate;
- social security or other public benefit lump sums;
- money from a lawsuit which has not yet been heard in court or settled;
- money for sale of property when the sale has not yet closed;
- retirement funds or workers compensation which are owed but unpaid;
- money promised by a friend or relative to help you out in tough times; and
- insurance money which has not yet been paid.

It is possible to include this money in your financial plan, but you need to be realistic about when the money may come and how much it will be.

If you are waiting for a lawyer to settle a case or an estate, it may be a good idea to call to let the lawyer know about the nature and urgency of your financial difficulties. There may be things which can be done to speed up legal processes, although in some cases there will be costs in the form of a decreased recovery. For example, the need for urgent settlement of a personal injury case can reduce the amount you are paid, particularly if the other side senses your situation.

Some money is certain to come in on a particular date. For example if your social security payments are due to start on a particular date, you can use this knowledge in making your financial plan. You can supplement your income from savings for a few months while you wait for the permanent change to kick in. Similarly, if a lump sum is guaranteed, you can plan to use that lump sum in a way which will cure your defaults on urgent debts.

On the other hand, it can be a poor choice to pin your hopes on money which is no more than a hope either in timing or amount. Payment that is too speculative should probably not enter into your plans at all.

Finally, some mortgage and car loan creditors will negotiate with you about a temporary delay in payments if you can show them that you have long term prospects for getting caught up. (This is not a negotiation which makes sense on your lower priority debts.) If you do want to use an expected change in income or a lump sum in negotiating with a particular creditor, you will need to gather the best documentation possible of the availability of the money, including a letter from the person who is handling the matter for you or who has oversight of the funds. Sometimes an affidavit will be required.

Balancing Your Budget With New Credit Card or Other Debt. If your expenses are more than your income, you may feel tempted to incur further debts to make up the difference. This is normally a bad choice. New debt will just put you further in the hole and create bigger problems, unless your situation turns around quickly.

While we never recommend your borrowing money to make your budget work if you are already in financial distress, some types of new loans will be worse than others in this situation. Incurring new unsecured credit, such as adding to your credit card debt, is better then incurring new secured debts. As described in Chapter One, the consequences of not paying credit card or other unsecured debt are unlikely to be as severe as if you do not pay a mortgage, car loan or utility bill.

Nevertheless, use of credit card debt to balance your budget can make your situation worse. Credit card debt is high interest debt. If you intend to make only the minimum payments each month on the bill, your debt will quickly compound — making it unlikely that you will ever get back on track.

Although credit card debt can usually be eliminated in bankruptcy, this may not be so if you run up big bills or cash advances just before filing. Creditors also argue, with some success, that if you use a credit card at a time when you did not have the ability to repay, you have committed a fraud which prevents the debt from being eliminated in the bankruptcy process.

Of course, there may be situations where you have to take out new debt. For example, you may need to buy a car to get to work. See Chapters Four and Six for advice on obtaining new credit and refinancing old loans while you are experiencing financial problems. If you do seek new debt, it is always a bad idea to misrepresent your situation in your application. This can lead to claims of fraud, giving rise to lawsuits and even, on occasion, criminal prosecutions.

Generally, Refinancing Will Not Help Make Your Budget Balance. You may be tempted, as a way to make ends meet, to consolidate many small loans into one larger loan, to refinance your home mortgage, or to take other steps to turn old loans into new loans. Chapter Four evaluates refinancing as a strategy to deal with your financial problems. In general, it is a bad option when you are already facing financial problems. It is always a bad idea to refinance unsecured debt into secured debt and to trade low interest rate credit for higher rate loans.

Balancing Your Budget By Borrowing From Friends and Relatives. Friends and relatives may offer to help out when you have financial problems. There is nothing wrong with accepting this help to get you through a tough period. Occasional problems arise, however, if you count on this help. Your friends and relatives may face their own financial difficulties and may withdraw their assistance — sometimes when you need it most. It is thus usually not a good idea to make help from others a cornerstone of your financial plan or to ask others to help you pay back debts which you would not otherwise need to pay.

When assistance from a friend or family member is part of your budget plan, and you need to verify this income for the purpose of getting a payment agreement on your mortgage or car loan, you may need to ask your friend for a formal statement of some type. If possible, use a signed letter for this purpose so that you don't put anyone in the uncomfortable position of contracting to loan you money.

Some creditors will push you to get a friend or relative to cosign with you when you are facing financial problems. You should avoid this whenever possible. The person who cosigns will be on the hook with you and your financial problems will become their's as well, if you cannot afford to pay. You don't want your friendships and family relationships to be on the line if your financial circumstances do not improve.

SOME OPTIONS FOR INCREASING YOUR INCOME

Introduction. This section points out ways to increase your income, the next section deals with medical and dental care, and a third section provides ideas about reducing your expenses. In reading through these sections, particularly the section on increasing your income through the Earned Income Tax Credit and certain public benefit programs, keep in mind that the law on these issues often changes. We try to point out some programs which are likely to be available for the foreseeable future, but you will need to get more detailed information to pursue these options.

You should take advantage of these programs when they are available. Each program was created to help people with financial problems and there is no reason to be ashamed to take this assistance. It is likely that you contributed financially to funding these programs either through tax payments or by payroll deductions.

You should also remember that most of the programs discussed here have appeal rights and procedures. If you are denied assistance which you think you are owed, consider taking your appeals. Professional help may be useful, but it is not required.

The Earned Income Tax Credit. The Earned Income Tax Credit is a frequently overlooked means of increasing your income if you are employed. Particularly if your income has recently decreased or you have been laid off, you can reduce your tax obligation and increase your take home pay. In some cases you can qualify for a refund even if you have no tax liability. Individuals who were laid off or had their hours reduced during the most recent tax year in particular may not realize that they qualify.

The amount of your tax credit is based on the amount of your income and your family's size. If you are employed and your total income falls below a threshold amount, you qualify for the credit even if you do not owe the government any money. Thus it is not a "credit" in the conventional sense of the word. You can get money back even if you owe little or nothing.

Because Congress has considered cutting back on this program, you should check with an accountant or other tax professional to determine if you are eligible. Obtaining the credit will require that you file the necessary tax returns.

Unemployment Compensation. You should always think about unemployment compensation when you have lost your job for any reason or when your hours have been significantly reduced. You should apply as quickly as possible after your employment is terminated or reduced.

The most common scenario for unemployment benefits follows a layoff. Benefits may not be available if you have been fired for cause or if you voluntarily quit. However, you may still be eligible for benefits even if your employer told you that you are fired rather than laid off. Similarly, you may qualify in some circumstances even if you quit your job. In general, it can't hurt to apply, although if you were fired or if you quit, you may first want to learn more about your state's benefit program.

Some lawyers and other professionals specialize in this area. In addition, there are several books and pamphlets available which discuss unemployment compensation. Call the personnel office of your former company, the state labor department, or the division of state unemployment. If you are a union member, ask the union if it provides help with unemployment compensation applications.

To expedite your receipt of unemployment benefits, assemble and bring all relevant documents to the *first* appointment.

Applying for Unemployment Compensation: The First Appointment. To expedite the award and receipt of unemployment benefits, you should assemble and bring all relevant documents to the first appointment, including *at least*: a Social Security card, a driver's license and other identification, a lay-off notice if you received one, and your four most recent pay-stubs. At the first appointment, you should be prepared to describe accurately the nature and cause of job termination or reduction.

This description should be worded carefully. Stating that the reason for leaving employment was voluntary will lead to denial of benefits. If you left work in anticipation of layoff or discharge, you should carefully set out the reasons why the lay-off or discharge was not voluntary.

Unemployment compensation applications can be denied if the state employee taking down the information misinterprets the reasons given for the discharge, and if you sign the statement as true without carefully reading and correcting it. For example, your statement that a supervisor began to verbally harass you and finally told you to leave and not return might be recorded incorrectly as: "The worker was verbally abusive and fired for cause." You should not sign this statement.

Steps to Take When Unemployment Compensation Benefits Are Denied. Unemployment Compensation can be denied for a variety of reasons, including that your employer is not covered by unemployment insurance laws, you were discharged for cause, or that you quit without a good reason. You can contest denial of unemployment benefits by requesting an administrative hearing. You should do so as soon as you receive a denial, because there are tight and strictly enforced deadlines.

After a hearing, if the claim is still denied, additional appeals are possible. Always make sure you meet the required deadlines. It may be wise to consult someone with experience in the unemployment compensation process after you file the papers, but before any hearing on appeal.

Food Stamps. If you are experiencing severe financial problems, food stamps can supplement your monthly food budget. To qualify, you must be below certain strictly enforced income limits which vary by family size. Emergency food stamps may be available in certain circumstances. Normally, applications will be taken by the welfare office in or near your community, although applications may be available by mail.

Food stamp offices may require the following documentation:

1. Identity and social security number of household members
2. Gross income and proof of income
3. Address (unless you are homeless, a migrant farm worker, or recently relocated)
4. Proof of age
5. Proof of the amount of your utility, rent, mortgage and other shelter expenses
6. Dependent care expenses
7. Medical expenses, and
8. Receipt of disability benefits.

Sometimes food stamp workers improperly deny a food stamps application because of their confusion about eligibility requirements or because of arithmetical mistakes. Do not take an initial rejection as final. Consider taking an appeal before the required time deadline expires.

Program requirements are subject to change. For more detailed information on the program, you may want to review program manuals and regulations, pamphlets available from the welfare office, or seek help from an advocate who specializes in food stamps.

Other Food Programs. Other programs for assistance with food may be available in your community. If your family includes a pregnant woman or a child under five, you should inquire about assistance from the Women, Infants and Children (WIC) program. Typically, WIC is administered by local public health departments and provides vouchers for supplemental foods important to the health of mothers and to the early development of their children. Eligibility for this program is based on family income and on whether the women, infants or children in the family are at nutritional risk. Welfare offices or health departments can provide information about WIC.

Many unions, churches and community groups have community cupboards or food pantries that distribute food for home preparation. Churches and social service organizations such as the Salvation Army maintain cafeterias to which families can turn. These programs can be located by contacting local church offices, United Way offices, or other social service agencies.

Other Welfare Programs. At present, all states administer Aid to Families with Dependent Children (AFDC) programs. States have great flexibility in setting eligibility requirements and benefit levels. A universal requirement is that the family include children — usually below the age of 18.

Application for AFDC can be made at a local welfare office, sometimes called a department of public assistance, department of social services, or department of human services. As with other programs, extensive documentation is requested.

If you qualify for the program, the amount of your benefits will be based on your other income and family size as well as certain other factors in some states. Job training or work requirements may also apply.

Some states have other emergency assistance or other welfare programs. Many states also have local General Assistance or General Relief programs. Benefits and eligibility requirements vary tremendously among states, but the programs are usually available only to people who are ineligible for any other form of assistance, and who have few or no resources.

Some general assistance programs cover only certain categories, such as children or the disabled. Some programs provide benefits for only a limited number of months each year. Most programs require that employable people participate in a work or job search program. Local legal services offices can provide more information about these programs.

Other Emergency Programs. Some states and communities have other emergency funds available to help with basic needs, such as food, shelter, medical care, clothing, or transportation. Often, these programs provide vouchers rather than direct cash.

Private social service groups and charitable and religious organizations sometimes have small funds available that provide limited grants or short-term loans to families lacking other available resources. The Salvation Army is a valuable resource in many communities, as are shelters and crisis centers.

Public and private funds are often difficult to locate. Some are listed in the social services section of the phone book. In many communities, one agency serves as an information clearinghouse or referral service for various sources of assistance.

Social Security and SSI Benefits. Although workers are eligible to receive Social Security benefits at age 62, many workers postpone receipt of these benefits because they will be eligible for larger monthly payments at a later date. While this strategy may make sense when the family's financial resources are adequate, it does not in a time of financial distress.

If you are age 62 or over, you may be eligible for Social Security benefits. The survivors of an insured worker may also be eligible for Social Security benefits upon the worker's death.

Social Security benefits are available only for those who have been employed a sufficient number of years in covered jobs, that is jobs contributing to the Social Security fund. Those aged 65 or over not eligible for Social Security may still be eligible for Supplemental Security Income (SSI). This is a federal program open to those whose income and assets are under established guidelines. Applications for Social Security and SSI, if you did not receive one in the mail, can be made at your local Social Security office.

Disability Benefits. You may also be legally entitled to Social Security disability benefits. Disabilities take many forms. Illnesses, physical and mental limitations, extreme pain, and depression or anxiety all qualify as disabilities. To qualify, the impairment or combination of impairments has to have lasted or be expected to last a year or more, and has to prevent you from engaging in substantial gainful activity in light of your age, education, and work experience.

Federal disability benefits are paid by the Social Security Administration. Social Security is a federally administered program, separate from the other public assistance programs discussed here. Applications are made at local Social Security offices.

If your past employment record does not qualify you for Social Security disability benefits, you can apply for SSI disability benefits. SSI is the federal Supplemental Security Income program for individuals whose income and assets fall below established guidelines.

Many applicants are initially denied disability benefits. You should fill out papers required to appeal at each stage and consider contacting a lawyer who specializes in disability benefit cases.

Workers Compensation. If you were seriously injured on the job, or if you suffer from serious job-related medical conditions, it is likely that you are entitled to workers compensation benefits. These may include medical benefits and monthly income payments until you are able to go back to work. If you are a union member, the union may help you qualify. Otherwise contact the worker's compensation board in your state directly. Your doctor's assistance in this process will be helpful. If you are having difficulties qualifying, you may wish to contact a lawyer specializing in workers compensation cases.

Child Support. You may be owed back child support by an ex-spouse. If you cannot obtain an attorney to press your claim for child support, a state agency should be able to help in the collection attempt. Contact the local welfare office to see which state agency assists families in the collection of child support and what type of assistance they can offer.

MEDICAL AND DENTAL CARE

Affording medical and dental care may be a significant problem when you are experiencing financial problems. This section provides advice on obtaining low cost and free care. How to handle back-due medical and dental bills is explored in other chapters, particularly Chapters One and Five.

Keeping Your Health Insurance After Losing Your Job. Ordinary preventive medical care, particularly dental care, tends to be postponed during times of crisis. Nevertheless, families sometimes suddenly confront large, unplanned medical expenses, and are caught with no medical insurance. Such nightmares can sometimes be prevented, particularly if you have just been laid off.

Within thirty days of being laid-off (unless the union or employment contract provides different terms), you should receive a notice from your former employer's health insurance company stating that your insurance has been terminated. The notice should specify a time period during which you can convert to an individual policy without any lapse in coverage.

If you can afford to pay the premium to convert to an individual family policy, you should do so, particularly if someone in your family has an existing medical condition requiring care. Often the only way to avoid restrictions on coverage of a pre-existing condition is to maintain coverage with the existing insurer.

Unpaid doctor and hospital bills should not prevent you from getting free or low cost medical and dental care.

Medicaid. If it is not possible to maintain private health insurance coverage, consider applying for a state or federally funded medical assistance program, known in many states as Medicaid. Qualification for Medicaid varies from state to state, but hinges on available family income and resources.

Medicaid pays the physician, the pharmacist, and any other service provider directly. Many states have co-payment systems, in which the Medicaid patient pays a small amount, usually only a few dollars, toward the service. Under current federal law, states must provide certain mandatory services, including inpatient hospital care, physician services, and skilled nursing services. States cannot deny service because of an individual's condition, although they can control service through a medical necessity review. A determination that a service is not medically necessary can be appealed.

States must also pay for transportation to necessary medical care. Optional services, which some states choose to cover, include prescription drugs, eyeglasses, dental care, psychiatric services, and private nursing. Most states provide lists of the services they cover.

As with other assistance programs, applications and information about medical assistance are available at local welfare offices. If benefits are initially denied, remember to exercise your appeal rights.

Other Medical Care Options. For applicants not qualified for Medicaid or for state medical assistance, Catastrophic Medical Assistance is available in some states to assist with major medical expenses. When medical bills exceed a certain percentage of an applicant's household income, the balance of the bill above that percentage is reimbursed.

Some hospitals have an obligation to provide free care to certain patients under either state or federal law. And all hospitals and doctors have an ethical obligation to deal with medical emergencies. In a crisis, you should use the emergency room of your local hospital and worry about the bill later.

Local service clubs also sometimes have programs designed to meet particular needs. The best known is the Lions Club, which helps to purchase eyeglasses for children.

Medical Prescriptions. Several options are available for families unable to obtain prescription drugs through Medicaid. Any patient receiving a prescription should ask whether or not a less expensive generic drug can be substituted. Doctors may have free sample supplies of medication available if you explain your hardship.

Additionally, most drug companies run programs which provide free medication for those in need. Find out the name of the company which makes the drug you need, and call telephone information for that company's "800" phone number. Call the company to ask whether there is a program for reduced cost or free supply of prescribed medication. You will have to document your need. Emergency one-time grants or small loans for drug prescriptions also can sometimes be obtained from private social service agencies or church organizations.

Low Cost Dental Care. Dental care often takes a back seat to more pressing financial obligations. However, there are several ways that families can obtain free emergency dental care or low-cost preventive care. First, some types of dental care are covered by health or dental insurance. Some dental coverage is included in Medicaid. Second, if neither insurance nor

Medicaid is available, many community college dental hygiene programs and university dental schools provide services for free or at negligible cost as part of their teaching programs. Some hospitals have low-cost oral surgery clinics.

SOME OPTIONS FOR
REDUCING YOUR EXPENSES

Everyone's expense needs are different. We are not going to suggest all of the ways you might consider economizing. However, we will list a dozen tips about possible expense reductions which are often overlooked by consumers. A combination of these savings can reduce your expense budget by several hundred dollars a month.

1. Real Estate Tax Reductions. If you own a home, many communities have a variety of real estate tax abatements, deferrals and hardship repayment plans. Most states have an abatement for older homeowners and many have a deferral process for people facing financial hardship. Less than half of those eligible take advantage of available real estate tax reductions.

2. Utility Conservation Measures. If you pay for your own utilities, you may be paying too much. Look into utility conservation assistance programs, many of which are offered free by utility companies. In addition, many books and pamphlets offer valuable tips. These can lower your utility costs by one half to one third. A variety of options to reduce your utility costs are discussed in Chapter Fourteen.

3. Reduce Your Telephone Expenses. Look into your telephone calling plan. You may want to change your local billing method or comparison shop among competing companies for long distance service. The types of calls you make and times you are likely to use the phone can greatly affect what type of calling plan works best for you. These issues are discussed in more detail below in Chapter Fourteen.

4. Reevaluate Your Homeowner's Insurance Needs. Many people pay more than necessary for their homeowner's insurance. If your property value has decreased, or if you are insuring for a value which includes the cost of the land your home is on, you are paying too much for homeowner's insurance. You also can consider eliminating unnecessary coverages or applying for special rate programs (such as reductions for using a smoke detector). Check with your agent; you may be able to cut your annual bill by hundreds of dollars.

5. Reevaluate Your Other Insurance Needs. Look into your life insurance and other coverages with the help of a trustworthy insurance agent. It helps for the agent to understand the nature of your financial problems. You may consider dropping optional coverages until your financial problems are solved. You might also consider converting a whole life policy to a term life policy in order to save money. Some policies may be "capped" or may include an option for deferring payments for a temporary period. Your auto insurance coverage is another area where it may be possible to save. Are all your coverages required in order to operate your car? Do you qualify for any savings plans?

6. Eliminate Discretionary Purchases. Although you will have to continue to pay for necessities, discretionary items can be eliminated from your monthly budget temporarily. Each purchase has to be evaluated to determine if it is more important to you than saving your home or car.

7. School-Related Expenses. If you have children in private school, you may have to consider a change during a period when you are experiencing financial problems. Private schools are expensive and public schools are free. If you decide to switch, you can tell your children that you had to choose between changing schools or loss of the family home. Family counseling may help with these difficult transitions. If you feel your children must stay in private school, you may want to speak with a school official or a financial aid officer. Special assistance programs may be available for families having temporary financial difficulties.

8. Religious Expenses and Charitable Contributions. If you are having financial problems and religious expenses are stretching your budget, consider talking to your priest, minister, rabbi, or imam. More often than not, special efforts will be made to help you through a tough financial time without affecting your membership or standing in the community.

9. Sliding Scale Community Services. Many community-based social service programs offer assistance for free or on a sliding scale. Low cost counseling on a variety of issues is widely available if you are persistent in looking for it. These programs are designed to help people in your situation in a confidential and effective way. You should not be embarrassed to get help.

10. Public Transportation vs. Driving. Automobiles can be very expensive. Between car payments, gas, repairs, and insurance, an automobile is some communities can be as expensive as a home. If you can find a way to get by without a car temporarily or permanently, you may find that you save many hundreds of dollars a month.

11. Unnecessary Payroll Deductions. If your income has gone down, you may be having excessive amounts deducted from your pay check for taxes. Check with your employer, or with an accountant if necessary. Similarly, you may have agreed to a payroll deduction for any one of a variety of reasons when things were going well. Check to see if these deductions can be eliminated.

12. Adult Children Living at Home. You may feel a great deal of obligation to dependents who share your home with you. However, if that person has income, it is certainly fair to ask for a contribution to the household expenses. Alternatively, it may be time to politely ask that person to find somewhere else to live permanently or temporarily. If you continue to pay the expenses of persons who can manage on their own, this may stretch your budget to the point that everyone loses their home.

DIPPING INTO SAVINGS AND SELLING YOUR ASSETS

You may have a lump sum of money in a savings account, a mutual fund account, a certificate of deposit, or a retirement account which you feel you can use to get you through a tough financial time. Similarly, you may have stocks, bonds, or other valuable property that you could sell to raise cash. It may be a good idea to sell assets which are easy to liquidate, like stocks and bonds, in order to give yourself more flexibility for meeting urgent financial needs. Sale of other non-essential valuable assets, like vacation homes and extra cars or even antique furniture and heirlooms, should be considered over the long haul. It is sometimes better to make a difficult choice in order to raise cash, rather than to lose everything.

There are several things you should keep in mind about using savings or selling off assets when you are having financial problems:

1. Think Carefully Before Spending Your Retirement Money. You may be tempted to dip into your retirement savings to get you through temporary financial difficulties. The most important consideration is whether you will have time to rebuild this savings so that you can live comfortably in retirement. If you are close to retirement age, you should look carefully at whether there are other ways to manage your financial difficulties which will allow you get over a difficult period with your retirement plan intact. On the other hand, if you are young and likely to have many productive years before retirement, use of retirement funds may make sense, if it helps you avoid loss of property or other hardship.

2. Using Your Savings or Selling Off Assets Should Be Part of an Overall Plan, Not Your Only Plan. If your income does not cover your expenses, you will need to use your savings or proceeds of an asset sale carefully. You should not use this money to finance an unreasonable lifestyle. For this reason, do not spend savings or other assets before evaluating your budget and cutting back on expenses. Your savings will go much farther if they are applied to the pared down expenses which you find essential to prevent true hardship.

3. Usually You Should Not Use Savings or Other Assets to Pay Low Priority Debts. This is because you may have more pressing needs before your financial circumstances get better. If your income does not meet basic expenses, your savings are a valuable resource which you should use only to protect important property or to pay for other necessities. You should not be pressured into using essential savings or your remaining assets to pay off your credit card bills or to get involved in a "get rich quick scam." Priority of debts is discussed in Chapter One.

4. Taking Loans Against Savings May Be a Bad Idea. Unless you can borrow money at a very low interest rate, borrowing against savings will be a losing proposition because you will be paying higher interest charges on the loan than you earn on your savings. This will eat into your budget (or your savings) more quickly then just spending down the savings account.

5. Spending Savings or Other Assets in a Lump Sum, Versus Spending Down Part Each Month to Meet Ongoing Expenses.

One difficult question you will face is how best to use your savings or the proceeds of an asset sale, in making your plan to manage your financial problems. You should consider two choices.

Some people use a set amount of their savings each month in their monthly budget to meet essential expenses. This can be the right choice if you have good discipline and if the savings will make the difference between meeting your essential expenses and falling hopelessly behind. As discussed above, you should not fall into the trap of using your savings to finance an unrealistic lifestyle. You will only postpone the day of reckoning.

The other choice about savings or other assets is to spend them in a lump sum for a particular purpose, like paying down a mortgage default. This choice may be necessary in order to postpone a catastrophic loss of property to foreclosure or repossession. However, you should be careful not to make this choice unless you have a longer term plan to get back on your feet. Paying many thousands of dollars on a mortgage to keep a home you cannot afford in the long term may be a waste of money.

In addition, if you plan to use savings to make a large payment on an existing mortgage or a car loan, you should probably avoid paying ahead. Use the saving to get caught up, and then keep any extra money to make future payments as they come due. This will give you more flexibility for the future.

If you feel you must pay ahead, make sure to make clear to the creditor in writing that you are paying future installments rather than contributing a lump sum toward the principal. Although in good financial times it may be a good idea to pay down principal due on a debt in order to reduce total interest payments, the opposite is true if you are having financial difficulties. A lump sum paid on the principal will not excuse you from future payments unless the loan is fully paid off. That is, even after you pay a lump sum as an advance on the principal, the next monthly or weekly payment will be due as scheduled. You will be in default if you do not pay it. Paying future installments rather than a lump sum toward principal also avoids prepayment penalties.

6. Do Not Talk About Your Savings with Bill Collectors. You should not tell bill collectors that you have savings. (That is, you should not tell those collecting on credit cards or other unsecured debts. On the other hand, you may need to let the bank which holds your mortgage or car loan know about your savings as part of a workout plan, as discussed in Chapters Ten and Fifteen.) Your choice about how to deal with your financial problems is personal. Bill collectors may use knowledge about your savings accounts in order to garnish the accounts or to pressure you into making wrong choices. More about dealing with bill collectors and protecting your savings from garnishment is included in Chapters Five and Seven.

> ### Never tell those collecting on credit card
> ### or other unsecured debt that you have savings,
> ### and don't use such savings to pay them.

7. How Best to Sell Off Assets. If there is an established market to sell certain of your assets quickly, such as most stocks and bonds, you can delay until you need money urgently to sell this type of property. For other types of property that is harder to sell, it is usually best to avoid panic sales at the last minute. Urgency will usually reduce the sale price. Plan ahead and try to get the best price possible by using the most common means that similar property is sold.

As discussed in Chapter Three, you should avoid pawn shops and other fringe businesses which buy or make loans on property. These companies are in the business of making money off your emergency need for cash.

DEALING WITH PRESSURES
CAUSED BY A TIGHT BUDGET

Financial difficulties can be emotionally draining. It is not uncommon for pressures to build up within families, which cause quarrels, temporary separations, or even divorce. Some studies document increases in physical abuse associated with money problems. As you make the difficult choices associated with your financial problems, you should be aware of the emotional pressures which may be building.

Mental health counseling, family therapy, and marriage counseling may be useful for managing the stress of financial problems. If you have health insurance, your policy may include free or low-cost mental health assistance. It can't hurt to ask your doctor. This type of assistance is also usually available from a variety of organizations on a sliding scale fee basis or for free. Call a local credit counseling agency or family services for a reference. You can also call and ask a therapist about low cost or free mental health counseling options available in the community.

Everyone has financial problems at one time or another. You should not be embarrassed to talk about your difficulties, either to seek help from a friend, or in the more formal process of therapy. Whatever course you choose, it is important that you remain aware of the additional stress you may be feeling and that you try to deal with it in the healthiest possible way.

As you struggle to get past your financial difficulties, keep in mind that better days will come. With careful planning to minimize short term hardship and some patience, you can put yourself in the best possible position to get a fresh start and to recover good financial health.

— 3 —

Choices That Could Get You Into Trouble

If you are in financial distress, you may feel pressured by creditors to repay them at all cost and you may have urgent needs to purchase items you cannot afford. Earlier chapters have described various effective techniques to make ends meet. This chapter lists seventeen options you should avoid. These options will only make matters worse.

Be particularly wary of anyone who advertises or solicits you with schemes to reduce your financial problems. These are usually scams or bad deals.

Some of these mistakes are steps you might be tempted to take out of a sense of desperation. But many of these mistakes will not be your idea, but rather choices some one else is trying to pressure you to take. Often unscrupulous businesses exploit people who have financial problems, believing that these people make desperate or poorly informed choices. These companies also know that people who feel that their options are limited are likely to be willing to overpay for credit and other services.

Unfortunately, even reputable companies have gotten into businesses which take advantage of consumers in financial trouble. You cannot assume that because a company is well known or because it advertises on TV that it will give you a fair deal. Also be leery of companies that use names which are designed to create confusion about their identity, such as using the name

"United States." Other companies use names very similar to legitimate organizations, such as calling themselves the AARC, instead of AARP.

This chapter lists a number of scams. However, new scams constantly arise and old ones change form. Whenever you deal with services aimed at people with bad credit or other financial problems, you need to be careful that you are getting good value for your money. When in doubt, just say no.

1. Bouncing Checks. It may be tempting to write a check when you know that you have insufficient funds in your account to cover it. At best, you may hope to make a deposit before the check is cashed. At worst, you may be deliberately using the check as a way to make the creditor temporarily happy.

However, bouncing checks is never the answer. Not only will you be charged a fee by the bank and by the creditor which will put you in a deeper hole, but you will open yourself up to criminal prosecution for false pretenses or fraud. If criminally prosecuted, you will have a number of possible defenses, but it is far better not to have to deal with this problem at all.

Whenever you are in doubt, ascertain your balance with the bank before writing a check. Remember that you may have written other checks that have not yet been deducted from your account. If you have a joint account, coordinate your check-writing carefully with any other person who has power to write checks and make withdrawals.

2. Post-Dating Checks. A post-dated check is one dated later than the date on which the check was written, with the expectation that it will not be cashed until that later date. Usually this is done with the hope there will be sufficient funds in the account by the time the check is cashed.

Never give a creditor a post-dated check. Even if you believe that you will have the money in your account to pay the check by that date, you may be wrong because something unexpected could happen. If that happens, you will bounce the check or you will not have the money for something else that is more important. Additionally, creditors occasionally deposit checks before their due date, and while this may be improper, it will cause you substantial problems. Finally, if you have given a post-dated check and later change your mind about paying that debt, stopping payment is difficult and expensive.

Creditors often encourage you to write post-dated checks as a collection tactic — often demanding that a check be dated with your payday. They want your check in hand as a way to get their money. You should resist the urge to give in to pressure to do this. You can offer instead to deliver the check on the day you write it — a day on which you have sufficient funds in your account. This preserves your choice not to deliver the check if your priorities change or you do not later have enough money in the account.

3. Selling or Giving Away a Creditor's Collateral. You may have property which serves as collateral for a loan from one of your creditors. A common example is a car which serves as collateral for your car loan.

It is a bad idea to deliberately sell or give away collateral, especially if you are experiencing financial problems. In some parts of the country, people are criminally prosecuted for "conversion" of collateral — meaning that you intentionally prevented a creditor from collecting its debt by disposing of the creditor's property.

If you have already lost, given away, or sold collateral, and if you are prosecuted by a state official or sued by the creditor, there are many defenses to such a suit. The most important defense is that your conduct was not intentional. In most cases, this means that you did not understand that the property was collateral or that you did know the consequences to the creditor of disposing of the property. In addition, most such prosecutions and lawsuits can be ended by payment of the value of the collateral either in installments or in a lump sum if you have it. Given overcrowding in most prisons and the technical nature of the supposed crime, jail time is rarely or never imposed.

4. Giving Away Property to Protect It From Creditors. If you are in debt and you have valuable property to protect from your creditors, it may occur to you to give it away to a friend or relative, or to sell it for a small percentage of its real value to someone who will later return it. Some people believe that this will protect the property from judgment liens and other creditor collection.

There are a variety of potential pitfalls in these types of property transfers. When you transfer property when your other assets are insufficient to pay your debts, creditors can have the transfer voided under your state's law concerning "fraudulent transfers" or "fraudulent conveyances."

To void the transfer, the creditor will have to bring a legal action, and this may delay or prevent the creditor's seizure of the property. But, if the creditor does challenge your transfer, this will increase the amount you owe the creditor. The creditor is also likely to sue the person to whom you have transferred the property. You also may have to pay additional damages and you can lose your right to bankruptcy protection. In rare cases, you could be criminally prosecuted.

A fraudulent transfer may be different than exemption planning. Generally, only certain types of property are exempt from seizure under your state's laws. Through exemption planning, you keep the total value of all of your property, but trade one type of property that is not exempt for another type that is. For example, the money in your bank account may not be exempt from seizure, but you could take that money and purchase a life insurance policy which is exempt from seizure. Small transfers of this type are usually acceptable, but state laws on these issues vary a great deal. You may wish to obtain expert advice before engaging in exemption planning.

5. Misleading Your Creditors. It is a bad idea to lie or mislead your creditors. However, you have no obligation to tell a debt collector anything, and in general it is a bad idea to give a debt collector too much information about your circumstances. The best rule of thumb is to refuse to answer any prying questions. For example, if you tell a debt collector too much about a new job, the collector may use that information to harass you at work. If you tell a debt collector about your bank account, it may use that information to seize money in the account after the collector obtains a judgment against you.

An exception to the rule of not volunteering information to creditors applies when you try to work out a deal with a creditor for a temporary change in loan terms, for installment payments in lieu of the creditor seizing your property, or for similar purposes. In those instances, the creditor will want and is entitled to information about your circumstances. When you are asking for help from a creditor, provide that creditor with accurate information.

Lying or misleading that creditor can not only get you into serious trouble for fraud, but also undermine the creditor's confidence in working with you to reach a mutually acceptable solution. Since much of the information you give to a creditor can be independently verified, your lie will be caught.

Occasionally, you may feel that a creditor wants you to lie in a written statement to qualify for a particular repayment option or refinancing. This is a good sign that the creditor is unscrupulous. The creditor may want a signed statement from you which misrepresents your financial situation for use in a later lawsuit against you if you fail to pay. These types of misstatements can also be used in some cases to prevent you from getting relief in bankruptcy.

6. Pressure-Related Spending Sprees. Some consumers respond perversely to pressure by spending money in irrational ways. Not only does this dig you deeper into debt, but some types of spending for unnecessary items or through cash advances on credit cards can cause problems if you later choose to file bankruptcy. There are counseling groups in many communities which can help you address uncontrollable spending habits. A credit counselor can usually point you in the right direction.

7. Unscrupulous Trade Schools. Many trade schools advertise aggressively that they can teach you a trade which will help you increase your income. Similarly, they claim you do not have to pay for the tuition until you obtain your high paying job, or that you never have to pay because of a government grant.

Many of these schools are rip-offs, and the fact that the school is accredited or approved by a government agency is *no* protection against the school being a fraud. Thousands of sham trade and vocational schools have received accreditation and government approval over the years.

The only sure-fire way of knowing whether a school's training is any good, and that the training will actually lead to a job, is to talk to employers in your area. Make sure you talk to employers you find on your own rather than to people recommended by the school. Ask them whether they would hire a graduate of that school, and, if not, what type of training they would recommend.

Often, a local community college offers the same course at a fraction of the cost. Or employers prefer to train their own people after hiring them at entry level positions. Other times, no short-term course will lead to employment in a particular field because there are no jobs available or because entry qualification requirements are much higher. Be particularly wary of a correspondence school or a school that starts through correspondence lessons and is completed with a residential portion. Find out what percentage of a school's students graduate, and steer away from schools with high drop-out rates.

Make sure you know what the tuition is, because often you will eventually have to repay it with interest. How does that tuition stack up with other alternatives? Find out also what you will have to pay if you drop out after a few weeks — you often have to repay almost all of the tuition.

Too often a trade school, even one with government approval, is a dead end, just getting you deeper into debt.

Making the wrong choice on a vocational school is much more serious than you think. Not only have you wasted valuable time, but you have incurred a loan that must be repaid. As described in Chapter Seventeen, failure to repay student loans can lead to tax refund intercepts, wage garnishment, large collection fees, and more. Perhaps most importantly, failure to repay the loan can make it difficult to obtain additional job training that may really be worthwhile.

8. Rent-to-Own. Rent-to-own has long been directed at people facing financial hardship. In a rent-to-own deal, you are supposedly renting property (usually furniture, electronics or appliances) for a period of time until you qualify for ownership. It is supposedly a way for people who do not qualify for credit to have use of an item while it is being purchased.

There are two major problems with rent-to-own. First, items purchased in this way are very expensive, often costing you more than three times the cash price. For example, a 19-inch color T.V. which costs $250 in the store is likely to sell at rent to own for more than $750 in total payments. On top of that, you may unknowningly have purchased a *used* T.V. that is only worth $150. Effective interest rates on rent-to-own can be over 200% and as high as 1000%.

The second problem with rent-to-own occurs when you can't keep up the payments. If you miss even one payment, the item can be repossessed. You will then lose any equity you have built up in the property. Many people have paid more than $1000 for property worth less then $500 only to lose that property for missing one payment.

If you need to buy furniture, appliances or electronic goods, and you can't immediately afford them, you should look at options besides rent-to-own. The best option may be to save money if at all possible and then to pay cash. Consider selling something you don't need to buy something you do. Also don't assume that you cannot qualify for more conventional credit. Stores may grant credit even to people with a bad credit record or they may have other ways for you to purchase at a reasonable rate of interest. Shop for the best possible cash price and the best possible interest rate.

9. Pawn Shops. For hundreds of years, pawn shops have made small loans in exchange for property. If the loan is not repaid, the pawn shop keeps the property. Pawn shops will always pay you less than the property is worth, so that they can get back their money if you don't pay. They also charge very high interest rates.

If you have valuable property you can live without, consider selling it in a more conventional way for its full value. When you get your financial circumstances back on track, you can buy a replacement.

A new type of "pawn" cropping up in some states is called an "auto pawn" where you borrow money at very high interest rates (for example, 240% or 360%) and put up your car title as collateral for the loan. This is also a bad idea — you can borrow money elsewhere at lower interest rates and without endangering your car.

10. Sale and Lease Back Rip-offs. Another way that some companies and individuals make money is to buy your property from you at a low price, and then to lease that property back to you at a high rental rate. These deals often are targeted at people facing foreclosure or repossession. Some companies get their leads by reading published foreclosure notices.

These businesses are rip-offs. Once you have sold your property to them, you no longer have the rights of an owner. You are likely to be overpaying in rent for something you formerly owned with no real way of getting it back. Additionally, there are many reported cases of fraud involving promises made in connection with these contracts. People have even been talked into transferring title to property without getting anything in return.

11. Auto Brokerage and Subleases. Another practice to avoid involves hiring a broker to sell or sublease your car to another person who will make your loan or lease payments for you. Often the broker arranges the transfer without the permission of your car lender or leasing company, making the deal illegal. In addition, the broker may not pass on the payments to your lender or leasing company. If the new car owner skips with the car, you will be left holding the bag. This form of auto brokerage is illegal in many states.

12. "Hard Money" Lenders. A variety of companies advertise loans supposedly designed for people with bad credit or as requiring no credit check. Other loan companies rely instead on a network of loan brokers to bring them business. These companies make money by lending to people in difficult financial situations on hard terms, including very high interest rates.

There is a whole industry of lenders preying on those in financial trouble, overcharging them and taking unfair advantage.

When you deal with such a lender, expect the lender to engage in some of the following shady practices:

- misrepresenting the loan terms — a 10% loan will turn into a 20% loan at the time of closing;
- making loans which the lender knows you cannot repay in order to seize valuable collateral, such as your home or car;
- charging unacceptably high interest rates;
- refinancing debts which are better off left alone;
- charging high hidden costs;
- paying loan brokers, car dealers and contractors incentives to mislead you about your credit options or to make inappropriate referrals;
- hiding ties to loan brokers in order to charge you illegal commissions;
- making loans on complicated terms, including negative amortization or balloon payments, in order to make an unaffordable loan look temporarily affordable;
- forming alliances with other sleazy businesses to finance

shoddy work or inferior goods, and then to share the profits
from doing so; and
- using high pressure sales tactics designed to get you to agree to
buy credit insurance or other unnecessary "tie-in" products.

Don't be suckered by hard money lenders. They have many techniques
designed to draw you into deals, and then make it almost impossible for
you to back away. You should never agree to refinance a low priority debt,
as discussed in Chapter Four. Ways to avoid refinancing scams are discussed
in more detail in that chapter.

13. Tax Refund Anticipation Loans. Another major scam aimed at
those in financial distress involves loans which are based on your expected
tax refund. The lender may even be the company preparing your tax return.
The loan is for a very short period of time between when your return is filed
with the government and when you would expect to get your tax refund.

For example, you might file a return with the government on March 15.
You would normally expect a refund, if you are entitled to one, within 30
days. In a tax refund anticipation loan, a company will give you the amount
of the refund less a fee on March 15, so that you don't have to wait until
April 15 for your refund check.

The fee you are charged is effectively interest on what amounts to a very
short term loan. Looked at in this way, you may be charged interest at an
annual rate of 200% or more. Some companies may try to fool you about
the annual interest rate by telling you the rate assuming that the company
will not be repaid for two or three months. Since the company is actually
getting the money back in one month, the real interest rate is two or three
times the number you are told. The best advice is to avoid tax refund anticipation loans, and be patient and wait for your full refund if at all possible.

14. Voluntary Wage Assignments. In some states you can voluntarily
assign some of your wages to a particular creditor, meaning your employer
automatically sends some of your paycheck to that creditor. A voluntary
wage assignment is different from a wage garnishment or an assignment
ordered by a court because it is something you do by agreement, rather than
something which is forced on you after a court judgment against you.

Creditors that have no other way to get payment will often pressure you
to agree to a voluntary wage assignment. This is almost always a very bad

choice. The wage assignment leap frogs these creditors ahead of your more pressing debts, such as your rent or mortgage.

If you do want to pay that creditor ahead of other creditors, go ahead and do so, but pay by cash, check or money order. The voluntary assignment will reduce your flexibility, because you will not be able to make other choices for use of that money if the need arises.

15. "For-Profit" Debt Counseling. While debt counseling may be a good idea, it is rarely smart to pay a "for-profit" counselor for this service. Many companies and individuals charge high fees for counseling which are not justified by the help they can offer.

If you choose a debt counseling option, try to find a qualified nonprofit counselor. Although some nonprofits charge a small fee, the fee is almost always less than what a for-profit business charges. Get a recommendation if possible. If you cannot get a recommendation from a friend or relative, try calling your state attorney general, a local legal services program, or a consumer help hotline.

It is not always easy to distinguish between nonprofit and profit-making credit counselors, because profit-making entities may adopt "non-profit" type names, such as "foundation" or "service." A United Way logo on the counselor's letterhead is usually a reliable indication that a counselor is a nonprofit, although not all nonprofit credit counselors are affiliated with the United Way.

It is also very important not to pay anything other than a fee to people who claim they will be able to help you. Some supposed debt counselors will tell you they can make an arrangement on a debt for you if you bring them cash for the creditor, or if you write a check to the counselor which will later be passed on. There are many reported cases of counselors absconding with this money rather than paying your debts.

16. Credit Repair Scams. Credit repair businesses have popped up all over the country, sometimes also going by names such as credit clinics or credit service organizations. These businesses charge unreasonable fees for services which they claim will help you improve your credit. At best, these business are charging you for work you can do yourself for free. More often, they are making promises to improve your credit which they cannot hope to keep. At worst, they will get you involved with rip-off businesses or even, in some cases, in schemes which can later cause you serious legal problems.

More discussion of credit repair is included in Chapter Six, including some simple steps you can take on your own behalf.

17. The Truth About the Lottery. People facing financial difficulties sometimes look to the lottery as a way to improve their financial situation. This is an expensive long shot at best. Spending substantial money on the lottery or other gambling can greatly compound your financial problems.

The lottery pays out only a percentage of the money it takes in. The percentage in some states is one half or less. This means that for every twenty dollars spent on lottery tickets, you are likely to win back only ten.

Very few people win big prizes. The chance of winning a million dollars is far less than one in a million. While you are experiencing financial difficulties, it is best to reduce or eliminate your expenses on the lottery, rather than to look at it as a way to solve your problems.

— 4 —

Refinancing Do's and Don'ts

• Twelve Simple Refinancing Rules
• Deciding When and When Not to Refinance
• Reverse Mortgages
• Refinancing Scams to Avoid

Refinancing is a process in which you pay off one or more existing debts with a new loan. It is sometimes suggested as a good way for people with financial problems to address their difficulties.

We recommend that you be very careful when refinancing debts. Refinancing an unaffordable amount of debt is one of the most tempting but risky steps you can take when you have financial problems. Many refinancing loans will hurt you more than they help.

Refinancing's attraction is that it seems to resolve your financial problems even though your income and your expenses do not change. The stroke of a pen pays off creditors who have been threatening action against you. After refinancing, you only have to make one monthly payment to a new creditor who is not (yet) threatening anything.

The disadvantages of refinancing are often hidden. Problems occur because of the complex mathematics which sometimes govern the refinancing process, including hidden fees and costs, and because the new loan may give the creditor new ways to force payment and seize your property that were unavailable under the prior loan. There are even times when a refinancing deal is nothing more than a scam to steal your home or other property. Each potential refinancing deal must be reviewed carefully on its merits based on the principles discussed in this chapter.

TWELVE SIMPLE
REFINANCING RULES

1. When in Doubt, Do Not Refinance or Consolidate Debts.
Refinancing deals almost always come with significant costs. These costs will usually just make matters worse in the long term.

2. Do Not Let Debt Collectors Pressure You Into Refinancing.
Debt collectors may try to scare you into refinancing because they have no other way to get their money. Better ways to address debt collection harassment are discussed in Chapter Five.

3. Never (or Almost Never) Refinance Unsecured Debt Into Secured Debt.
For example, do not take out a mortgage on your home to pay off credit card or medical bills. Unsecured creditors rarely can do anything to seriously hurt you if you fail to pay. By trading in such a loan for a mortgage loan, you face loss of your home if you continue to have financial problems. Do not refinance unsecured debt into secured debt even if this allows you to lower the interest rate you are paying.

4. Do Not Refinance Utility Debts.
Work something out with the utility company instead; most utility companies have flexible repayment plans. Even if this is unavailable, it will almost always be cheaper to get the utility turned back on then it will be to pay the refinanced debt. For more information on utility bills, see Chapter Fourteen.

5. If You Have an Existing Debt With a Finance Company or High-Rate Second Mortgage Company, Do Not Refinance that Debt With the Same Company.
Ask the company to agree to lower payments on the existing loan, but do not allow the creditor to refinance that loan, which may involve prepayment penalties, new closing costs, and perhaps even a higher interest rate. Never allow the company to add new security — such as your home.

6. Do Not Turn Your Car Loan Into a Second Mortgage Unless You Would Rather Lose Your Home Than Your Car.
Repossession is bad, but foreclosure is worse.

7. Do Not Refinance a Loan with Household Goods Collateral into a Second Mortgage Loan. Not only is your home worth more than your household goods, but it is very hard for a lender to repossess your household goods. See Chapter Sixteen.

8. Do Not Refinance Low Interest With Higher Interest Loans. The "APR" (Annual Percentage Rate) of the new loan must be lower than the *stated interest rate* of the old loan, that is the rate stated in the note, or you will be losing money. You have already paid for certain up-front fees in the old loan, and the new loan with those fees (and also insurance, closing costs, and other up-front fees not treated as interest) must be cheaper than the old loan after those fees have been paid off.

9. Do Not Include Your Long-Term First Mortgage in a Refinancing Package. Do not let second mortgage lenders pay off your first mortgage and give you a new mortgage equal to the first mortgage plus the new loan amount. The only exception is if the new mortgage is for the equivalent length of time and the interest rate is significantly *lower* than the old first mortgage — to offset prepayment penalties and fees and charges.

10. Do Not Refinance Loans When You Have Valid Legal Reasons Not to Pay That Debt. If you have a legal defense to repayment of a debt, you can raise that defense in court. If you refinance with a new lender, the defense will not be available against the new creditor. You should get legal help to see if you have a valid defense *before* entering the refinancing deal.

11. Watch Out for Scam Refinancing Companies. Refinancing involves great potential for hidden costs, fees, even hidden collateral, and other unfair loan terms. Even some reputable lenders make unfair refinancing deals. When in doubt, get help in reviewing the loan *before* you sign anything. You can walk away from a bad deal even at the last minute. A lender that is unwilling to let you get outside help should not be trusted. Another way to avoid scams is never to let a contractor or salesperson arrange financing for you and be wary of mortgage brokers. Unfortunately, many brokers find refinancing deals which involve big commissions for them rather than good loans in your best interest.

12. You Can Cancel Any Refinancing Deal That Involves a Mortgage on Your Home. In most refinancings in which you give the lender a mortgage, federal law gives you the right to cancel for any reason for three days after the date you sign the papers. If you change your mind about taking out the loan, make sure you cancel in writing before the deadline. You can, but need not, use the cancellation form provided by the lender.

DECIDING WHEN
TO REFINANCE

As summarized by the twelve rules described above, many refinancings are bad deals that will make matters worse for you. This section goes into more detail about the factors you must consider before deciding to refinance your debt. The rule of thumb is that when in doubt, do not refinance even if you are behind on a debt.

Unsecured and Secured Debts. Most debts are called "unsecured." This means that a home, car, or other property is *not* collateral for the loan. Good examples of unsecured debt are hospital and doctor bills, lawyer bills, and most credit card debt. Utility debt is also unsecured. As described in Chapters One and Five, you have relatively little to fear from non-payment of your unsecured debts. To recover anything, the creditor will have to go to court, and even then may have difficulty collecting.

It is almost always a bad idea to refinance unsecured debt into secured debt, such as happens when you use a home equity line of credit or a second mortgage to refinance your debt. When you put up your home, car, or other property as collateral on a loan, this is a secured loan and the creditor has a "security interest" in your property. Secured debt will pose serious problems for you if you get behind in payments because the creditor has the right to quickly seize the collateral.

Also do not "trade up" on security. For example, do not refinance a car loan into a second mortgage, or turn a loan secured by household items (which creditors rarely if ever seize) into a home mortgage loan.

Be sure to look at the loan documents and disclosure statements in any refinancing to see what property you are putting up as collateral. These documents will describe whether you are giving the creditor a "security interest" in any of your property.

Utility Bills. Utility debts should not be refinanced. While you do not want your heat or electricity shut off, there are many preferable ways to prevent a utility termination or to get service turned back on (see Chapter Fourteen) than to refinance your utility debt with a new lender.

Refinancing a utility debt can begin a downward spiral. If you are having trouble paying the utility bills, refinancing these low or no interest debts will not improve matters. Instead, you will have to pay both the *old* bills now refinanced and your current monthly utility bills. Particularly unwise is folding a utility debt into a home mortgage debt. Not only are you paying more in interest, but the risk in the event of default is much more serious. Even if you are facing shut-off, there are always better ways to deal with the back debt than to refinance.

If you are having trouble making ends meet, *never* refinance low interest or unsecured debt into high interest debt or debt that takes a mortgage on your home.

Low Cost vs. High Cost Credit. When you are having financial problems, refinancings or loan consolidation often converts low cost loans into high cost loans. This makes these debts more unaffordable for you. Many of your existing bills charge you *no* interest or charge only minimal late charges. A mortgage loan you took out to purchase your home also usually has a relatively low interest rate.

Refinanced loans, on the other hand, will often be high cost loans. Not only will the stated interest rate be high, but the creditor will assess points, closing costs, insurance charges, maybe even broker's fees or hidden charges. In addition, the loans you are paying off may include penalties for early payment (prepayment penalties).

One way of determining the real cost of the new loan is to look at the "disclosure statement" explaining all the terms for the new loan. The federal Truth-in-Lending law requires that creditors provide this statement before you sign the loan papers. You should look at the APR (annual percentage rate) of the new loan rather than the amount of the payments.

Lenders have numerous ways to make payments look artificially low, even when the loan is at a very high cost to you. For example, in some variable rate loans, your monthly payments will climb after the first several months. Monthly payments will also be artificially low when there is a large, lump sum "balloon" payment at the end of the loan. Similarly, some loans require monthly payments that are less than the monthly interest due so that the principal amount keeps going up even though you keep on making payments (this is called negative amortization). Other times you will pay high closing costs and up front fees, but not realize this because they are deducted from your loan amount.

You should examine all of the loan terms before you sign any papers. Do not look at the monthly payment as the only issue. If loan terms are not favorable, shop around for another loan. You can always walk away from signing loan papers, even at the very last minute. Definitely walk away if the lender tries to change loan terms from what you had been originally offered. Remember also that if you have to put up your principal residence as collateral for a refinancing, federal law allows you to cancel the loan *for any reason* up to three days after signing the loan.

Here are some items to look at in the loan's disclosure statement. What is the Annual Percentage Rate or "APR" (that is, the interest rate)? What is "the finance charge" (the total interest payments over the life of the loan)? You can compare these amounts to the costs of your existing debts as well as to alternative loans.

The "amount financed" is supposed to be the money the creditor is giving you. However, often much of the amount financed never goes to you or to pay off your obligations, but instead goes to purchase credit insurance or to pay various fees and charges. You will need to carefully review the disbursements or "itemization of amount financed" in order to identify fees and costs being paid to others. As far as you are concerned, the amounts going to credit insurance, attorney fees,closing costs, etc. are really part of the finance charge, making the true interest rate higher than the stated rate.

If you are unclear about the distribution of the loan funds, request an itemization of the amount financed which will explain where your money is going and why. If this statement is different from what you expected, walk away from the loan. Most importantly, ask questions or seek professional help to review the paperwork if the loan terms are unclear to you.

The "payment schedule" shows not only the amount of your first payment, but also describes the ways that your monthly payments may change. Make sure all of the payments on the loan will be affordable. Do not rely on the creditor's oral promise to refinance again when your scheduled payments go up.

Bank Loans vs. Finance Company Loans. In general, do *not* refinance a bank loan with a finance company loan. (In fact, try to avoid finance companies entirely.) Finance company loans tend to be at higher interest rates and may include unnecessary insurance, fees, and hidden charges.

Many consumers think only finance companies will make loans to them, that banks will not make a loan because of a bad credit history. Do not make assumptions — ask a few banks. Also beware of finance company loan "flipping." Many finance companies encourage frequent refinancings, each time making the loan *less* advantageous for you and each time assessing prepayment penalties on the old loans.

Long Term vs. Short Term Credit. Always look at the length of a loan and whether there is a balloon payment (that is, a very large payment that is due as the last payment). You should not refinance a loan you are paying out over 15 years with a loan you have to pay off in four years.

Particularly watch out if the monthly payments for the shorter loan are the same or lower than the longer term loan. This almost invariably means the shorter term loan has a large balloon at the end. You may not be able to pay the balloon payment when it comes due. If you are later forced to refinance the balloon, you will have no leverage and you will be stuck with whatever loan terms the creditor wants to offer. If the creditor will not refinance the balloon, and you cannot find another way to pay off the balloon, the lender may seize any collateral it has taken, including your home.

Variable vs. Fixed Rates. You will be offered either a fixed or variable rate loan if you refinance. In a variable rate loan, the interest rate you pay can go up or down during the life of the loan. The interest rate in a fixed rate loan stays the same for the full term of your loan.

Whether your variable rate interest goes up or down will usually depend on whether other interest rates in the economy are going up or down. For example, your rate may be set at five percentage points above the current interest rate for one year United States Treasury Bills.

You need to exercise care when refinancing from fixed rate loans to variable rate and sometimes *vice versa*, because it is difficult to compare loans of the two types. A good rule of thumb is never to refinance from a fixed rate into a variable rate, because of the risk of increased payments which a variable rate requires.

Occasionally, a variable rate option is the right choice, but you must first make sure you know what you are doing. Getting help from an expert is good advice. Check the loan documents. The lender is required to tell you the maximum rate which could ever apply to your variable rate loan. Make sure you can afford the loan even if the rate increases to the maximum.

One other problem to watch out for in variable rate loans is low "teaser rates." These are rates designed to be low for the first months of the loan, but which often then dramatically increase. Pay less attention to the stated teaser rate then to the Annual Percentage Rate (APR) disclosed for the whole term of the loan. If you are not good at understanding interest rates, it is best to avoid teaser rates and variable rate loans entirely. The more a particular lender pushes variable rate loans as an only option over your objection, the more you should consider dealing with a different lender instead.

Beware of lenders trying to change the loan terms at the last minute. Whenever you have doubts about loan terms, your best course is to walk away.

Another trick of unscrupulous lenders is to change an offered loan from fixed rate to variable rate at the last minute. This is a sure sign of a bad loan. If any term of the loan is changed at the last minute from what you expected, do not sign the loan papers. Either have a professional review the papers to make sure they don't include unfair terms, or walk away from that lender entirely.

Points, Broker's Fees and Other Up-Front Charges. When you refinance one or more loans into a new loan, you often have to pay points, broker's fees, or other up-front charges. Since you have already paid for any such charges on your old loans, these charges are an extra cost of the new loan. Even if the new loan's interest rate appears lower, these added charges may make the new loan more costly.

Make sure the "APR" (Annual Percentage Rate) on the new loan is lower than the *interest* rate stated on the old loans. The "interest rate" (as opposed to the APR) on the old loan will not reflect points, broker's fees, closing costs, and other up-front fees. The stated interest rate reflects the continuing cost of the old loan *after* up-front costs have been paid. The APR is a measure of the total cost of a loan with all of these up-front costs factored in.

Insurance and Other Extras. Consumer debt frequently is loaded up with a lot of extras. Just as some auto dealers make their real profits selling expensive rustproofing and service contracts, so, too, lenders sell overpriced extras or tack on fees and charges to their loans. Unless you have a special reason for wanting these extras — they are usually highly overpriced and a very bad deal — you should not purchase them. That sounds easy, but often you do not know what extras you are buying and lenders have sophisticated techniques to sell unnecessary products.

One of the most offensive extras is credit life and credit accident and health insurance. These policies are supposed to pay off your loan if you die or become disabled. To sell this coverage to you, the lender will need you to initial a statement that you want this coverage. You should not do so. Only a small percentage of these insurance premiums are ever paid out as losses to policyholders.

Additionally, many such policies are designed so that companies can deny coverage to you even when it appears you have a valid claim. For example, the insurance may not cover many types of accidents which you would expect it would cover. Any benefits that are paid out are limited to the amount left on the loan, so that you never actually receive cash on the policy. You will always be better off buying insurance from other sources.

While you have the legal right to turn down credit insurance and many other extras, you are likely to be compelled to pay for certain other charges if you want a loan from a particular lender. Examples are property insurance on the collateral and title examination fees. However, you may be able to negotiate about the amount of these fees.

If mandatory charges seem overpriced to you and the lender is unwilling to negotiate, shop around for another lender. You will find significant variation among lenders as to closing costs and other charges. In addition, you should always factor in the cost of all extra charges when you are trying to decide whether you are saving or losing money by refinancing existing loans with a new loan.

Prepayment Penalties. When you pay off old loans through refinancing, there are almost always significant prepayment penalties on the existing debt. These penalties should be treated like extra charges on the *new* loan. Add them to the finance charge on the new loan and consider that they increase the interest rate on the new loan accordingly.

You will find it difficult to measure the size of these penalties, but they almost always exist. Even if the creditor does not have an explicit prepayment penalty, some states allow creditors to compute payoff figures using a fudge factor significantly to the creditor's advantage. Additionally, if you purchased credit-related insurance on the old loan, that insurance will be canceled and you will receive less than a full rebate. (The creditor will then try to sell a new insurance policy with the new loan.) If you have difficulty computing the prepayment penalties, assume that they exist and that they are a significant disadvantage to refinancing.

Consumer Defenses. You may have legal grounds not to pay a debt. These include, for example, that the goods were never delivered or that repair work was shoddy. If this is the case, never refinance such a loan with a different creditor, because you may lose the ability to raise these defenses against the new creditor. The more removed a creditor is from the original seller, the harder it is to raise defenses.

Backing Out of a Refinancing. If you change your mind about a refinancing deal in which your home is collateral, federal law allows you to cancel the loan within three days of signing the loan papers. If you decide to cancel, you fill in and mail the cancellation form that the creditor is required to provide you at the time you signed the contract. It is important that you do so by the three day deadline. Federal law also provides other grounds for canceling refinancings if your home is put up as security. See Chapter Twelve for more details.

Of course, any time you are considering a refinancing, whether or not your home is collateral, you can always back out before the papers are signed. You should never feel embarrassed to walk away from a bad deal even if you are being pressured. Some lenders will threaten penalties or legal action if you do not sign papers which have already been prepared. These threats are false, because you have no responsibility to pay if there is no binding agreement. There is no binding agreement until you sign the papers.

REVERSE MORTGAGES

Reverse mortgages are increasingly available as a refinancing option for older homeowners who have built up substantial equity in their property. For most reverse mortgages, you can draw down your home equity without having to repay that loan for quite some time. Some reverse mortgages have no repayment obligation as long as you remain in the property — no matter how long you stay.

In most reverse mortgages, the lender will look at your age, the amount of equity you have in your home, and the prevailing interest rates in order to determine the amount it will lend you. You will then be able to receive your loan amount in one of the following ways:

- Fixed monthly installments that will be paid to you for a set period of time. This is called a "term" plan.
- Fixed monthly installments (smaller ones) that will be paid to you for as long as you live in the home (this is usually called a "tenure" plan).
- As a line of credit to be drawn at your convenience. This may also be combined with a term or tenure plan.

A reverse mortgage may be a good way to get some money now based on the value of your house whether or not you are having financial problems. If you are interested, look for a bank or mortgage company in your community who offers this product. However, a good deal of caution is required for a number of reasons.

Most importantly, you can only borrow against your equity once. If you have taken a reverse mortgage and spent the money, you will not have the financial resource of home equity available again to you in the future. For example, if you use your home equity as a resource for a reverse mortgage or another loan at age 65, the equity will not be available to help pay for home health care later if you should need it.

Other potential drawbacks to a reverse mortgage include:

- The costs involved in getting a reverse mortgage can be very high. Some reverse mortgages include up-front fees as high as $5,000 or more. You should shop around for the loan product with the smallest total fees.
- The amount of cash you get may not really meet your needs. For example, a 65 year old with $50,000 in home equity may get as little as $100 per month on a term mortgage. (This calculation varies for different lenders and it depends on a variety of factors, including regional loan limits, interest rates, and the amount of the closing costs.)
- A reverse mortgage can affect your eligibility to receive certain government benefits such as SSI and Medicaid. (Social Security payments are not affected.)
- Some shady lenders offer very unfair reverse mortgages or conventional mortgages that look like reverse mortgages. You should only work with a reputable lender in an established program.
- A reverse mortgage makes it difficult to pass your home on to your heirs after your death, and instead the home usually will go to the lender when you move or if you die. This may change your expectations about what you will leave to your heirs.

Reverse mortgages provide an orderly way to spend whatever equity you have in your home. But there are expenses, pitfalls to avoid, and disadvantages.

Reverse mortgages are not for everyone. You should work with a knowledgeable counselor if you are at all in doubt, especially since free counseling is an element of most reputable reverse mortgage programs. If you do take out a reverse mortgage, set up a plan to use the money wisely. You will not be able to tap your home equity again.

REFINANCING
SCAMS

Tips to Avoid Refinancing Scams. Many unscrupulous companies prey on people in distress, because financial emergencies make people vulnerable to poor decisions and rip offs. Here are twelve tips to help you steer clear of frauds:

1. *Be wary of anyone who contacts you about refinancing or loan consolidation,* particularly if the solicitation does not come from an established financial institution in your community. Be skeptical of any solicitation from a finance company, even if the company has helped you out before. Well known finance companies have engaged in serious frauds.
2. *Definitely avoid anyone who solicits loans via a "door to door" visit of your home.* It is very expensive to market anything door to door, and odds are someone coming to the house to help bail you out of trouble is really coming to get you in deeper.
3. *When in doubt, check out the lender.* If you have any reason to suspect someone you are considering doing business with, check with your state's attorney general, banking commission or consumer complaint hotline. If there are complaints on file from other consumers, you want to know about it. Check both the business's name and the names of any individual you are dealing with, because some individuals change their company names on a repeated basis to avoid becoming well-known in the community. (If you do check on a business, remember that the absence of complaints does not necessarily mean that the business is reputable. You still need to pay attention to the other scam avoidance techniques discussed here.)
4. *Never sign documents without knowing what is in them.* If you own a home, you should be especially wary, because odds are any deal to "help" you will involve your giving up a mortgage or other rights to your home.
5. *Avoid any offer that you sell your home, with an option to buy it back.* This will always be the quickest way to lose your home and any equity you have built up. Any sale of your home means that you no longer have the rights of an owner.

6. *Be careful of advertised schemes to save homes from foreclosure or personal solicitations to help you avoid foreclosure.* "For profit" foreclosure assistance has a very poor track record. Many financially strapped consumers pay money for short term help or no help at all. Non-profit counseling or bankruptcy assistance are usually better alternatives.

7. *If your regular banker or credit union cannot help you, odds are lenders and brokers who advertise cannot get you a good deal either.* Most loan brokers and some lenders advertise as offering help to people who are credit risks. These advertisements will usually get you involved with people who are known as "hard money lenders" and who will almost always make your situation worse. Brokers are often expensive to use. Many will shop for a loan which includes a big commission to them, rather than the best terms for you.

8. *Beware of anyone who wants to consolidate all of your debts into one loan.* This *never* makes sense. The solicitation shows that the person suggesting the loan consolidation is not out to help you, but to fleece you.

9. *Do not send an "application" or "processing" fee to a lender who advertises "Bad Credit, No Problem" and then asks you to call an 800 or 900 number.* This may just be a scam to make off with the fee. Any "900" number call will also cost you money which is very hard to get back.

10. *Do not refinance repeatedly with the same lender.* Encouragements to refinance regularly can only mean that the lender is looking to make a large profit at your expense by taking advantage of hidden costs of refinancing.

11. *Do not refinance to take advantage of offers of small amounts of cash or to get a gift.* These deals are almost always designed by lenders to be very costly to you. Cash or a gift is offered in order to convince you to make a deal which has no real financial advantages for you.

12. *If it is too good to be true, it is not true.*

Steps to Take If You Are Victimized by a Refinancing Scam. It is much easier to avoid a refinancing scam than to get your money back. Do not expect a business which is ripping you off to easily agree to return money or to be responsive to your complaints. However, you should always take action if you are ripped off, both to try to get your money back and to help prevent the same thing from happening to other consumers.

Your first step should always be to ask for return of any money you have lost in a refinancing scam. There is some hope that the lender does not want to alert law enforcement officials and is willing to "buy off" one victim with the hope of snaring more. For this reason, threats to go to a state Attorney General's office or district attorney or the local press may help.

A second step is to not just threaten, but to actually complain to your attorney general, your state commission overseeing banks, and to your local better business bureau. Consumer complaint hotlines, the press, and neighborhood non-profits can also be useful. You may find that other people have made similar complaints and that legal action is pending or can be brought. At a minimum, a complaint to a public official or complaint hotline will be on record and will help prevent your neighbors from being duped as well. You should keep all paperwork and make records of all conversations with the scam operator.

Your best course is usually to enlist the aid of an attorney who will represent your interests. Although some lawyers will not want to handle a consumer fraud case, they may tell you if you have a good claim and may make a referral to someone who does handle consumer law cases. You will want an attorney who is willing to pursue your case aggressively. As discussed briefly above, there may be grounds to cancel the mortgage which has been placed on your home and to undo the whole agreement. The lawyer may be able to take other action as well that reduces your obligation on the loan.

Filing bankruptcy is another strategy. It will stop a scam operation's attempt to foreclose your home in its tracks. To be effective in the long run, though, your bankruptcy attorney must aggressively challenge the scam operator in the bankruptcy proceeding, something not all bankruptcy attorneys are prepared to do.

Responding to Debt Collectors

• What Debt Collectors Can and Cannot Do To You
• Seven Ways to Stop Debt Harassment
• Illegal Debt Collection Practices and What to Do About Them

DO NOT LET COLLECTORS PRESSURE YOU

Do not let debt collectors push you around. Chapters One and Four showed you which bills to pay first and when to refinance. It is the job of some bill collectors to persuade you to pay the wrong bills first and to refinance bills that should not be refinanced.

Do not let debt collection harassment force you into making wrong decisions that will hurt you later. If a certain bill is less important, explain to a creditor why you are not paying and when you propose to pay:

> *"I have to pay my rent and utility bills first. I just got laid off, but when I get a new job I will do my best to meet my credit card debt. I understand that you will want to cancel my card, and I will pay you when I can."*

If the creditor or a bill collector still calls at all hours and writes threatening letters, use the tips in this chapter to stop debt collection harassment.

COLLECTORS CANNOT
LEGALLY DO MUCH
TO HARM YOU

Debt collectors are experts at making threats about the dire consequences of nonpayment. It is important to know what a debt collector can and cannot legally do when you get behind on a particular debt. Most debts, such as virtually all credit card obligations, doctor bills, small amounts owed merchants, and many small loans are "unsecured." This means you have not put up any collateral, such as the family home or car, to secure the loan's repayment. An *unsecured* creditor can legally do only the following three things:

1. Stop Doing Business With You. For example, a credit card issuer can cancel your card or a dentist whom you owe money might refuse to let you continue as a patient. Usually, though, there are other merchants or professionals from whom you can obtain the same goods or services on a cash basis or even on credit. The threat of stopping business with you is only serious where a particular creditor has a monopoly in your community, such as the only doctor in a rural area. Utilities also usually have a monopoly, and dealing with utility bills involves special issues discussed in detail in Chapter Fourteen.

2. Report the Default to a Credit Reporting Agency. The fact that you are behind on your bills almost certainly will end up on your credit record. You cannot stop this, short of always being current on all of your bills. While this is unfortunate, you only make matters worse by paying a particular bill first just because that collector is threatening to ruin your credit record.

The reason you make matters worse is that the collection agency threatening to ruin your credit is almost always bluffing. If a creditor reports delinquent debts to a credit bureau, your delinquency is already in your credit record even before the collector starts making threats. If the creditor does not routinely report information to a credit bureau, collectors who threaten you almost never go to the bother of doing so themselves.

Other creditors who may never threaten to ruin your credit record automatically report by computer to a credit bureau your every payment and non-payment *on a monthly basis*. So if you pay the first creditor instead of the second, the second creditor will report your delinquency automatically. That way, you now have two delinquencies on your credit record instead of one. Why threats to ruin your credit record should not be taken too seriously is explained in more detail in Chapter Six.

3. Begin a Lawsuit to Collect the Debt. This is the threat that may worry you the most. But there are four reasons why the threat of a lawsuit is far less serious than you imagine. First, it is hard to predict whether a particular creditor will actually sue on a past due debt. It is expensive to take you to court. Many creditors will not do so for small debts, say under $1000, although some creditors do take even small debts to court. Still other creditors do not take even large debts to court. How aggressively a collection agency threatens suit is no indication whether the creditor will actually sue, even if the threat appears to come from an attorney.

Second, if the creditor sues you, you have a right to respond, to explain why the money is not owed. You need not let the creditor win by default. You do not have to hire an attorney to respond to the lawsuit. Often when a creditor sees that you will contest the action, it will stop pursuing the lawsuit. How to respond to a lawsuit is detailed in Chapters Seven and Eight.

Third, even if the creditor does pursue the lawsuit and eventually wins, the worst that can happen is that a court judgment will be entered against you. You will *not* automatically be in contempt of court for failure to pay the judgment. The judgment only gives the creditor the legal right to *try* to seize your property or wages or to seek a court order requiring payment.

Fourth, if you are "judgment proof," you have nothing to fear from even these special collection techniques. You are "judgment proof" if all your assets and income are protected by law from a creditor trying to enforce a court judgment.

You may thus want to know whether you are judgment proof or whether the creditor can legally seize either your income or property after prevailing in its lawsuit. State exemption laws usually protect a certain amount of your property from seizure pursuant to a court judgment. A local legal services program, an attorney, or a credit counseling agency can provide a list of exempt property in your state and advise whether your state's laws allows your home or any other valuable property to be taken and sold by a creditor with a judgment against you. Often the information is also available in pamphlet form.

To be judgment-proof, your wages or other income must also be exempt from seizure. Federal law limits the amount of wages that a creditor can seize. In all states the first $127.50 a week of take home pay is protected, and only a portion of the amount over $127.50 can be seized. (The $127.50 amount is 30 times the minimum wage of $4.25. For example, if the minimum wage goes up to $5, then $150 a week would be protected from garnishment.) Moreover, in certain states no wages can be garnished at all; in other states more than the first $127.50 is protected. Finally, Social Security and other government benefits cannot be seized at all. More on state exemption laws and protections from wage garnishment can be found at Chapter Seven.

As can be seen, the threat of a court action on an unsecured debt is not nearly as real or dangerous as the threat of a landlord's eviction action, a bank's foreclosure on a mortgage, a car's repossession, or a utility's termination of gas or electricity service. These latter four actions usually happen quickly with a minimum of legal process and expense to the creditor.

Remember the cardinal rule about debt collectors — unless they work for your landlord, utility, mortgage holder, or other secured creditor, they often have no bite behind their bark.

Debt Collectors Cannot Legally Take Other Actions to Collect on Unsecured Debts. A creditor, if it chooses to, can stop doing business with you, report a default to a credit bureau, or sue on the past due debt. A collector's veiled threats to do anything else on an unsecured debt are deceptive and violate federal law. The collector cannot seize your wages or property before the creditor has obtained a court judgment, nor can it send you to jail or send your children to foster care. Collectors cannot publish your name in a newspaper, report a debt to your neighbors, or seek to collect from other family members, unless they cosigned the debt or a court order is entered which makes the family member responsible. Creditors who growl the loudest should not drive you into the teeth of a creditor with real bite.

DEALING WITH
GUILT FEELINGS

You are not a deadbeat when circumstances outside your control prevent you from paying your debts. If you have excess debt burdens, you must repay your most important debts first, and postpone payment of other debts.

Believe it or not, the collector knows this even better than you. Creditors know from long experience that most people pay their bills and, when they do not, it is because of job loss, illness, divorce, or other unforseen events. Creditors take this risk of default into account when they set the interest rate — creditors make enough money off you and others in good times so that when you default, the creditor is covered.

Do not be fooled by collector statements to the contrary. Debt collectors are *instructed* to ignore your reasons for falling behind on your debts, to show no sympathy, and not to listen to reason.

You have no moral obligation to pay one debt at the cost of not paying another debt, particularly where the debt not paid is more central to your family's survival. Creditors know this. They should not be rewarded for trying to pressure you to pay them off at the expense of another creditor.

SEVEN DIFFERENT WAYS TO STOP
DEBT COLLECTION HARASSMENT

Because bill collectors have no bite behind their bark, they will bark very loudly, hoping to intimidate. Do not let them. This section lists seven different approaches to stop debt harassment.

Keep in mind that the effectiveness of any of these approaches may depend on whether the creditor is doing its own collection (for example, the doctor's office is calling you up) or whether the creditor has hired a debt collection agency or attorney. You usually have more rights if you are dealing with a debt collection agency or an attorney.

The key federal law regulating debt collection, the Fair Debt Collection Practices Act (FDCPA), applies only to debt collection agencies and attorneys, and generally does *not* apply to creditors collecting their own debts. Nevertheless, most states have laws which regulate creditors collecting their own debts, and the seven approaches listed here generally will work with creditors collecting their own debt, and not just with collection agencies.

1. Head Off Harassment Before It Happens. When you have more bills than you can afford to pay, you obviously cannot pay all your bills. While you should pay your most important bills first, you should not totally ignore any of your bills, such as by tossing a series of warning letters in the trash. Instead, there are steps you can take short of payment which will make it clear to the creditor that you are not ignoring the bill.

Creditors will not forget about a bill just because you fail to respond. The creditor will hire a collection agency or turn the matter over to an in-house collection bureau. The job of these collectors is to get you to notice the bill, and sometimes they are not very nice in the methods they choose to attract your attention.

To avoid this result, before the creditor refers a loan out to a collection agency, and before the debt gets into the machinery of the collection process, call up the creditor and explain your situation. Promptly contacting the creditor is most important with hospitals, doctors, dentists and similar creditors who would otherwise quickly turn a debt over to a collection agency. Although retailers, banks and finance companies are more likely to have an in-house collection arm, it still pays to try to avoid the transfer of the debt to that office.

You can say that you have to pay the landlord or mortgage, utilities and certain other bills first. You have not forgotten the creditor and will pay when you can. Make it clear that you cannot afford to pay the bill, and will not pay a collection agency either. Do not overpromise, but be polite and honest.

Make sure the creditor understands you will pay the creditor when you can and there is no need or advantage to go to the expense of hiring a collection agency. You will not pay a collection agency any sooner than the creditor.

The creditor then has a financial interest *not* to turn the matter over to a collector. Collection agencies usually charge the creditor a fee of approximately one third of what they collect, or sometimes charge the creditor a flat fee per debtor. The creditor can avoid this fee by sitting tight.

You also have a financial interest in heading off referral of a debt to a collection agency. Creditors are generally more flexible than debt collection agencies, and are more willing to work out payment plans. You may waste a lot of time trying to negotiate with debt collectors, where you would have been more successful dealing directly with the creditor. In addition, the costs of collection can, in some cases, be added to your debt.

One danger of calling the creditor is that the creditor might convince you to start making reduced payments that you cannot afford to make. For this reason, a counselor or friend might help you in talking to the creditor.

2. The Cease Letter. Assuming you fail in explaining the situation to the creditor, and you are being harassed for the debt, the simplest strategy to stop collection harassment is to write the collector a cease letter. Federal law requires collection agencies to stop their dunning after they receive a written request to stop. The federal law does not apply to creditors collecting their own debts, but even these creditors will often honor such requests.

The letter need not give any special explanation why the collector should cease contacts. Nevertheless, it is generally a good idea to explain why you cannot pay and your hopes for the future. The letter might also describe prior abusive tactics of the collector's employees and your resulting distress. It is very important to keep a copy of the written request.

Here is an example of such a letter (delete references to billing errors, debt harassment, or any other statements that do not apply to you. A simple request to stop collection contacts is sufficient):

Sam Consumer
10 Cherry Lane
Flint, MI 10886

January 1, 1996

NBC Collection Agency
1 Main Street
Flint, MI 10887

Dear Sir or Madam:

I am writing to request that you stop communications to me about my account number 000723 with Amy's Department Store as required by the Fair Debt Collection Practices Act, 15 USCA § 1692c(c). [*NOTE: Delete reference to the Fair Debt Collection Practices Act where the letter is to a creditor instead of to a collection agency.*]

I was laid off from work two months ago and cannot pay this bill at this time. I am enrolled in a training program which I will complete in March and hope to find work that will allow me to resume payments soon after that.

Please note that your letters mistakenly list the balance on the account as $245. My records indicate that the balance is less than that.

You should be aware that your employees have engaged in illegal collection practices. For example, I received a phone call at 6:30 a.m. from one of them last week. Later that day I was called by the same person at my training program which does not permit personal phone calls except for emergencies. My family and I were very upset by these tactics.

I will take care of this matter when I can. Your cooperation will be appreciated.

Very truly yours,

Sam Consumer

cc: Better Business Bureau
    10 Main Street
    Flint, MI 10887

3. The Lawyer's Letter. You do not need a lawyer to send a cease letter. Believing that they have serious legal problems, people often go to lawyers, when all they actually need is relief from a few abusive bill collectors. When such relief is all that is needed, you can send a simple cease letter without the cost of legal assistance. If these letters do not stop the abuse, a letter from a lawyer usually will.

Collection agencies must stop contacting a consumer known to be represented by a lawyer, as long as the lawyer responds to the collection agency's inquiries. Even though the federal Fair Debt Collection Practices Act requirement does not apply to creditors collecting their own debts, these creditors also will generally honor requests from a lawyer. A collector's lawyer also is generally bound by legal ethics not to contact you if you are represented by a lawyer.

4. The Work-Out Agreement. Probably the most common consumer strategy, though not the best, to deal with debt harassment is to work out a deal with the collector. Collectors will generally stop collection efforts after you work out a payment plan with the collector.

Many collection agencies and creditors claim initially that they must receive payment of the balance in full. They will urge you to borrow from a loan company or from relatives to pay off the debt. As described in Chapter Four, this is almost always a bad idea.

If you resist this suggestion, eventually most collectors will agree to an installment plan. Again, collectors initially will ask for payments beyond your financial capability. If you stick to your guns, the collector will agree to a realistic plan, one that often greatly reduces the amount of the debt.

In some locations, credit counseling agencies offer help in obtaining workout agreements on unsecured debts. Although these agencies can be helpful if you can afford to pay some but not all that you owe, you should not use a consumer counseling plan if it requires payments which exceed your ability to pay or if you have better options for dealing with your creditors, as discussed elsewhere throughout this book. You should be especially careful not to agree to a credit counseling plan if it requires that you pay low priority debts at the expense of not meeting your high priority obligations.

While you may feel flushed with victory in negotiating a large debt down to small monthly payments, even this may be offering too much to the collector. As described in Chapter One, you must prioritize your debts. Even a small payment to an unsecured creditor is unwise if this prevents payment of your mortgage or rent. There are other, better ways to stop debt harassment.

5. Complaints About Billing Errors. Collection letters are sometimes in error, mistaking the amount due or the account number, or billing the consumer instead of his or her insurance company. Occasionally, you may even receive collection letters aimed at someone with the same or a similar name. When a collection letter contains a mistake, write to request a correction. Collection agencies, by law, must inform you of your right to dispute the debt. If you then dispute the debt in writing within the next 30 days, the collection agency must stop collection efforts while it investigates.

If the dispute involves an open end account, a credit card, or an electronic transfer of money, you have the additional legal right under the Federal Fair Credit Billing Act to require the creditor to reexamine the bill. You must write a letter pointing out the mistake within 60 days of receipt of the disputed bill. Your rights to correct billing errors are periodically included with credit card statements.

Although other creditors are not required by this law to investigate errors, they usually do so as well. Even after deadlines have passed, most collectors will stop their collection efforts and investigate.

6. Complaining to a Government Agency. Another strategy is to write to government agencies responsible for enforcing laws that prohibit debt collection abuse. A government agency is not likely to investigate immediately unless it has other complaints against the same collector, a fact that probably cannot be known beforehand. Nevertheless, sending a copy of the complaint letter to the collector often produces good results.

The complaint letter should be sent to the Federal Trade Commission, Bureau of Consumer Protection, Washington, D.C. 20580. Copies of the letter should be sent to the consumer protection division within the state attorney general's office, usually in the state capitol, and also to any local office of consumer protection listed in the local telephone book. Addresses can be obtained from a local better business bureau or office of consumer affairs.

If the collection tactics include abusive telephone calls, a copy of the same letter should be sent to the local telephone company and to the public utility commission in the state capitol. If the collector's abusive behavior appears part of its routine practice, either because of form letters or because of lack of provocation, this should be pointed out to the agency. An example of such a letter follows:

Sam Consumer
10 Cherry Lane
Flint, MI 10886

January 25, 1996

Federal Trade Commission
Bureau of Consumer Protection
Washington, DC 20580

Dear Sir or Madam:

I am writing to complain of abusive debt collection tactics used by ABC Collection Agency, 1 Main Street, Flint, MI 10887, which I request that you investigate.

I was laid off by U.S. Steel two months ago and have not been able to maintain all payments on all my bills. ABC began contacting me in

December about my account with Amy's Department Store in Flint. ABC's abusive collection tactics have included:

1. Telephoning my sister asking her to lend me the balance when she does not have anything to do with this account.
2. Calling me at 6:30 a.m. at home and using offensive language, calling me a "God damned deadbeat."
3. Writing that they would sue me if they did not receive payment in ten days (this was a month and a half ago) whereas all they have done since then is to call and to write. (A copy of that letter is enclosed).
4. Continuing to contact me after I sent them a letter asking them to stop. (Enclosed is my letter to them and a later letter from them).
5. Billing me for $245 when no more than $185 is owed on the account.

My family and I are doing our best to get back on our feet, and this abuse is very distressful. Your assistance will be appreciated.

Very truly yours,

Sam Consumer

cc: Attorney General's Office
Bureau of Consumer Protection
Lansing, MI 10826

Flint Office of Consumer Affairs
14 Main Street
Flint, MI 10887

ABC Collection Agency
1 Main Street
Flint, MI 10887

Upper Michigan Telephone Co.
36 Main Street
Flint, MI 10885

Public Utility Commission
Lansing, MI 10826

7. Bankruptcy. When you file your initial papers to institute a personal bankruptcy, this instantly triggers the automatic stay. This stay automatically stops all collection activity against you, from collectors, creditors, or even government officials. No further collection activity can proceed unless a particular collector obtains permission from the bankruptcy court, and the bankruptcy court will not grant this permission to collectors seeking to contact you about unsecured debts. Filing for bankruptcy is thus a very effective means of stopping debt harassment.

Nevertheless, as a general rule, a bankruptcy filing is not your best strategy where your only concern is debt harassment. Bankruptcy should be saved for when you have more serious financial problems, because debt collection harassment is usually easily stopped without having to resort to a bankruptcy remedy. In fact, be wary of any attorney offering to file bankruptcy for you where the only problem is debt harassment.

ILLEGAL DEBT
COLLECTION CONDUCT

This section lists many types of illegal debt collection harassment. This will help you to demand that the collector stop its harassment. If you suffered financial, physical, or even emotional harm from the illegal collection harassment, you can sue the collector to recover all your damages, no matter how large they are. You can also sue the collector for up to $1000 plus all of your attorney fees, even if you are not damaged by the illegal collection activity.

The major law specifying illegal debt collection conduct is the federal Fair Debt Collection Practices Act (known as the "FDCPA"). The FDCPA requires collection agencies to take certain actions:

• The collection agency must stop contacting you if you so

request in writing or if you dispute the debt in writing.

- The collection agency, in its initial communication or within five days of that communication, must send you a written notice. That notice identifies the debt and the creditor, and gives you the right to dispute the debt or to request the name and address of the original creditor, if different from the current one. If you raise a dispute, the collector must suspend collection efforts on the disputed portion of the debt until the collector responds to the request. (Note that your failure to dispute a debt is not an admission of liability. The collector would still have the burden of proof in any court action to collect the debt.)
- Any lawsuit by a collector must usually be brought in the same county or other judicial district where you reside or signed the contract.

The following collection agency conduct also violates the FDCPA:

- Communicating with third parties, such as your relatives, employers, friends, or neighbors, about a debt unless you or a court has given the collector permission to do so. Several narrow exceptions to this prohibition apply. Collectors may contact creditors, attorneys, credit reporting agencies, cosigners, your spouse, and your parents if you are a minor. Third-party contacts are also permitted if the contacts are solely for the purpose of locating you and do not reveal in any way the contact's underlying purpose.
- Communicating with you at unusual or inconvenient times or places. The times 8:00 a.m. to 9:00 p.m. are generally considered convenient, but daytime contacts with a consumer known to work a night shift may be inconvenient.
- Contacting you at work if the collector should know that the employer prohibits personal calls, or contacting you at other inconvenient places, such as a friend's house or the hospital.
- Contacting you if you are represented by a lawyer, unless the lawyer gives permission for the communication or fails to respond to the collector's communications.

- Contacting you when you write a letter asking the collector to cease communications. The collector is allowed to acknowledge the letter and to notify you about actions the creditor or collector may take.
- Using obscene, derogatory or insulting remarks.
- Publishing your name.
- Telephoning repeatedly and frequently.
- Telephoning without disclosing the collector's identity.
- Making communications that intimidate, harass or abuse you, such as a threat to conduct a neighborhood investigation of you, or telling you that you should not have children if you cannot afford them.
- Making false, misleading or deceptive representations in collecting debts, such as pretending that letters carry legal authority.

It is illegal for a collector to contact your employer or neighbors about your debt, call you late at night, call you at work, call you repeatedly, make false threats, misrepresent who is contacting you, or engage in any other form of deceptive conduct or unfair harassment.

- Falsely representing the character, amount or legal status of a debt, or of services rendered or compensation owed.
- Falsely stating or implying a lawyer's involvement, such as where form letters written on an attorney's letterhead and bearing an attorney's signature in fact came from a collection agency and were not reviewed by a lawyer.

- Threatening arrest or loss of child custody or welfare benefits.
- Stating that nonpayment will result in arrest, garnishment or seizure of property or wages, unless such actions are lawful, and unless the creditor or the collector fully intends to take such action.
- Threatening to take actions that are illegal or that are not intended. To verify a collector's intention to file suit, you could ask the local court clerk to help you check the plaintiff's index to see whether the company making the threat has a history of filing similar suits. Suit is less likely the smaller the debt (e.g., less than $500), the more distant the collector, and the stronger your basis to dispute the debt. Other common threats that may be false are that the collector will refer the action to a lawyer, harm your credit rating, or repossess household goods.
- Using any false representation or other deception to collect or to attempt to collect any debt or to obtain information about you.
- Failing to disclose in communications that the collector is attempting to collect a debt.
- Using unfair or unconscionable means to collect debts.
- Collection of fees or charges unless expressly authorized by the agreement creating the debt and permitted by law.
- Depositing post-dated checks before their date. The collector also must give at least three days but not more than ten days notice before depositing the postdated check, or using the check for the purpose of threatening or filing criminal charges.
- Causing expense to another party while concealing the purpose of the communication, for example, by making collect telephone calls and sending collect telegrams.
- Threatening self-help repossession without the legal right to do so, or if the collector has no present intent to do so.
- Using any communication, language, or symbols on envelopes or postcards that indicate that the sender is in the debt collection business.

SUING DEBT COLLECTORS
FOR THEIR ILLEGAL CONDUCT

Why Sue the Debt Collector. Families in financial distress are subjected to more debt collection harassment than most families. Such harassment is illegal and you should be compensated for any injury suffered. You are already experiencing difficult emotional issues, and you do not need further harassment by debt collectors. Obviously, any money collected — or any amounts written off existing debts in settlement of a harassment charge — will be particularly welcome. At the same time, any money collected will deter future misconduct by debt collectors.

Suits for Up to $1000 and Your Attorney Fees For Even Minor Collector Misconduct. Even when you are subjected to only minor forms of illegal collection action that is more of an annoyance than a real injury, you can sue the collector and recover up to $1000 and all of your attorney fees for any violation of the FDCPA. You can recover up to $1000 even if the conduct did not in fact cause you any injury.

On top of the $1000, you can recover for any damages that were caused you by the illegal conduct. Courts may award actual damages for such emotional injuries as loss of happiness, loss of energy, loss of sleep, tension headaches, crying spells, and marital problems. Consumers have been awarded as much as $6,000 for emotional distress when the stress aggravated pre-existing medical problems.

Where the collector's conduct is seriously improper, you may also be able to recover large punitive damages on top of your actual damages. Examples of such conduct are threats to throw you in jail, to deport you, or have your children put in foster care. The punitive damages are meant not just to compensate you, but to punish and deter the collector from future misconduct.

When you win an FDCPA case, the collector must pay your attorney fees, which may encourage a private attorney to take the case on a contingent fee basis, particularly where the claim appears strong. In fact, the collector may end up paying more in attorney fees than in damages.

Even though many debt collectors are small operations, you can usually recover your judgments against the collectors. Many collectors carry professional liability insurance to protect themselves against consumer claims. The existence of such insurance is often important in settling claims. You thus have a lot of leverage in dealing with a collector that violates the FDCPA.

Finding an Attorney to Sue a Debt Collector. It is not always possible to find an attorney to handle an FDCPA claim. Families with low incomes and limited assets may be eligible to obtain free legal services from a neighborhood legal services office, and those offices may pursue such claims. Other consumers can contact bar association pro bono attorneys who might handle the case. A few cities also have lawyers who regularly handle debt collection harassment cases. In other areas, you can seek a personal injury lawyer willing to pursue the case on a contingent fee basis. The key to convincing a private attorney to take the case will be the availability of an attorney fee award paid by the collector if you win the lawsuit.

Another aid is that private attorneys unfamiliar with the FDCPA can find everything they need in the National Consumer Law Center's *Fair Debt Collection* (3d ed. 1996) to allow them to pursue a FDCPA claim with a minimum of expenditure. This book is the most thorough resource for bringing cases under the federal FDCPA as well as under other debt collection laws. The manual analyzes the statute, agency interpretations, court decisions, and reprints the statute, legislative history, agency interpretations, sample court documents, interview checklists, damage awards, and other important practice aids. Much of this is on a computer disk, allowing the attorney to quickly edit all documents which must be filed.

What You Should Tell Your Attorney. Once an attorney is found, your job is to document the extent of collector misconduct and the impact on your family. Although you may not want to discuss your feelings about the harassment, it is key to determining what kind of legal case you have. All symptoms of emotional distress should be discussed: anxiety, embarrassment, headaches, nausea, indignation, irritability, loss of sleep, and interference with family or work relationships. Did you consult a doctor? Are there symptoms of psychosomatic illness brought on by the harassment? One survey of 1300 consumer judgment debtors revealed that just less than half suffered psychosomatic illness as a result of their financial distress and about a quarter of them consulted a doctor.

Out-of-pocket losses should also be listed, ranging from loss of employment to loss of wages because of time taken off from work to try to resolve the dispute. In addition, telephone charges, transportation, medical bills, and counseling services could all be part of your actual damages.

Keep a record of all expenses related to the collection effort. Prepare a statement describing your physical and emotional response to the collection efforts, and list all costs incurred as a consequence of that response. If a doctor or counselor had to be consulted, that expense should be included. Supporting statements should be obtained from family members, relatives, friends or co-workers.

A verbatim telephone log of collection contacts would also be helpful. Pen and paper should be kept near the telephone to record all telephone contacts.

The Federal FDCPA Applies Only to Certain Debt Collectors. The FDCPA applies to collection agencies and lawyers; it does not generally cover creditors or their employees collecting their own debts. That is, the FDCPA applies to an independent debt collection agency hired by a creditor to collect its debts. It also applies when a creditor hires an attorney to collect its debts.

On the other hand, the FDCPA does *not* apply to collection attempts by a creditor's employees or officers collecting for the creditor and in the creditor's name. Other than this serious restriction, the Act applies broadly to most attempts to collect consumer debts. The debt need not arise from the sale of goods on credit. For example, the FDCPA applies to collection agencies and lawyers' attempt to collect medical bills, rent, utility bills, loans, and dishonored checks.

The Act does not apply to sheriffs, marshals, and other state and federal officials when collecting a debt in the performance of their official duties. However, private collection agencies who are collecting debts owed to a state or federal agency (such as student loans) are subject to the Act.

What if the FDCPA Does Not Apply? If the FDCPA does not apply to collection efforts, you still have legal remedies for debt collection harassment. These remedies will mostly involve state law, not federal law. While there will be variations from state to state, in every state there will always be at least some remedy for debt collection harassment. For more detail on these other state remedies, see the National Consumer Law Center's *Fair Debt Collection* (3d ed. 1996).

— 6 —

What You Need to Know About Your Credit Rating

• *Addressing Threats to Damage Your Credit Rating*
• *Coping With a Bad Credit Record*
• *How to Get a Copy of Your Own Credit Report*
• *Cleaning Up Your Credit Record*

THREATS TO DAMAGE YOUR CREDIT RATING

Debt collectors often threaten to ruin your credit rating if you do not pay them. There is little substance to this threat. Most likely, the creditor has already reported to a credit bureau the exact number of days your account is delinquent. The collector is unlikely to provide any additional information to the credit bureau. In some cases, a creditor does not have an arrangement to routinely supply account information to a credit bureau, and has not reported your deliquency. But even in these situations, the collector will rarely provide such information on you if you fail to respond to its threats.

How Delinquencies Are Reported on Your Credit Record. You can see why such threats are usually false by understanding what information is on your credit record and how it got there. Almost every adult American has a credit file with the three major national credit bureaus, TRW, Equifax, and Trans Union.

Your file has basic personal information on you and your spouse — social security number, birth date, current and former addresses and employers, etc. The report will also list individually, for many of your debts, basic account information, including the latest activity on the account, the current balance, and the amount past due. Most importantly, each account includes a code which explains whether the account is current, thirty days past due, sixty days past due, ninety days past due, or if the account involves a repossession, charge off or other collection activity.

The report will also include a summary of your past credit experience, such as the number of times that any account was 30, 60, or 90 days delinquent, the date of the most recent delinquencies, and the date of the most severe delinquency. The report will also list any accounts that have been turned over to a collection agency, any court judgments against you, tax liens, foreclosures, and bankruptcies.

Most major creditors subscribe to one or more credit bureaus. Subscribing to a credit bureau is a two way street — the creditor agrees to continuously supply the credit bureau with current account information on the creditor's customers in exchange for the right to find out information about other credit applicants. Usually creditors supply information to credit bureaus by computer. Each month the creditor gives the credit bureau access to a computer tape of the status of thousands of accounts, and the relevant information from this computer tape automatically flows into each borrower's credit file, replacing the current status of that particular debt.

Every *month* credit bureaus insert two *billion* new pieces of information into consumers' credit records. The credit bureaus also scour public records to add another 2 million pieces of information about tax liens, bankruptcies, foreclosures, and other legal judgments.

Your credit report is thus an up-to-date, reasonably objective description of the status of many of your credit accounts. It does *not* include personal comments or subjective opinions about you from creditors or debt collection agencies, such as a notation that you are a deadbeat or a lousy credit risk.

Why Collectors Cannot Ruin Your Credit Record. Your file at a credit bureau is constantly being updated with the current payment status, the amount owed, how many days a debt is delinquent, and what collection actions have been taken. This happens automatically. Creditors do not withhold information from a credit bureau to give you another chance to pay. Each month, the exact status of your debts is updated.

Consequently, for most credit card issuers, banks, finance companies, and other major lenders who subscribe to a credit bureau, threats to report a debt to a credit bureau are hollow because the creditor has already provided the debt's status, and there will be nothing else for the creditor to report. (When the account is turned over for collection or written off, that information will also be supplied to the credit bureau.)

Doctors, local stores, and other smaller creditors are less likely to subscribe to and supply monthly information to credit bureaus. If a creditor does not regularly report account information on its customers, it would be most unusual for the creditor to supply information on you individually. Moreover, the credit bureau may not accept the information from a non-subscriber.

It is even more unlikely that a collection agency hired by a creditor will report information on you to a credit bureau just because you do not respond to the agency's collection attempts. It is the rare collection agency that will go to the expense and bother of supplying information to a credit bureau on those who do not pay that collector.

Collectors that do supply information on consumers to credit bureaus will entangle themselves in a detailed federal law regulating reporting agencies. Collection agencies supplying information are really just passing on information supplied them by the creditor that hired them, and under federal law, the collection agency is thus treated and regulated as if it were a credit bureau.

It is particularly a mistake to stop paying Creditor "A" so that you can pay Creditor "B" who is threatening to damage your credit record. The delinquent debt that is subject of the threat has already been reported to a credit bureau or is likely never to be reported. On the other hand, it is very likely that your stopping payment to Creditor "A" will result in a new delinquency on your credit record.

Debt collection agency threats concerning your credit record should not just be ignored. The threats are probably deceptive and thus illegal under the Federal Fair Debt Collection Practices Act (FDCPA). You can sue the collection agency under that statute and receive as much as $1000 even if you are not injured by the threat, and the debt collector will have to pay your attorney's fees. Such suits against debt collectors are described at Chapter Five. If a creditor itself is doing the threatening (not an independent agency hired by the creditor), then the FDCPA does not apply, but you may have other legal ways of challenging the creditor's conduct.

Don't Worry If the Collector and Credit Bureau Seem to Be the Same Company. Sometimes a threat to ruin your credit rating (or even just an inquiry about a debt) takes on an added bite because it appears that a credit bureau is doing the threatening. Do not give any special notice to such threats.

Credit bureaus do not collect debts and do not threaten to ruin your credit record. An entity doing so is a debt collector or a creditor, not a credit bureau. A debt collector or creditor misrepresenting itself as a credit bureau is violating federal law, and you can sue for up to $1000 plus any injury caused to you plus your attorney fees. (See Chapter Five.)

Even if a collection agency is affiliated with a credit bureau, the collector's threats to supply information about you to a credit bureau is generally a bluff. Collection agencies rarely supply information about debtors to credit bureaus, and this is still the case even if the credit bureau and collection agency are corporate affiliates. As with any debt collector, information on your account generally is supplied by the creditor that hired the collector, not by the collector. When such a collector affiliated with a credit bureau does threaten you, you have the right under federal law to obtain a free copy of your credit report from the credit bureau.

COPING WITH A
BAD CREDIT RECORD

If you are experiencing financial problems that make it impossible to pay all of your bills on time, it is unavoidable that your credit record will indicate these problems. This section explains what a bad credit record does and does not mean for you, and how you should deal with it. The next section presents several strategies to improve your credit record.

Renting an Apartment or Home. Your credit record is of limited relevance when you are leasing a residence. Most landlords do not look at your credit record. Larger landlords, landlords specializing in low-income housing, and larger city landlords are more likely to pull your credit record. If you are unlucky enough to pick a landlord who looks at your credit record and turns you down, try another landlord. The odds are generally with you that the next landlord will not look at your credit record.

Utility Service. Your credit record will have no impact on your ability to obtain utility service, and generally does not affect the size of the security deposit you must offer. The only important precondition to your obtaining utility service is that you do not owe that particular utility company any money. You can obtain utility service even if you owe back bills to other utilities or other creditors.

Home Mortgages. There are several reasons why you might want to take out a new home mortgage in times of financial distress. You may want to refinance an existing mortgage, take out a second mortgage, or sell your home and buy a less expensive home with smaller mortgage payments. Unfortunately, a bad credit report will make it difficult to obtain a home mortgage, unless you can obtain a creditworthy cosigner.

Many conventional mortgages follow Fannie Mae or Freddie Mac guidelines. Under these guidelines, a foreclosure on your credit record will make it extremely difficult to obtain a mortgage for about the next three years, and will impact your ability for seven years. You should try to establish at least a year of on-time mortgage payments and pretty close to on-time payments for your other loans before applying for a new mortgage. Also pay off any judgments, liens, and the like. It is difficult to obtain a mortgage for at least two years after you obtain a bankruptcy discharge.

VA, FHA, and FmHA mortgages have looser guidelines than Fannie Mae or Freddie Mac. Even then, you should have no current defaults and a one or two year period since any bankruptcy discharge. You may also find other mortgage lenders with more flexible guidelines than those for Fannie Mae or Freddie Mac. Nevertheless, it is important to avoid con artists and hard money lenders that charge outrageous interest rates for high risk mortgages. As discussed elsewhere in this book, such desperate choices are likely to make your situation worse.

If you want to take out a home mortgage despite your bad credit record, several steps should be taken. First, obtain a copy of your own credit report from several of the major credit bureaus several months before you apply for the mortgage. (How to obtain copies of your own report is described later in this chapter.) In many home sales, time is of the essence, and you should already be dealing with your credit rating problems before you apply for the mortgage.

Try to clean up the report as much as possible, by seeking corrections for inaccurate information, bringing all debts current or renegotiating a payment schedule for those debts, paying off liens and judgments, and the like. The next section provides tips for cleaning up your credit record. When the mortgage company questions an aspect of your credit record, try to explain any extenuating circumstances. You can also provide favorable information not present on your credit record, such as an excellent history of rent and utility payments. (Most landlords and utilities do not provide this information to credit bureaus.)

Shop around for a mortgage company that says it can accept your credit history. Sometimes you may have to pay a slightly higher rate. For example, some legitimate lenders are now rating their applicants as A, B, C, or D, and then charging a slightly higher rate for each step in the scale. But definitely avoid extraordinarily high rate lenders that prey on those in financial distress. They charge unaffordable interest rates as high as 13 to 25%, plus hidden fees, brokerage charges, points, and the like. Another good rule of thumb is to avoid any lender that solicits you, particularly door-to-door or over the telephone. Also be mindful of the rules about refinancing discussed in Chapter Four.

Leasing vs. Buying a Car on Credit. Despite popular belief to the contrary, it is not easier, when you have a bad credit record, to lease a car than to buy the car on credit. In either case, you will have to convince the company that you will make regular monthly payments.

Because you are not building up any equity, lease payments are usually less than credit payments. But leasing may be more expensive in the long run, particularly if you terminate the lease early.

There are many types of car lenders and lessors, and it is hard to predict when your credit record will result in your being turned down for a loan or a lease. Do not assume that a bad credit rating will lead to credit denial, and if one creditor turns you down, the next may not. Nevertheless, you should not go overboard in applying for credit because denials of credit are likely to show up on your credit record.

In general, you should more easily be approved despite a bad credit record the higher your down payment is and the lower the car price. While high interest lenders should accept more risky loans, sometimes the local bank that you have dealt with for years will be more generous. It is always a good idea when buying a car to use reputable dealers and lenders, and to avoid car loans involving unusually high interest rates. Such loans are often associated with lemon cars, hidden fees, and excessive prices.

If a husband and wife are seeking a loan or lease, and only one spouse has a bad credit record, you can apply in the name of the other spouse, relying exclusively on that spouse's income and assets. Then the creditor is not allowed to look at the other spouse's bad credit record.

You can almost always lease or buy a car on credit with a creditworthy cosigner. Bear in mind though the risks borne by the cosigner if you default. They will be as responsible for the debt as if they bought the car themselves. A cosigner has been described as "a fool with a pen."

Credit Cards. If you are in financial trouble, you should limit what you buy on credit, and it may be a good idea to get rid of all of your credit cards. Nevertheless, credit cards are often a convenience, and sometimes they are necessary. For example, credit cards may be essential when purchasing or making reservations over the telephone, when you do not have a checking account, when you need proof of identification, or when you need to leave security when renting a car or video tape. You are also better off buying appliances or other items with a credit card from reputable merchants than getting involved with a rent-to-own dealer or other merchant that will grossly overcharge you.

One way to get a credit card is to open your mail. If a card issuer solicits you, it cannot deny you the card because of your credit rating.

Even when you have terrible credit and have lost all of your old credit cards, you may still be able to obtain a new credit card. One of the best ways is to just sit back and wait to be offered a credit card in the mail. When a direct mail solicitation offers a credit card to you, the creditor has already reviewed your credit history and by law cannot then turn you down based on your credit record.

If you do not receive credit card solicitations in the mail, you could apply for a few cards and see what happens. It may be easier to obtain a store credit card than a VISA or MasterCard.

Another option is to seek a "secured credit card" that is offered by a number of nationwide banks (Bank of America, Bank One, Chase Manhattan, Citibank, First Consumers, Wells Fargo, to name just a few). You deposit cash in the bank, and then they give you a MasterCard or Visa with a credit limit generally equal to the amount you deposited. Usually the minimum amount you can deposit is $500, but some banks let you deposit less (with a correspondingly lower credit limit). A few banks even give you a credit limit somewhat higher than the amount deposited.

Your deposit will earn interest. When you fail to pay your credit card bill, the bank will dip into your amount on deposit to pay your bill. A secured credit card thus does not provide you with new credit, but does give you the convenience of a credit card. Banks offering secured credit cards will be less picky about your credit record, but the bank may still turn you down if you have significant debts when applying for the card.

Your secured credit card payments will be reported to credit bureaus, and can thus build up your credit record. After a year of good payments, you can also ask the card issuer to graduate you to a regular credit card with a higher credit limit and to release your deposit.

When you look around for a secured credit card, keep in mind that there are good and bad secured credit cards. While a recent survey of annual fees for these cards found annual charges in the $18 to $50 range, *no* legitimate card issuer will also charge you an application fee. Avoid any card offered to you with an application fee.

Legitimate secured credit cards have interest rates under 20% and a few are as low as 10%. You will also want a MasterCard or Visa, and not a card that works only at a few stores. Be skeptical of a secured credit card company that solicits you. Shop around for the best deal.

Do not take out a credit card that puts your home or other property up as collateral for your card purchases. That type of card puts your home or other property in immediate peril every time you miss a credit card payment.

A final approach to obtaining a credit card is to become an authorized user on someone else's card. Your credit rating will not affect the principal cardholder. But you do put that cardholder at risk if you do not make payments or reimburse the cardholder for your own purchases.

Student Loans and Grants. For most student loans and grants, your credit record is irrelevant. (The one exception is Unsubsidized Loans which require students with bad credit records to have a creditworthy cosigner.) The key issue instead is whether you are in default on a prior student loan. How to obtain new loans and grants even when you are in default on earlier student loans is explained at Chapter Seventeen.

Your Credit Record Will Not Damage Your Friends, Relations, and Need Not Even Affect Your Spouse. Your credit report has no impact on the ability of your friends, associates, or even family members to obtain credit or employment. A creditor is not allowed to look at your credit record if, for example, your spouse, child, or parent applies for credit, and they are not relying on your income or assets in the credit application.

Your Credit Record Will Not Damage Your Reputation in the Community. No one can obtain your credit record for curiosity, gossip, or to determine your reputation. Your credit record can only be used to consider your application for insurance, credit, employment, and certain benefits and other business transactions. Federal law prohibits both credit bureaus and collection agencies from placing your name on a bad debt list that is circulated to the public.

> Your credit record is just between
> you and creditors — your neighbors
> and friends should never see it.

Your Credit Record Cannot Be Used in Divorce, Child Custody, Immigration, and Other Legal Proceedings. Normally, no one can use your credit record in a divorce or in a proceeding to determine child custody or child support. Credit reports generally also cannot be used in other legal proceedings, such as immigration proceedings, applications for citizenship, or as a basis to deny your ability to register to vote. Government agencies can only receive a credit report on you if they are permitted by a court order.

Insurance. Although insurance companies can look at your credit record, insurers generally are not interested in your credit history. They may ask a reporting agency for information on your medical history and any insurance claims you have filed. If you are turned down for insurance because of information in your credit report, the insurer must notify you of this fact.

Insurers may not even be concerned about your credit rating when they permit you to pay your insurance in installments. If you miss an installment, the insurer can easily cancel the policy and not lose much on your default.

Employment. Employers sometimes look at your credit report, although you will generally be notified before they do so. Employers who look at your credit report are generally less interested in your credit history than in public record information, such as your arrests, convictions, or any court judgments against you. If you apply for a job that involves access to large amounts of money, or if you are going to be "bonded," an employer may look at your record more carefully. Some employers are also interested in other information about your character which is not found in your credit file, and will ask an agency to interview your former employers, friends, and acquaintances to create an "investigative consumer report." However, if you are turned down for a job because of information in your credit report, the employer must notify you of this fact.

Public Assistance. Those considering your application for eligibility for public assistance may review your credit report as well. But their reason for doing so is not to see if you have unpaid bills, but only to see if you have hidden income or assets.

CLEANING UP
YOUR CREDIT RECORD

The last section provided advice on how you can live with your bad credit history. This section provides tips on how to, and how not to, improve that credit record. One of the reasons to put this section last is so that you can understand that your credit rating is not your most important concern in times of financial hardship. More important is trying to save your dwelling, utility service, car, and other essential possessions. You can go forward with your life even if you have credit card and hospital bill delinquencies on your credit history.

The strategies included in this section are summarized from the National Consumer Law Center's *Fair Credit Reporting Act* (3d ed. 1994). Refer to that volume for more detailed information.

Stabilize Your Situation. In the long run, the most important thing for you to do to re-establish a good credit rating is to stabilize your employment, income, and debts. This will prevent new delinquencies from being reported. While your past delinquencies can stay on you record as long as seven years, creditors are likely to ignore older debt problems if your situation becomes stable, and if you start paying your present obligations.

For example, continuous employment for the last two years may be a better indicator of your ability to repay a loan than a debt that was once delinquent for several months four years ago. Similarly, a creditor may be more likely to extend credit to you if you have a reasonable debt level, even if one or two accounts are delinquent, than to someone with excessive debt, even if that individual has not yet defaulted on any loan.

Creditors know that virtually all delinquencies are based on your inability to pay, and not your intent to avoid legitimate obligations. Unless a credit record shows a pattern of intentional avoidance of valid obligations, the creditor will be more concerned with whether you will have the present and future ability to repay the loan.

Once you get back on track, each year your older debt problems will have less of an impact on your ability to obtain credit. Seven years will come around sooner than you might think, and then there will be no record of your problems at all.

Look At Your Own Credit Record. If you want to take additional steps to clean up specific items on your credit record, your first step is to find out exactly what is on your credit record so you know exactly what you have to clean up. You will also catch any errors on your report.

Not all credit information is supplied to credit bureaus, and information that is supplied to one bureau may not be supplied to other bureaus. The only way to see what your credit record actually looks like at a particular bureau is for you to see a copy of your actual report at that bureau.

In practice, you will want to see your credit report from one or more of the three major national credit bureaus. TRW offers one free report per year. You can call with questions about the procedure at 1-800-392-1122 or 1-800-682-7654. Requests for your report should be sent to TRW

Information Services, PO Box 8030, Leighton, UT 84041-8030 with your full name (including middle initial, Junior, etc), year of birth, social security number, spouse's first name, addresses with zip code over the last five years, and a photocopy of a utility bill, a billing statement from a major creditor or your driver's license.

TRW will send you your credit report for free; Equifax and Trans Union charge $8, although less in some situations

---

For Trans Union and Equifax, you can only obtain a free report if you have recently been denied credit because of information in one of their reports. Otherwise, there is an $8 charge in most states.

You can call Equifax at 1-800-685-1111 or write to Equifax Credit Information Services, PO Box 105873, Atlanta GA 30348 with your full name (including middle initial, junior, etc), date of birth, social security number, and addresses for the last five years. You must include a copy of a current utility bill or your driver's license.

You can call 1-800-916-8800 for information on obtaining reports from Trans Union. You will have to send a signed request to Trans Union Corporation, PO Box 390, Springfield PA 19064-0390, with your full name and your spouse's, current address and other addresses over the past two years, social security number, spouse's social security number, date of birth, employer, and phone number. For husband and wife, Trans Union charges $16 and requires both signatures. If you have been denied credit, insurance, or employment within the last sixty days because of a Trans Union report, you can obtain a free report just by calling 800-916-8800. Have the denial letter handy when you call.

Supplying Positive, But Unreported Payment History. Your credit record may not indicate your regular payments to your landlord, utility, doctor, a local merchant, or others. These creditors may not subscribe or furnish information to any credit bureau. If you have a good payment record with these creditors, your credit record would be improved by getting credit bureaus to include this information.

This is generally difficult to do. The credit bureau is not legally required to include this information, and may not accept your statement. Sometimes a credit bureau will allow you to include this information for a fee. You can also try to have the landlord, utility, or other creditor supply information on your payment history. A better strategy may be to supply this information yourself directly to the creditor from whom you have applied for credit.

Explaining Damaging Items. Credit bureaus are not required to include in your file your explanation of why you were delinquent, although they may agree to do so. However, they are required to accept at no charge your explanation why their entry is inaccurate. For example, they may not have to include your letter that explains that you were sick or lost your job. But they must include a letter that states that you were not delinquent because the creditor agreed to postpone payments until you could return to work from your illness.

A better approach may be to explain the delinquency to the lender from whom you are applying for credit. Federal law requires that creditors at least consider your explanation. Similarly, Fannie Mae requires its mortgage lenders to review any letter you provide explaining your credit blemishes.

Correcting Errors. The odds are almost 50% that there is incorrect information in your credit file. You have the legal right to correct this information and should do so. You have enough trouble with accurate damaging information. You do not also need inaccurate damaging entries. You should correct errors by sending a written dispute to each credit bureau that has this incorrect information. If you do so, the credit bureau by law must reinvestigate the entry and correct erroneous information. Even after the entry is corrected, periodically check to make sure that this incorrect information has been deleted permanently. Inaccurate items have a habit of popping up again even after being corrected.

Cleaning Up the Current Status of Accounts. Probably the most important aspect of your credit record is the current status of your credit accounts — a listing for each of your accounts detailing how much is owed, how many months it is delinquent, and whether special collection action has taken place, updated on a monthly basis. You can clean up this part of your record, even though it will be more difficult to deal with the historical portion of your report that indicates every time you were delinquent in the past.

While you are still experiencing financial difficulty, the wrong way to clean up your current account listing is to pay up everything you owe on all of your accounts. You should instead make sure you pay your high priority debts first, such as your rent or mortgage, and let other debts stay delinquent if necessary.

Nevertheless, there may be a way to bring your accounts more current without a significant expenditure of money that you cannot afford. Since this information is replaced each month by more current data from your creditors, all you need to do is have your creditors report to the credit bureau that the debt is no longer delinquent.

Having seen your own credit report, you will know which creditors supply information to credit bureaus and which do not. If your goal is to clean up your current account status on your credit record, you should only worry about those creditors that supply account information on you.

The trick is to get those creditors to report your account as current even when you have not brought that account fully current. Instead, try to negotiate a repayment plan with the creditor for amounts less than the scheduled payments. It may be that the creditor will accept one half or less of the amount due, paid out over a series of months, rather than receive nothing.

It is critical though that you only agree to modified payment schedules that you can meet, while still being able to keep current on your other loan and financial obligations. Falling behind again will only make things worse. A creditor may be less likely to agree to a second repayment agreement if you fail to make payments as negotiated.

Any negotiated repayment agreement should require the creditor to supply updated account information to all relevant credit bureaus indicating the account is now current. Only when you miss a payment pursuant to the repayment agreement can the creditor report the account as delinquent. Sometimes, it may be simplest for the creditor to mark the old account paid in full, and set up a new account with you under a new number, and report that new account status to the credit bureau on a monthly basis. But avoid any type of refinancing where the total amount of your obligation does not decrease, unless the repayment terms are more affordable.

In negotiating with a creditor, you may want to enlist the aid of someone you trust to provide moral support and to make sure the creditor does not talk you into a bad deal. It helps to have a maximum repayment figure you can afford written down in advance, and then not to agree to a repayment plan which exceeds that figure. When negotiating, be sure to raise any reasons why you do not owe the amount in full.

Alternatively, contact a nonprofit consumer credit counselor, whose job is to negotiate repayment agreements with creditors. Consumers should never contact *for-profit* credit counselors, who are often scam operators. Even nonprofit consumer credit counselors may receive funding from creditors and cannot be expected to advocate too aggressively for you or point out legal defenses you may have.

In any negotiation, do not be affected by threats to turn accounts over to a debt collector for collection (collectors cannot do anything to you that the creditor could not). Similarly, the threat to furnish a negative credit report should not be effective because the creditor has already done so, and the issue in the negotiation is what type of payment will the lender accept in return for cleaning up the credit record.

Disputing Negative Entries Concerning Your Credit History. While your current account status is an important part of your credit file, creditors will also look at historical information about how often in the past you were delinquent or had a foreclosure or repossession. Working out a repayment agreement will not alter this credit history portion of your file. This is more difficult to clean up than your current account status.

An important method of clearing up your credit history is to dispute with the credit bureau negative items appearing in your file. You should dispute all items that are inaccurate or that do not tell the whole story. For example, you could dispute a debt being listed as delinquent if the creditor orally permitted you to make late payments. Or you may have paid late because you refused to pay until problems with the item purchased were resolved.

Credit bureaus will usually reinvestigate items, and will not delete an item simply because you dispute it. Sometimes agencies will refuse to reinvestigate because the dispute appears frivolous or irrelevant. To avoid this, make sure not to use a form provided by a credit repair agency because credit bureaus may ignore these forms completely. Instead, use the reporting agency's own form or your own simple letter. Do not dispute everything in the file, unless you have a valid basis to do so, but specify certain items with clear reasons why the items themselves are inaccurate or incomplete.

If a dispute is not frivolous or irrelevant, the agency must reinvestigate, at least by asking the original sources of the information what they think of your dispute. If the source cannot or does not verify the original item, your view must prevail. In fact, the older a debt, the greater the difficulty the credit bureau is going to have in confirming the information with the original source. The creditor may be out of business or may not have saved files going back four or five years.

Cleaning Up Your File With the Help of the Creditor. As described above, your dispute can delete unverified information that a particular debt was ever owed. Of course, this will not work if the creditor insists you owed the money and verifies that fact to the credit bureau. In that situation, you will need the creditor's help in deleting this information.

In trying to persuade the creditor that its information was inaccurate, you should supply whatever proof you have. If your proof is insufficient to resolve the matter, you may have to agree to pay part or all of the debt, either immediately or in installments. You may have a chance (particularly if you are persistent and talk to supervisors) to obtain an agreement with certain creditors for installment payments amounting to anywhere between 45 and 75 cents on the dollar owed, in exchange for their correcting information in your credit file. Other creditors, though, may refuse to change what they have already told a credit bureau.

If a creditor does agree to delete information, it can contact the credit bureau to request the deletion. For example, the creditor could tell the credit bureau that there was good reason for your late payment and the payment had not in fact been delinquent. Second best, the creditor can agree not to verify its original information if asked by the credit bureau. Then, when you dispute the item, the information will not be verified on reinvestigation, and it will have to be deleted.

Be sure that any agreement with the creditor to remove historical information is clear and in writing. Otherwise, creditors may not, in fact, follow through in deleting the information.

Student Loan Defaults. If one of your more troubling delinquencies on your credit record is a student loan default, there are certain special steps you can take, as described in more detail in Chapter Seventeen. If you qualify for a closed school or false certification discharge (described in that chapter), the fact that you were ever in default on the student loan is deleted from your credit record.

You can also consolidate or rehabilitate a defaulted student loan (as described in Chapter Seventeen), so that you are no longer delinquent. Nevertheless, the fact that you were in default on that loan at one time will remain on your credit record.

Public Record Information. The most damaging information on your credit record is sometimes found from public records, such as arrests, convictions, judgments, foreclosures, tax takings, liens and the like. The best way to remove this information from your file is to do so at the source, and then make sure the corrected information is updated in the credit bureau's files.

For example, you may be able to come to an agreement with a creditor to remove a default judgment against you in return for a promise to enter into a repayment plan. You can then dispute the information in your file, and the credit bureau will have to remove the entry because it can no longer verify the accuracy of its entry of a default judgment.

Filing Bankruptcy. Filing bankruptcy sometimes may actually improve your credit record. A bankruptcy discharge gets you off to a fresh start and should reduce your debt burden. It should also enhance the stability of your employment and income. Wage garnishments, continuous collection calls, car repossessions, telephone disconnections, and other consequences of an unaffordable debt burden are eliminated, and this should help you find and hold steady employment.

The resulting stability of your income and lowered debt burden may be more important to a potential creditor than the fact that certain older debts were discharged in bankruptcy. Another advantage of bankruptcy is that it will clear up the current account status of most entries in your file. The credit bureau will have to list the outstanding balance as "0" for each item. While the bankruptcy will be listed in your file, and while the historical summary will list that certain debts had been delinquent at one time, the current account information should be much improved. This is a key part of any lender's review of a credit report, and the deletion of numerous outstanding balances should make it more likely you will receive new credit.

For some creditors, the listing of a bankruptcy will be a black mark. These creditors will refuse to extend you credit or do so at higher rates. But other creditors look at the fact that you cannot file a second chapter 7 (straight) bankruptcy for another six years, and that fewer debts are now competing for your stream of income. In addition, certain government agencies will not provide a government-backed mortgage if you have outstanding defaults, but will do so if you have discharged your debts in bankruptcy. Usually you will only have to wait a year or two after the bankruptcy to become eligible for the mortgage loan.

Bankruptcies stay on your credit record for ten years from the bankruptcy filing, while the underlying debts are usually only reported for seven years from the delinquency. Thus, if your delinquencies are generally five or six years old, bankruptcy may not be the best option to deal with the credit record issues. The debts will have to be deleted from credit reports within another year or two, while the bankruptcy will stay on your record for a full ten years from the date of the bankruptcy.

File Segregation Is Not Recommended. Some consumer self-help manuals and credit repair services suggest file segregation as a means to clean up your credit record, but we recommend strongly against it. Under this approach, you try to confuse the credit bureaus about your identity so that a new, clean file is created for you. You then put as much positive credit history as possible in the new file and apply for credit under the new identity. If the intent is to defraud creditors, this approach is illegal. In addition, the credit bureaus have instituted new programs that may catch you, and this will reflect poorly in your credit file.

Avoid Credit Repair Agencies. Avoid these companies that promise to fix your credit record for a fee. They usually call themselves credit repair, credit service, credit clinic or similar names. These agencies usually cannot deliver what they promise, and you can generally do a better job cleaning up your credit record at no cost, just by following the advice in this book.

There are also widespread reports of credit repair agencies engaging in fraud, misrepresentations, and other consumer abuses. Additionally, in some cases, credit repair strategies recommended by these companies may make matters worse for you or occasionally may even cause you other legal problems.

Collection Lawsuits

Threats by a creditor or collection agency to sue on a debt can be very frightening. However, most threats of lawsuits are just that — threats. These threats should be viewed with skepticism and should not lead to special efforts to pay that debt unless there is some way in which a lawsuit can hurt you. If you are sued, this chapter provides advice on how to respond and explains what can and cannot happen to you if you lose the lawsuit. Here are the basic rules for dealing with lawsuits and threats of lawsuits:

1. *Not all threats of lawsuits will be carried out.* Many creditors and collection agencies threaten to sue as a way to scare you into paying back money which they could not otherwise collect. A threat is used because that collector has no good way of getting paid unless you choose to send in payments. A threatened lawsuit should not cause you to change your priorities about dealing with your debts.

2. *If you are actually sued, you should respond to court deadlines. You may want professional help to evaluate whether you are at risk of losing property in the legal process.* Ignoring a lawsuit can have unintended consequences. These include loss of your right to argue that you do not owe some or all of the money. Liens on your property can also result. Generally, it is safe to ignore a lawsuit only if you have no defenses and if there is no possibility of being forced to pay a judgment if one is entered in court. You

may want professional help to figure this out.

3. *The best way to deal with a lawsuit is to win it. You may have a defense to a lawsuit which can be raised in court.* You may have a good argument that you don't owe money which a creditor is trying to collect. This can offset, in whole or in part, the amount which the creditor is claiming due. Sometimes just raising a defense will lead the creditor to drop the case. More information about possible defenses to a lawsuit is in Chapter Eight.

4. *If you lose a lawsuit, there are a variety of ways the creditor can try to use the court judgment to force you to pay. You must remain alert to these tactics and deal with them as they come up.* Enforcement of a judgment against you can lead to garnishment of your wages or attempts to sell your property. You have exemptions which will prevent this from occurring in many cases. You may need to raise those exemptions in order to benefit from them.

Courts also may have special procedures to require you to make payments. You need to comply with orders to appear in court or to make payments. However, you can raise defenses to payment in court if you cannot afford to pay. You can also consider using the bankruptcy process, because you may have more rights to deal with judgments in bankruptcy than in state court. These may include eliminating the judgment entirely in many situations.

WILL THE CREDITOR ACTUALLY SUE YOU?

Creditors frequently threaten to sue to collect on overdue debts, and this may cause a great deal of anxiety. Usually it is clear that you *can* be sued, but the more important question is *will* you be sued? More often than not the answer is "no," even if there are repeated threats of a suit.

Creditors do not always make rational decisions. However, the following are good indications that a creditor will *not* sue:

- Creditors typically will not file a lawsuit if they have a more effective remedy available. The lawsuit process is slow, somewhat expensive, and, as will be detailed later in this chapter, often unprofitable as a way to recover money from people who have few assets. If the creditor can do something else more effective, it will. For example, a creditor usually will not go to court initially to sue you if, instead, it can repossess your car, foreclose on your house, or terminate your utility service.

- Creditors are unlikely to file a collection suit when the amount of the debt is small. Most creditors rarely sue on debts under $1,000 and some don't sue unless a debt is much higher than that.
- Creditors are unlikely to sue if you dispute the debt and threaten to raise a reasonable defense.
- Creditors are unlikely to sue when you are making small payments even if they are less than what the creditor demands.
- Creditors are not likely to sue when that creditor has no history of filing suit. You can check with the local court clerk or legal services office to see if certain common creditors in the area — for example large retailers or finance companies — have a reputation for filing suit or not.
- When a creditor is out-of-state, it is even more unlikely that it will sue over a small amount, particularly if you have informally raised a defense.

Certain types of threats to take action against you can also be discounted. For example, a collection agency's threat to garnish your wages is often deceptive because the collection agency cannot garnish wages unless it obtains a court judgment. When the same collection agency in its next letter threatens a lawsuit, that statement should be viewed with skepticism because the collector has proven to be untrustworthy. Frequent threats are often a signal that the creditor has no real remedy and is trying to intimidate you into paying an otherwise uncollectible debt voluntarily.

HOW TO RESPOND TO A COLLECTOR'S LAWSUIT

Always Pick Up Your Certified Mail and Accept Notices About Court Actions. You will not escape the consequences of a lawsuit by hiding from notice about that action. Court judgments can be entered against you, even if you don't pick up your mail from the post office or accept delivery when it is brought to your home. You will need a copy of the notice in order to respond appropriately.

Get Professional Advice If You Think You Do Not Owe the Money Or If You May Have a Defense. It is important that you not ignore a lawsuit. Professional advisors may be able to make suggestions about the best way to respond. In many cases, a lawyer can take steps that will significantly improve the outcome for you; doing nothing usually is the worst tactic.

If you cannot get the needed advice from a lawyer or counselor, see if a self-help manual has been written for your state on how to defend a lawsuit. It is likely that someone has published a pamphlet about how you can represent yourself in court, particularly in small claims court. Make sure you get a manual for *your* state. Check with the clerk of your local court.

In general it is a good idea to contact the clerk of the court. Court offices are not just for lawyers — you have as much right to ask questions as someone with a law degree. You should be sure to understand the necessary response requirements and deadlines. The job of the court clerk includes providing help on these issues.

In some busy courts, clerks may not be very helpful. In others, the advice they give may not be accurate. You may find that the officers in the individual courtrooms are more accurate than the employees in the clerk's office. It certainly cannot hurt to ask several clerks the same question and compare their answers. Whenever relying on information from a court clerk, write down the clerk's name and the answer you received.

Carefully Read All Court Documents You Receive. To start a lawsuit, the creditor files a document with the court. Usually this is called the petition or the complaint. In this chapter, we will use the word "complaint" to refer to the document which a creditor uses to begin a case. The complaint asks the court to enter an order or judgment that you owe the creditor a certain amount of money.

Along with the complaint filed with the court, the creditor usually must prepare another document, to be delivered to you. This document informs you that a lawsuit has been filed against you. It is often called a "summons" or "original notice". We will use the word "summons" here. The summons usually tells you what kind of suit is being instituted, what the creditor wants, and the actions you must take to respond to the lawsuit, including the deadline for responding.

The summons must be delivered to you according to state procedure. Sometimes a sheriff or constable must personally deliver the summons. Sometimes mail is sufficient. Dropping the summons on your doorstep is not sufficient.

Never hide from a court summons, always read it carefully, follow the instructions, meet all deadlines, and attend all hearings.

Each court has its own procedures for responding to a summons. The summons should tell you what steps are proper to respond to a lawsuit *for that particular court*. Do not assume that a response appropriate for one type of court will be correct for another court or another type of case. Instead, read the instructions on the summons or seek help from the clerk's office. Be especially careful to meet the deadline. Responses received after the deadline can be ruled invalid.

Summonses are sometimes written in legal jargon that is difficult to understand. Carefully read all the documents, noting any deadlines. If something is unclear, ask a lawyer or someone familiar with legal documents to explain what the document means. As described above, a court clerk may or may not be helpful in explaining the documents. In using a publication to understand the notice, make sure the publication is current, deals with your state, and with the particular court at issue.

Check Which Court Is Hearing the Case. You will want to read which court issued the summons, so that you can direct all questions and your responsive documents to the correct court. Knowing about the court where the case will be heard will also be critical in determining if you can handle your own case and how much legal help you need.

The most common court used by creditors to sue is "small claims court," a court designed to decide claims for relatively small amounts of money. For example, in some states the small claims court can only handle cases seeking $5,000 or less. Other states have higher limits. If the creditor is seeking more money than the small claims court limit, the suit must be filed in the state's general, all-purpose court. These courts have different names in different states.

Because small claims courts are designed to handle claims for small amounts of money, the procedure is usually simple and less formal. In many small claims courts a lawyer is not required; in fact, in a few states, lawyers are not permitted. If a creditor can sue in small claims court, it will often do so without hiring a lawyer. You should also feel confident appearing in that court without a lawyer.

A state's other courts usually follow more formal procedures. Creditors are represented by lawyers, and formal rules of pleading and evidence apply. Although you can represent yourself in this type of court (this is sometimes called appearing "*pro se*" or "*pro per*"), your wisest course may be to use a lawyer.

How to Answer the Summons. To avoid the creditor winning the lawsuit by default, you *must* follow the instructions on the summons. If those instructions are unclear, a lawyer (not the creditor's lawyer) or other professional should be consulted. Another alternative is to contact the clerk of the court where the suit was filed. The summons will tell you to appear at a hearing, to file a written response, or to file an appearance at the clerk's office. If a written response is required, there will also be a deadline in the summons. If the summons has both a deadline for a written response and a date to appear in court, you must file your written response by the deadline or you may risk losing by default and having your court date canceled.

If the summons requests you to appear at the hearing, the summons usually specifies a time, a date, and a place at which the hearing will be held. In more formal courts, it is unusual for a hearing to be scheduled immediately, without allowing time for you to file an answer. In some states hearings are scheduled right away for small claims courts cases. Whatever the court, eviction cases and demands for the immediate possession of property are also usually handled promptly.

A summons often will tell you to file a written answer to the summons, also sometimes called an "appearance," within a certain number of days, usually less than thirty. Although the summons may say "appear and defend," this may not mean that you must physically appear on the date mentioned, but only that a written document must be filed with the court by that date.

Many small claims courts that require written answers provide prepared answer forms, which only need to be signed and returned to the court clerk. The answer form states that the defendant (you) deny the plaintiff's (the creditor's) claim. You should return these by the appropriate deadline if you wish to dispute the case. Other small claims courts require no written answer.

In more formal courts, there are usually no prepared answer forms. For these courts, the answer should usually be written by a lawyer, and should include reasons why you deny being required to pay all of the creditor's claim. If you do not wish to hire a lawyer, you may draft an answer on your own, but you should do your best to follow the court's procedural requirements. Although answers not written by lawyers are accepted by courts, they may be found insufficient on technical grounds.

If you need more time to find a lawyer or to prepare an answer, a time extension is usually allowed, either by written agreement with the creditor's attorney or by a court order. If you reach an agreement for an extension of time (or any other type of agreement) with the creditor or the creditor's attorney, you should confirm the agreement in writing.

Most courts require that you send a copy of the answer and any other document you file with the court to the creditor or the creditor's lawyer, if the creditor is represented by a lawyer. You should indicate on the original court document filed with the court clerk that a copy was mailed to the creditor or its lawyer. Of course, you should also keep a copy of what you file, stamped and dated by the clerk.

Respond to the Court Summons in a Timely Manner. It is important that you scrupulously meet all time deadlines set out in the summons, whether the deadline is to appear at a hearing, to file an answer or to file an appearance. (In many states there is no distinction between filing an answer and an appearance.)

If the deadline is missed, a default judgment can be taken against you. This means that the court will order you to pay the money, plus court costs and, in some cases, any attorney fees, even though there was no hearing on the lawsuit. You will have no opportunity to raise any defenses or explain why you should not have to pay. Instead, the creditor will be granted whatever it requested.

Fewer than 10 percent of consumers who are sued file answers, even though 50 percent or more have good reasons to dispute some or all of the creditor's claim. It is important that you respond. Filing an answer will also slow down the court process and may result in the creditor either ceasing to pursue the lawsuit or agreeing to a reasonable settlement. The creditor may be counting on the case being among the over 90% that result in a quick default judgment in the creditor's favor.

Merely by answering, you change the creditor's evaluation of the case. The cost of actually trying the case and the possibility of losing may persuade the creditor to drop the case or to settle for less than the full amount claimed. Certainly if you want to settle the case, you will obtain a much better deal just by answering the summons and contesting the case than if you let the creditor win by default.

If you informally reach an agreement with the creditor, it is still important to file an appearance and answer. Creditors have been known to proceed with a case and take a default judgment despite having previously reached an agreement with you. Any agreed-upon payment plan or other settlement should be in writing and there should be a clear written statement that the creditor will drop its lawsuit.

An oral agreement with the creditor is not a substitute for filing an answer to the summons and cannot alone prevent a default judgment. In fact, the safest course is to file a copy of the written agreement with the court clerk to be entered into the court record.

Submit Defenses and Counterclaims to the Court. You can tell the court why the creditor should not collect on a debt by presenting a defense, a counterclaim, or both. A defense is a reason why you need not pay the creditor, in whole or in part. A counterclaim is a claim that the creditor owes money to you, regardless of whether you owe the creditor on the debt.

Sometimes the difference between the two is only technical. For example, where a dealer finances the sale of a car that turns out to be a lemon, you might use the car's defects both as a defense and as a counterclaim against the dealer.

It is extremely effective to raise defenses and counterclaims in debt collection lawsuits, particularly if the amount at stake is small. Frequently, creditors do not want to be bothered with a case and will let it drop just because you raise a defense.

Creditors often find lawsuits cost-effective only if large numbers of cases can be disposed of quickly, usually where the debtor never shows up and the creditor wins by default. Creditors may not want to bother with a case that includes a defense because the defense takes time — do not forget the creditor's attorney may be billing out his or her time at $100 dollars an hour or more. Just waiting for a trial to be called may create attorney costs greater than the size of the debt.

Many attorneys take debt collection cases on a contingent fee basis, meaning they keep about a third of the debts they collect. When the attorney takes the case on this basis, often it will be the attorney who will not want to pursue a lawsuit if you can raise valid defenses. Since the attorney's recovery is capped at one-third of the debt, it will not pay to put several hours into a small case.

The creditor is counting on you to give up; creditors often drop lawsuits if you put up a contest.

Each state and each type of court will have its own procedures as to how you present a defense or counterclaim. Some courts require a written statement filed at the beginning of the case specifying your defenses and counterclaims. Some small claims courts require only that you raise the defenses and counterclaims in your statements at the trial.

A wide variety of defenses are possible, for example:

- failure to deliver the item purchased or to provide proper services under a contract,
- defects in the item or services,
- misrepresentation or duress in the creation of the debt,
- that money was paid by you, but not credited to your account,
- that the debt is not owed or that you are current on your payments,
- that the creditor is collecting more than you agreed to pay,
- that you never agreed to pay the debt at all (if, for example

someone fraudulently used your name),
- that the debt has been discharged in bankruptcy,
- that the debt was incurred so long ago that under state law the creditor has waited too long to bring the lawsuit, or
- that the creditor has violated applicable laws in making or collecting the debt.

An important type of defense involves challenging the creditor's calculation of the amount due. The creditor may be seeking attorney fees or collection costs that are either excessive or not allowed by law. For example, the loan contract may not require that you pay fees and costs. The creditor may also have improperly computed the loan's payoff figure. For example, incorrect rates of interest may be applied.

You can raise not only defenses, but also counterclaims that the creditor owes you money. In consumer cases, counterclaims frequently arise when creditors or debt collectors violate consumer protection laws. Claims can also be based on a seller or creditor engaging in unfair or deceptive conduct. Remember that if you have had subsequent problems with the goods or services purchased, you have a defense because you did not receive full value for your money.

Chapter Eight details available consumer claims and defenses. Remember to look at all stages of the transaction, from the original sales solicitation all the way through to the creditor's debt collection procedures.

Attend All Court Proceedings and Respond to All Papers You Receive. In small claims court, you generally only have to go to court once to resolve the case (unless the hearing is rescheduled). When a case is rescheduled, you need to return to court on the rescheduled date.

In more formal courts, a case could be more complicated. The creditor could, but rarely does, take your deposition or send you other paperwork (called "discovery") which you must answer. If your deposition is taken, the creditor's attorney asks you questions, under oath, before the actual trial date and without a judge present. If you get requests for documents or questions about the case (usually called "interrogatories"), you will need to respond to the best of your ability, in writing. Keep copies of any responses you provide. As a participant in the case, you also have a right to hold a deposition or to send discovery to the other side. Because the requirements for doing so are technical, usually you will need a lawyer to set this up for you.

In more formal courts, before the trial, either side can ask for a judgment if there are no important facts in dispute. This is usually called a "motion for summary judgment." If you receive a copy of a motion, you will need to respond to it. Otherwise, it may be granted automatically by the court. Some consumers lose cases because they ignore motions or other paperwork which requires a response filed with the court. When you do file a response, always send a copy to the creditor or to the creditor's lawyer if they have one.

When any type of a hearing or deposition is scheduled, you should attend. A default judgment probably will be taken in your absence, even if you filed an answer or appearance earlier. If you cannot attend, you should send someone else to ask for a delay (usually called a "continuance"), explaining the reasons why you could not attend the hearing that day. This will usually be allowed if you had a good reason for not attending (such as illness, family emergency, preexisting and unavoidable work conflict, or unusual transportation problems).

Whenever possible you should let the creditor or the creditor's attorney know in advance if you have a good reason for not attending the hearing. Often they will agree to a delay in the case. If a delay is agreed upon, you should put it in writing, in the form of a letter, a statement confirming the agreement.

The hearing is the opportunity for both parties to tell their story to a judge or magistrate. In many small claims courts, the hearing is informal. Usually, the creditor first explains why it is suing. In most cases, the creditor gives the judge a copy of the purchase contract and the accounting records that shows any missed payments.

Next, you will present your response. To be most effective, you should consider consulting a lawyer for advice about presentation of your case. At a minimum, since court can be frightening, you should make notes about what you plan to say, so that you do not forget an important issue at the last minute. You should not hesitate to ask for a delay in the court date if needed to find an attorney.

How to Prepare for a Court Hearing. Here are some tips to help you prepare for a court hearing:

- *Bring all relevant documents.* It is unlikely that you will have another chance to present documents except at the hearing.

Remember that courts generally pay a lot of attention to written documents. It will be helpful to have extra copies available, because the court and the creditor will keep copies of the documents you present. In more formal courts, you may need to bring someone to identify the documents and prove they are authentic unless you have personal knowledge of what the document is and where it comes from.

- *Bring witnesses if there are any.* You have the right to present witnesses, and their impact may be important, especially if they are not a friend or relative. For example, if the dispute is about an item which does not work properly, a mechanic or another witness can testify from their own experience in using that item.
- *Do not rely on written statements of your witnesses,* because the court usually may not allow them into evidence. Have the witnesses attend the trial.
- *Consider going to court beforehand to orient yourself* as to where the courtroom is, how the court works, how people dress, when to stand, how to tell when your case is called, where you sit during the hearing, whether a microphone is used and how to use it, the judge's personality, whether an interpreter is available, etc.
- *Take a companion to the actual hearing* to offer emotional support, to give you feedback and other help, to keep track of your documents, and to offer a second opinion if you must respond on the spot to a settlement offer.
- *Prepare a written chronological report of events in advance,* together with a checklist of points to make, and a checklist of documents to be given to the court, and take the checklist with you.
- *Assume that the judge has not read any of the documents* already presented to the court and knows none of the facts of the case. Start at the beginning and tell your story in a clear and organized fashion in the order it happened. Sympathetic facts should be brought out and repeated if necessary.
- *Do not be afraid to be forceful, but do not make personal attacks on individuals,* including lawyers, witnesses, or the judge. A display of anger will usually hurt more than it helps.

DEALING WITH A DEFAULT JUDGMENT

As explained earlier, by not filing a written answer or appearance within the specified time, or by failing to attend the hearing, or by missing other deadlines, you may lose the opportunity to raise your defenses. This is usually called a "default." It is important that you not lose by default unless a lawyer has evaluated your case for you and determined that you will lose nothing by allowing a default to be entered.

Nevertheless, if a default has been entered against you, you may still be able to set aside the ruling and receive another chance to be heard. Specific court rules govern these opportunities. Usually, a default can be set aside only for specific reasons and within a short time after the judgment has been entered into the court records.

Reasons for setting aside a default commonly include not having proper notice of the case or other unavoidable circumstances that made you unable to answer within the required time. In some courts, you will also have to tell the court briefly about your defense or counterclaim so that it will know that you have a chance to get a different result if the default is lifted. Usually, a request to "remove," "lift," or "set aside" a default has to be made to the court in writing. A copy of your request should always be mailed to the creditor or to its lawyer.

THE JUDGMENT AND YOUR APPEAL RIGHTS

The judgment is what the court orders after hearing the case. If you win, you will get a court order that says you owe nothing (or a reduced amount). If the creditor wins, the judgment gives the creditor the right to force payment by a variety of methods. You cannot be forced to pay unsecured debts until a judgment is entered.

Once the judgment is entered, if you do not pay, the creditor has special rights to seize your property or income (unless this property or income is protected by federal or state law). However, you may have certain rights to prevent payment of a judgment even after it is entered.

A party that loses a lawsuit at the first court level can appeal to a higher level. For cases heard in small claims court, that usually means appealing to the state's general purpose trial court. This may be the only appeal that is allowed from a small claims court decision. Further appeal can be granted only if a higher court specifically says that it wishes to hear the case.

If a case starts in a more formal trial court, the losing party can appeal to another court which has power to hear appeals. In some states, more than one appeal is possible because there are several layers of courts. Deadlines for filing an appeal are generally short and strictly enforced. Procedures for what papers to file in an appeal may be quite technical and may also be strictly enforced.

The costs of an appeal vary widely, but can be significant. Typical costs include a filing fee, fees for a transcript of the trial, and posting a bond to cover the judgment being appealed. In some circumstances, a party unable to afford these fees can request that some of them be waived.

If there is an appeal, in most cases, it will not involve a completely new presentation of the case. Usually, an appeal court will review the case on the record made in the court below.

CREDITORS' ATTEMPTS TO COLLECT COURT JUDGMENTS

Significance of a Court Judgment Against You. Even if you lose a lawsuit, this does *not* mean you must repay the debt. If your family is in financial distress and cannot afford to repay its debts, a court order to pay may not really change anything. If you do not have the money to pay, the court's decision that you owe the debt will not make payment any more possible.

What the court order does do is let creditors use several special collection tools to try to squeeze money from you. How effective these tools are will depend not only on how much income and property you have, but on the *types* of income and property involved. In some cases these tools are effective in recovering money and may even result in loss of your home. In other cases, these special tools will have *no* impact on you. In still others, the creditor will not take further action against you despite the judgment, because of the cost or time involved in using these special collection tactics to enforce a judgment.

Where losing a lawsuit has no adverse effects for you, you are called "judgment proof." Your assets and income are small enough and are of a type that federal and state law fully protects them from seizure by creditors. In that case, you do not really have to worry about the judgment unless your financial situation substantially improves. You should ignore the judgment and save your income to pay bills whose payment is critical to your survival, such as a mortgage, rent, or utility payment.

Even a court order cannot make you pay a debt if all your income and property is exempt from seizure.

If you are faced with a collection lawsuit, you should know in advance whether you are judgment proof, that is whether the creditor can use the judgment to hurt you. If you can be hurt, that creates even more incentive to defend against the lawsuit.

If you do not know whether you are "judgment proof" under the laws of your state, you can consider consulting a lawyer on this limited issue. The most important consideration in determining whether you are judgment proof is whether the creditor can force you to pay with one or more of the special creditor remedies discussed below.

Creditors may be able to utilize any of four different types of special remedies to obtain involuntary payment if they obtain a court judgment against you. These remedies vary a great deal on a state by state basis. If any of the remedies produces only partial payment, the creditor can continue to resort to the same or a different remedy to try to recover the full amount. The remainder of this chapter discusses these special remedies in general terms. You will need to get specific information about practices in your state.

Attachment and Execution. A creditor with a court judgment can arrange for the sheriff to seize certain of your property. Because the creditor is armed with a court judgment and is asking the sheriff to do the seizure, the creditor can seize your property even though the creditor had not taken that property as collateral for its loan. After seizure, the sheriff sells the property at public auction, and applies the proceeds to the judgment by paying the creditor.

These auctions are usually poorly attended and bring low bids. For this reason, creditors rarely seize used household goods, which will have minimal resale value. If property is sold at auction, you or your friends can attend the auction and purchase back the possessions at a bargain price.

The right of a creditor to take your property is limited. State law specifically protects certain types of your property and/or certain amounts of your property. Protected property is called "exempt". You can prevent the seizure of exempt property by filing a notice of exempt property, or by taking similar steps specified by your state law. In some states, you will need to file papers with the sheriff or a public official by a certain deadline in order to get the benefit of an exemption. In other states, the sheriff gives you permission to set aside exempt items at the time of seizure or sale.

Additionally, the sheriff cannot seize property in your possession which does not belong to you. To stop its seizure, the property's rightful owner may have to file a declaration of ownership with the appropriate office. More discussion on your rights to protect property from seizure are discussed later in this chapter under "Exemptions May Prevent Creditor From Seizing Property."

Judgment Liens. Any unpaid judgment generally becomes a lien on real estate owned by you in the county where the judgment is entered (or statewide in some states). Creditors also may have the right to transfer judgments or otherwise to make them applicable to your real estate in other locations.

Unless the real estate is legally exempt from execution, creditors can force its sale in much the same manner as they can force the sale of other property. Later in this chapter, there is a discussion as to when real estate is exempt from execution.

Even if the real estate is exempt from execution, the creditor's lien on your property usually remains in effect until you sell it. In most states, when you sell the property, mortgages are paid off first. Then you get to keep what is left, up to your state's maximum exemption amount. Anything over that amount goes to satisfy all or some of the creditor's judgment against you. Even if your property is exempt from seizure today, if the property's value increases enough in the future, the creditor can then recover its judgment from the sale of the property.

One possible way of getting rid of judgment liens is to file for bankruptcy. To the extent the property is exempt when you file for bankruptcy, the lien can be permanently removed.

Garnishment. A creditor with a court judgment against you has the right to "garnish" money belonging or owed to you that is in the hands of a third party. In this context, to "garnish" means to take. Most often, garnishment takes money from your wages or bank account.

Garnishment usually can only take place *after* the creditor obtains a judgment against you. After obtaining a judgment, the creditor can file a request for garnishment with the court clerk, sheriff or another local official depending on state practice. A notice is then issued to the "garnishee" (a bank, an employer, or another third party holding your property), directing that party to turn over the property at a specified time.

You must be given notice of the garnishment. You can then request a hearing to prove that state or federal law protects the funds at issue from garnishment. Federal and state law protect you from garnishment in two ways:

1. *A portion of your wages is protected from seizure.* Current federal law provides that the first $127.50 from weekly take-home pay, after taxes and Social Security are deducted, cannot be garnished at all. (The $127.50 amount is 30 times the current minimum wage of $4.25. For example, if the minimum wage increased to $5, the amount of weekly wages protected would increase to $150). If the weekly take-home pay is more than $127.50, an employer, in response to a garnishment order, must pay no more than the *smaller* of the following amounts:

   • the weekly take-home pay (after withholding) minus $127.50, or
   • twenty-five percent of that take-home pay.

A higher amount can be garnished if the debt is for child support or alimony.

The standard described above is based on federal law and sets out minimum wage protections for debtors in all fifty states. In addition, in some states, you have even greater protections against wage garnishment. Some states prohibit all wage garnishment or allow a smaller amount of wages to be garnished than the federal standard. Moreover, federal law and some state laws forbid employers from firing employees solely because their wages are being garnished.

2. *Certain types of income, primarily government payments, are completely exempt from garnishment.* Even if your income is large enough so that a portion may be garnished, certain sources of income are *completely* protected under federal or state law. For example, federal law completely exempts Social Security payments, Supplemental Security Income, and veterans' benefits. States with AFDC and unemployment insurance programs usually exempt those benefits from garnishment as well. If you place these funds in your bank account, the money remains exempt from seizure. However, problems sometimes arise when your bank account includes both exempt and non-exempt money. It is hard to trace which part of the funds is exempt.

Usually, your first $127.50 a week in take home pay and all your Social Security or other government benefits are completely exempt from seizure.

Federal and state law do a better job protecting wages than bank accounts. If you are threatened with a court judgment, you must weigh the benefits of a bank account against the risk of having the money seized. Creditors will have more difficulty finding and seizing a bank account in another state or in another individual's name.

If a significant amount of your income or cash in a bank account is subject to garnishment, you may wish to work out a deal with the creditor rather than allow your money to be taken. The creditor may be just as happy to accept a certain amount a month instead of going through the garnishment procedures. The creditor's motivation to settle is increased in states where part of the amount garnished goes to pay court costs and the employer's administrative costs, and does not go to the creditor. More information on garnishments and available defenses is contained in National Consumer Law Center, *Fair Debt Collection*, Chapter 9 (3d ed. 1996).

Debtor's Examination. After obtaining a judgment, a creditor can ask a judge to order you to appear in court to answer questions about your income and assets. The purpose is to find income or property that is not protected by law and which the creditor may seize.

In some states this procedure is called a debtor's examination, but the procedure goes by other names in other states. Some creditors routinely request a debtor's examination. Others never do. Three important things to remember about a debtor's examination are:

- It is a court-ordered appearance. Failure to show up can result in arrest, citation for contempt, and a jail sentence.
  A notice to appear for a court examination should *never* be ignored. You should appear or make a written request to the court for a postponement. The court will usually grant a postponement if the creditor agrees to the request or if you have a good reason.
- Your answers are made under oath, and often are recorded by a court reporter. Lying under oath is perjury, a crime punishable by jail.
- If the creditor which holds a judgment does find assets or income not protected by law, the creditor can obtain a court order requiring you to turn over those assets to the creditor. Failure to comply with the order could be considered contempt, and could result in jail.

Because of all the various ways a debtor's examination can get you into trouble, it is a good idea to obtain legal representation promptly.

The first step in responding to notice of a debtor's examination is to review your assets *well before the examination*. Determine if all your property is protected by law and if all your income is exempt from garnishment. If so, immediately tell the creditor. This may be sufficient to get the creditor to drop the request for an examination since it will just be a waste of everyone's time. If the examination is canceled, be sure to get this in writing; do not rely on the creditor's oral promise that it will drop the examination.

If there is property that legally can be seized, you may consider "exemption planning," just like wealthier families engage in tax planning or estate planning. Exemption planning involves maximizing the protection of existing laws by converting property that could be seized (for example, cash) into property that cannot be seized (for example, household goods or equity in the home).

By way of example, suppose you are a homeowner with $10,000 in cash and $10,000 equity in your home. Assume the homestead exemption is $20,000 and other property exemptions allow you to exempt only $3,000 in cash. In this example, at least $7,000 in cash can be seized. But, if the cash is used to prepay the mortgage in part, the increased equity in the home is fully protected by the homestead exemption.

This type of planning is a better approach than giving non-exempt property to relatives or friends. This latter type of transfer will be frowned upon and can be set aside by a court. If you cannot account to the court for transfers of large amounts of your property, you may be accused of fraud, and this would compound your legal problems.

If there is property important to you that a creditor can seize, you can approach the creditor about a "workout" agreement. You can offer to pay all or a portion of the amount due over a period of months or even years. The amount you offer to pay should be directly related to what the creditor could seize after the debtor's examination. Do not offer to pay $3000 over 12 months when the only items the creditor could seize have a market value of $500.

There are two important points about workout agreements. First, always get the agreement in writing. The writing should excuse you from attending the debtor's examination, and contain the creditor's promise not to use wage garnishment or execution on your property as long as you continue to make payments. (You can also ask for an agreement to waive the remainder of the debt if part is paid. Some creditors will accept partial payment if they know they can't get payment in full. From the creditor's perspective some payment is better than none.)

Second, finalize the agreement before the debtor's examination. Failure to show up at the examination could lead to a contempt of court citation and make any subsequent settlement with the creditor that much more difficult.

A final option to avoid your loss or property after a debtor's examination is to file for bankruptcy. The bankruptcy will immediately stop any seizure and may allow you to keep your property permanently. Since bankruptcy is a right under federal (national) law, your rights in the bankruptcy process will take precedence over the state court collection process. Chapter Eighteen discusses consumer bankruptcy filings.

EXEMPTIONS MAY PROTECT YOUR PROPERTY FROM SEIZURE

State exemption laws protect certain types of your property from seizure after a court judgment and permit you to keep the basic necessities of life. However, exemption statutes provide little or no protection from a creditor seizing *collateral.* For example, if you put up a home or car as collateral on a loan, exemption laws do not prevent the creditor from seizing the home or car if you get behind in your loan payments.

Exemption statutes do provide significant protections against property being seized by *unsecured* creditors with judgments against you. Exemption statutes give you important rights if you have not put up any collateral when taking out a loan, but where, *after a court judgment,* the creditor seeks an order to seize your property.

Some exemption statutes specify dollar amounts of property that are exempt from seizure. For example, the statute may specify that $8,000 worth of your personal property is exempt from seizure. Such a statute would allow you to choose which items of your personal property you want to keep, as long as what you keep is worth $8000 or less. Such a statute will apply to your personal property, and not your home, which is considered real estate. What types of property are considered your personal property will be specified by your state statute.

Exemption amounts stretch a long way because the exemption amount relates to your equity in property, not to the property's value.

Homestead exemptions protect your residence, and can be as high as $100,000 or more, but can also be significantly less in other states. Under some exemption statutes, if husband and wife own property, they may be entitled under the exemption law to double the amount of protection. To benefit from the homestead exemption in some states, a declaration of the homestead must be filed with the property registry in your community. In a few states this paper must have been filed before the credit was granted. You should always file your declaration as early as possible if you live in a state where a declaration is required. In other states protection is automatic.

One of the best things about exemption protections is that an exemption for only a few thousands of dollars may in fact be sufficient to protect your home or car worth significantly more. The key is that if you have a mortgage or other lien on the property, your equity is less than the full value of the *property*. The amount that may be exempted refers not to the dollar value of the property, but to the value of the your *equity* in the property. Equity is how much the property is worth in excess of mortgages, tax and water liens, liens from home improvement work, or other secured debts.

For example, consider a state homestead exemption of $30,000 and a home worth $150,000. If you have a $100,000 first mortgage and a $20,000 home equity loan, you have $30,000 in equity. Since the homestead exemption is $30,000, the home is completely exempt from execution by a judgment creditor.

In addition, because execution on property is usually expensive, many creditors will not seize property even if there is non-exempt equity. Instead they will wait to collect on their lien until you sell the property. They will then expect to be paid from the proceeds of the sale.

Some states specify that certain of your property is totally exempt from seizure, no matter how much money it is worth. The list of totally exempt property typically includes such items as tools and supplies required for your occupation, clothing, a car (usually with a value under a specified amount), a bible and household goods. Texas and Florida also totally exempt a principal residence on a certain size plot of land.

If a homestead or other exemption allows you to exempt only a certain portion of your equity in the property, the creditor can force a sale. You would retain the amount of the exemption from the sale proceeds. In the prior example, if the home's value increases to $200,000, a creditor with a court judgment could force a sale. The first $100,000 would go to the mortgage holder, the next $20,000 to pay off the home equity loan. The next $30,000 of sale proceeds would be kept by you. Only the last $50,000 of sale proceeds could be used to pay the creditor initiating the sale. (Of course, if the creditor is owed less than $50,000, you get the balance.)

If you file for bankruptcy, in some states the property that can be exempted from seizure is increased because you can choose the federal bankruptcy exemptions. These may or may not be better than your state's exemptions. But some states have "opted out" of the federal exemptions, meaning that even in a bankruptcy, you must rely on your state exemptions.

Some creditors try to force you to turn over property that is exempt under law from seizure. The creditor will point to small print in the contract in which you agreed to waive rights under state exemption laws. These blanket waivers are now illegal under federal law.

Even if exemption laws fully protect your property at one point in time, you may be at risk if your equity in your property increases. Court judgments remain on the books for many years. If your equity in a home or other property increases beyond the exemption limit or if a household acquires nonexempt income or property, creditors may be able to reach it. At that point, if the judgment is still unpaid, you will have to work out a payment plan with the creditor or reconsider a bankruptcy filing.

State exemption laws can be very complicated. This is an issue for which you may want to get professional help. At a minimum, you should try to find a publication which addresses your state's laws. This type of publication may be available from the local bar association, a legal services office, or a consumer credit counselor. Make sure anything you read is up to date.

Fighting Back

- *Reasons You Should Raise Your Defenses*
- *Identifying Your Legal Claims*
- *How to Pursue Your Legal Claims*

You may not have to repay all of your debt. You may have complaints concerning the conduct of lenders, salespersons, collectors, contractors or service providers, and these complaints may reduce the amount you owe.

Misconduct and errors by creditors and sellers help cause your financial problems. Many examples are discussed below. Your complaints about this conduct create important legal rights for you, in the form of legal claims against your creditors. These claims can be used to eliminate the obligation to pay some or all of your debts. The fact that you have fallen behind on your payments doesn't prevent you from raising your defenses to repayment. Fight back whenever you have a chance; the best defense is usually a good offense.

WHY FIGHT BACK?

You should take the offensive and raise all your legitimate claims in the debt collection process for three reasons:

1. There May Never Be Another Chance. If you do not raise your claims in response to a debt collection lawsuit or other collection action, you may never have another chance to do so. If you wait to begin an affirmative case, the court may say that the action was brought too late and is barred under court rules. Similarly, a court may throw out your lawsuit, saying that you should have raised the issue at the same time the collector brought its case — that it is a waste of the court's time to hear the same case twice. Also, it is hard to find time and resources to begin a lawsuit. You may lose the drive and initiative to sue over a consumer problem if you wait to file a separate suit.

Raising claims immediately in response to a debt collection action will avoid all of these problems. You will be highly motivated — no one likes to pay a debt when treated unfairly. It is cheaper and easier to respond to a lawsuit than to initiate your own suit. (Usually there are no fees for defending an action. In states where there are fees, you may be able to get them waived if you cannot afford to pay.) Additionally, courts may allow you to raise even very old claims if they are raised as a defense to a collection action, as opposed to a separate lawsuit.

2. You Should Be Compensated If You Have Been Hurt. If you have a good claim, you are entitled to recover for any injury suffered. Many consumer laws also allow you extra damages to discourage sellers or creditors from engaging in this misconduct. In some cases this may include punitive damages, which are special damages designed to punish a party which is responsible for especially serious misconduct. If you pursue these claims aggressively, rather than pay the creditor, it may turn out that the creditor owes you money.

When your injury is very small, some consumer statutes still award you $100 or even as much as $2000 as a way of encouraging you to pursue the problem. If you cannot afford to pay a debt, raising even small claims against the creditor may help cut the debt down to size.

3. Raising Claims Helps to Get Good Settlements. Creditors collecting on relatively small consumer debts depend on you not contesting the debt. This allows them to collect their money quickly and inexpensively. When you raise claims in response to a collection action, the economics of collection change dramatically. Not only does the collector have to factor in the value of your claim, but also the time and expense it will take to finally resolve the case.

Often collectors will drop cases when you present strong claims. Other times they will agree to settlements very advantageous to you. Of course, not every creditor will cave in at the merest mention of your claim. Some creditors are more willing to face a court trial than others.

IDENTIFYING CLAIMS YOU MAY HAVE

Consumers do not always realize all the different claims they can raise relating to a debt. You may want to see a lawyer or non-profit counselor to find out if you have a defense. In doing so, you should bring any documents you have concerning the debt or the sale that created the debt. Sometimes the documents will provide a good basis to reconstruct any problems you had with that creditor or seller.

Nevertheless, it is not only the documents which are important. Oral promises and other statements made to you can also be the basis for a claim. You should explore all of the following six stages related to a transaction.

1. The Original Sale of Goods or Services. Most debts arise from the purchase of goods or services. In the case of loans, the money often is earmarked for the purchase of particular goods or services. Additionally the loan itself should be thought of as a service which the creditor provides.

A first question is always what statements (and written advertisements) were made to encourage you to buy the goods or to clinch the deal. Were the seller's statements false? Did the written documents jibe with the seller's oral statements? Were high pressure tactics used? Did the seller hide key information?

You may feel that you will lose in a contest with the seller, that a court will always believe an established business person over an individual who is fighting a debt. Quite the contrary, used car dealers, aluminum siding sellers, and other merchants may have very low believability for judges and juries.

Without getting into legal technicalities, any relevant oral or written misrepresentation, non-disclosure, or high pressure tactic is likely to lead to a legitimate consumer claim. Anything that you find to be outrageous, unfair, unjust, or fraudulent is likely to form the basis of a case.

Pay special attention to door-to-door sales. High pressure tactics and oral misrepresentations are common in those transactions. In addition, such sellers have to give you a right to cancel the sale for any reason within the first three days. Were you given such a notice?

The National Consumer Law Center's *Unfair and Deceptive Acts and Practices* (3d ed. 1991) provides the best description of the many types of claims and legal theories available to consumers relating to sales abuses. The book lists thousands of practices, categorized by type of sale, that have been found to be deceptive or unfair.

2. Warranties. After receipt, goods or services often do not turn out as expected. The goods are later discovered to be defective, work is not completed, or the work is found to be substandard. These problems provide a strong basis for claims.

A common mistake consumers make is to assume that, when a product is sold "as is" or "without warranties," that they cannot complain about problems with the product. In fact, "as is" disclaimers often do not prevent you from winning court awards from sellers.

Of course, you should always raise claims when goods or services are not delivered, the wrong services are performed, or the work is not completed. Similarly, when goods or services come with a warranty, the seller's failure to comply with the warranty should be actionable. For more detail on consumer claims based on the performance of the goods or services, see two National Consumer Law Center publications, *Sales of Goods and Services* (2d ed. 1989) and *Unfair and Deceptive Acts and Practices* (3d ed. 1991).

3. Loan Terms. Most debts begin with a loan contract — often called a "note." Anything that you find to be outrageous, unfair, unjust, or deceptive about the terms of the loan agreement is likely to form the basis of a valid claim. Oral misrepresentations made to encourage you to enter into a loan agreement also may be a basis for claims, as should a lender's attempt to confuse you or hide important terms. High pressure tactics should also be challenged.

You may also have a claim where a creditor signs you up for a loan which the creditor knows you cannot afford or where the creditor knows that a refinanced loan will be worse for you than sticking with the original debt. Bogus charges, double-charging, sale of useless insurance and the like may also be actionable.

A common problem arises when two or more businesses team up to mislead you. For example, a home improvement contractor may have set up a high rate loan for you to pay for home improvements, because that contractor gets a commission from the loan company. Similarly, some loan brokers will arrange bad deals in order to take advantage of a high commission. In these types of cases, claims can be made based on the relationship between the parties. In many cases both parties can be sued based on the actions of either one. You should not assume that you have no claim when the party who took advantage of you is no longer in the picture.

In addition, the Federal Truth in Lending Act, state installment sales laws, and other state credit legislation create various requirements as to what the creditor must tell you about a loan. Violations may lead to as much as $2,000 in special damages in addition to any actual damages you have suffered. You also may be entitled to rescind some types of mortgage loans, as discussed in Chapter Twelve. These statutes are technical and you may need the assistance of a lawyer. The National Consumer Law Center's *Truth in Lending* (3d ed. 1995) is the best volume available about your rights under the Federal Truth in Lending statute.

Many states have usury laws that set maximum interest rates and limits on certain types of credit charges. Creditors violating these "usury" statutes will have to pay significant damages, but again a lawyer is usually necessary to press such claims. NCLC's *The Cost of Credit: Regulation and Legal Challenges* (1995) fully discusses a variety of types of credit overcharges.

4. Creditor's Subsequent Conduct. You can also raise claims and defenses based on a creditor's conduct after a deal is completed. You should check whether payments have been properly applied, whether escrow amounts are handled correctly, and whether late charges are appropriate.

Creditors often purchase property insurance for you if your own insurance coverage lapses. Make sure this substitute coverage was not purchased for periods when you had your own insurance in place, did not contain unnecessary coverages, and was not sold at an inflated price. These problems are especially common now because many big companies which loan money also have interests in insurance businesses.

Determine if the creditor's employees made false promises that the creditor would not repossess the collateral or call in the loan if certain payments were made. If the creditor assigned the loan to a second creditor, were you clearly notified of a new address to send payments?

5. Debt Collection Tactics. Chapter Five discusses what types of debt collection practices are illegal. Even when your primary concern is a repossession, a debt collection lawsuit, or a foreclosure, do not forget to consider *earlier* debt collection contacts. If these earlier contacts were illegal, they will form the basis for legitimate claims against the creditor or collector. You may be able to obtain $1,000 in damages for collection agency misconduct even if your actual injury from the harassment is hard to determine.

6. Attempts to Enforce a Court Order or Security Interest. You may have problems with the way a creditor attempts to collect on a judgment, repossess a car, seize household property, foreclose on a home, evict you, or terminate utility service. Creditors often are sloppy in the way they sue, garnish wages, repossess or seize property. Their failure to follow proper procedures may lead to legal claims. In most states, these claims give rise to special damage awards. Your rights in these areas are spelled out in Chapter Seven and Chapters Eleven through Sixteen.

Sometimes raising all your defenses
and counterclaims to a collection lawsuit
will both cancel your debt and result in a
cash recovery for you and your attorney.

An Example. Ms. P was sued for the balance owed on a car loan after her car had been repossessed and sold. The car had never worked properly, and a loan which was promised at 8% had turned into a 15% finance company loan. Ms. P received no notice prior to repossession and she was sued, not where she lives, but rather in the next county.

In defending the lawsuit, Ms. P should raise all of her available claims. These might include the seller's misrepresentations about the car and the credit terms, problems with the car's performance and the seller's failure to repair the defects. The creditor may also be responsible for an illegal repossession and for failure to give required notices. Finally, the lawsuit itself may violate federal law by not being brought where Ms. P resides.

All of these claims may be used to offset the amount Ms. P owes the creditor on the debt. In fact, it is not uncommon for an aggressive attorney to be able to settle a case like this one so that Ms. P owes the creditor nothing, and instead the creditor pays her several thousand dollars and also her attorney fees and court costs. On the other hand, if these defenses and counterclaims are not raised, the creditor might get a judgment against Ms. P which it could enforce by garnishing her wages or selling other property. (See Chapter Seven.)

HOW TO RAISE YOUR CLAIMS

When to Raise Your Claims. Usually you will want to raise all available complaints as early as possible in the debt collection process. Waiting too long may diminish your credibility. Warning a collector at an early stage that you have significant claims to offset a debt may be sufficient to get the creditor to drop collection activity. If the you wait to raise the claims during a creditor's collection lawsuit, the creditor may be less likely to drop the case because the creditor has already invested resources in the action.

Consequently, every time a creditor contacts you about payment, mention your claims. If the creditor still pursues a lawsuit on the debt, raise the claims at that point also. Chapter Seven explains how to raise counterclaims and defenses to the creditor's lawsuit.

Your claims should also be raised against a lender bringing a court action to foreclose on your home. It is harder to use your claims to stop a "non-judicial foreclosure" of your home or a self-help repossession of your car. In both of these actions, the creditor seizes your property without a court proceeding, so that there is no hearing for you to object to the taking. When such non-judicial actions are threatened or have occurred, you may want to obtain an attorney to bring your own court action to try to stop or undo the seizure based on your claims.

After a seizure of property, a creditor may seek the remainder due on a debt, after crediting you with the sale price. This is called an action to collect the "deficiency." You may also raise all your claims in response to such a deficiency claim.

Put Your Complaints in Writing. If you believe you have claims against a creditor, you may want to put the basis for your claims in writing and mail them to the creditor and to its attorney, if any. This is especially important if you believe that you have warranty or similar claims. Don't forget to keep a copy of anything you mail. This will prevent the creditor from later claiming that it did not know you were dissatisfied. You generally should try to put your complaint in writing as early as possible. However a letter to the creditor does not substitute for the formal process of raising your claims in a court action. You will need to file the appropriate court papers as well.

Complaints About the Sale Should Be Directed to the Collector as Well as the Seller. Often the creditor collecting a debt is not the original seller who provided the goods or services to you. Debt collectors usually do not want to hear about problems you had with the seller or with a prior creditor involved with the debt. The collector may tell you to go talk to the seller or that prior creditor.

Although the collector might not want to hear about your complaints, you should tell the collector anyway. The very fact that the collector does not want to hear about these problems is a good indication of how important it is to press these claims.

There are several reasons why it is critical that you press available claims against the collector, instead of just tracking down the original seller or creditor. By the time you get a court order against the original seller, the seller may be bankrupt or may have skipped town. Also, a court order against a seller may take years to obtain, and involve costly filing fees and legal bills. Finally, an award against the seller will not by itself stop a collection action brought by someone else. You can win against the seller, but lose in a separate case brought by the collector.

On the other hand, when you raise defenses against the creditor collecting on the debt, it is the collection action that may take years to resolve. Raising your claims as a defense to a collection suit is also usually free because the party bringing the lawsuit, not the person being sued, pays the court fees. Additionally, bringing claims against the collector may deal with the pressing problem of payment on that debt.

Despite their protests to the contrary, creditors are often liable for whatever problems you have with the seller.

If you obtain legal representation, your attorney may decide to sue not only the creditor bringing the action, but also the seller, the original creditor, or even the debt collection agency. But the key thing to remember is that it is always better to defend the creditor's attempt to collect a debt than to give the creditor the money and try to get it back from someone else. When the creditor tells you to go talk to the seller, firmly answer "no thank you, I am raising my claims against you."

The Creditor Is Often Responsible for the Seller's Misconduct.

Creditors collecting on a debt are usually responsible for the actions of the seller, original creditor, and any debt collector or repossessor. In most cases the loan documents will say that any collector of the loan is subject to all claims and defenses that you have against the seller. In other words, the very loan the creditor is trying to enforce will say that you can raise the seller's misconduct as a defense.

Another legal principle is that you can usually raise against a subsequent collector of a loan any defense you could raise against the original lender. What this means is that if one creditor transfers the loan to another creditor, all your defenses against the first creditor are also available against the second creditor. It is easy to see who the first creditor is by looking at the loan documents and seeing who is identified as the lender.

Where the seller is the original creditor, which is often the case where goods or services are purchased on credit, you are in a good position to raise the seller's misconduct as a defense to the loan. For example, where a car dealer or home improvement contractor is the original creditor, you can raise as defenses on the loan anything you could raise with the car dealer or home improvement contractor, no matter who is trying to collect the loan.

Sometimes creditors try to claim they are "holders in due course." This special status would free them of any responsibility for the conduct of an earlier creditor. Fortunately, the law in recent decades frowns on the holder in due course status in consumer matters. Creditors are not usually able to avoid responsibility. For this reason, you should assume you can sue the person or company that is suing you, even if they are not the one who originally caused you harm.

9

Saving Your Home: An Overview

- *Twelve Tips for Dealing with Mortgage Problems and Foreclosure*
- *How to Use This Book to Defend Your Home*
- *How Foreclosures Work*

TWELVE TIPS FOR DEALING WITH MORTGAGE PROBLEMS AND FORECLOSURE

Potential loss of your home is the single most urgent problem you may face if you are having financial difficulties. For many people, foreclosure means not only loss of shelter, but also loss of many years investment to create home equity and a livable family environment. For this reason, you will almost always want to deal with a foreclosure problem as your highest priority if are having financial problems and you own a home. Here are twelve important tips for preventing foreclosures:

1. Reexamine Your Budget. Can You Cut Expenses or Increase Income if It Means Saving Your Home? If you are facing foreclosure, make a special effort to eliminate unnecessary expenses. Food, mortgage payments, utilities, essential transportation and unavoidable health related expenses should be your highest priorities, though even those expenses can be examined to see if reductions are possible. (See Chapter Two.) On the other side of the budget, look at whether there are ways to increase your income, including loans from pension plans, food stamps, fuel assistance, property tax abatements and unemployment or disability income. (See Chapter Two.)

2. Make Timely Home Mortgage Payments, If Possible. If you cannot pay all of your bills, you should make mortgage payments first after food and utilities. This is because the mortgage company has the right to foreclose and take your home while other creditors generally do not.

3. If You Fall Behind on Your Mortgage and the Creditor Returns Your Partial Payments, Save as Much of This Money as Possible Each Month Toward Your Mortgage. When you fall behind on payments, the mortgage company has the right to refuse partial payment. If you can afford partial payments, but the mortgage company refuses to take them, the money should be put aside rather than used for other bills. The money that is set aside will help you negotiate with the mortgage company later, and even if nothing can be done to save your home, you will have some money saved for moving expenses.

4. Resolve Any Disputes You May Have Concerning the Amount Due. Use Legal Assistance If Necessary. Some foreclosures occur because of mistakes made by the mortgage company. When you disagree with the amount the mortgage company says you owe, you should immediately try to address the problem by contacting the mortgage company. Provide the documentation they request and keep copies for yourself. If you are not satisfied with the result (or if there is an unreasonable delay), you may want to get legal assistance. You also may have legal defenses to repayment of some mortgages, especially those with high interest rates or unusual terms. See Chapter Twelve.

5. Ask the Mortgage Company Whether It Will Agree to a Temporary or Permanent Change to Your Mortgage Terms (Called a "Workout"). A workout is often the best solution to your financial difficulties because it allows you to resume your mortgage payments. There are many different types of workouts, including repayment agreements (getting caught up over time) and loan modifications (changes to loan terms which do not change the total debt, but which reduce monthly payments). The mortgage company will ask you to send them documents which set out your monthly income and expenses. They will also need supporting information like recent tax returns. Not all workout proposals will be accepted. For a discussion of how to arrange a workout, see Chapter Ten.

6. Evaluate Your Refinancing Options. Particularly if you have equity in your home, refinancing may be an option to avoid foreclosure. There are some loan programs, including reverse mortgages for older homeowners, which will reduce or eliminate your monthly payments. Refinancing options should be evaluated carefully, possibly with professional assistance. Avoid high rate refinancing loans and do not consolidate other substantial debts with your existing mortgage. (See Chapter Four.) These choices will only make your problems worse in the long term.

7. Consider Selling Your House Before Foreclosure. It is a good idea to list your home for sale if you are behind on your mortgage. This is true even when you are pursuing other options. The reason to consider a sale is that the foreclosure process is not likely to bring the best possible price for your home. You will almost always get a better price if you sell your home on the open market instead of letting it go to foreclosure. If you owe more to the mortgage company than the home is worth, you will need to get the mortgage company's permission to sell at that lower price.

8. Keep Track of Foreclosure Deadlines. If there is a court case, you will want to take steps to prevent the foreclosure before the court takes final action. You will *always* want to take steps to prevent foreclosure before a foreclosure sale is held. Once the sale is held, you will no longer own the property and in most states, it is impossible to keep your home. If you have applied to the mortgage company for a workout, do not let them wait until the last minute to give you an answer. This prevents you from examining your other options. If you are considering getting help from a lawyer or non-profit counselor, do so as far in advance of the sale as possible so that you can get complete advice.

9. If You Are Unable to Arrange a Workout or Other Satisfactory Solution, Consider Getting Legal Help to Prevent the Foreclosure. Chapter 13 bankruptcy is one of several legal options you have which may solve a foreclosure problem. (Chapter 7 bankruptcy will delay but not prevent a foreclosure.) If you decide to obtain legal help, do it early so that the lawyer will have enough time to advise you properly.

When selecting an attorney, be careful to find someone you trust even if the fee is slightly higher. The best way to do this is through recommendations from friends or family. If no recommendation is available, contact the Lawyer Referral Service of your local bar association and ask for a list of attorneys who handle foreclosure defense and bankruptcy.

10. Be Realistic About What Is Possible. If you are unable to afford the house for the long term, your best option may be to sell the house. If you have no equity in the house, you may choose to walk away from it by giving it back to the mortgage company. You should not waste money which you can use to move, trying to salvage an impossible situation.

11. Avoid Foreclosure Scams. By law, foreclosure of your home will be advertised to the public. Unfortunately, there are people who read these advertisements, and then offer help to people facing foreclosure in order to rip them off. You should avoid sale/leaseback schemes and high rate loans which are offered as a way out of foreclosure. They will only make things worse. Requests for high fees or for money to pay the mortgage (payable to someone other than the mortgage company) are also indications of scams. In addition, offers of new mortgages as a way out of foreclosure can lead to disastrous deals which will make your situation impossible to resolve. If you do sign a mortgage under pressure of foreclosure, remember that you have three business days to cancel.

12. Get Counseling Help. The foreclosure process can be very compli-cated. In every community, there are *non-profit* counselors who may be able to help you avoid foreclosure. If you cannot afford or cannot find a lawyer, non-profit counseling may be a good alternative. However, non-profit fore-closure counselors are not always easy to find. You can call a local nonprofit housing organization and ask if they do foreclosure counseling. You can also try to get a referral from your mortgage company or local officials. If some-one offers to help, make sure you are dealing with a legitimate non-profit with experience in default and delinquency counseling.

HOW TO USE THIS BOOK
IN PROTECTING YOUR HOME

The next three chapters provide a variety of strategies you can use to protect your home from foreclosure. In cases where foreclosure prevention is not possible, the chapters also list some steps you can take to recover your equity, or to minimize the amount still owed to the lender after the foreclosure.

This chapter, on the other hand, provides an overview of what is in those other chapters and gives you some general information about how foreclosures work. You should first read this chapter, and then read the relevant portions of the other three chapters.

Chapter Ten: Workouts. Most foreclosures are straightforward. They occur because homeowners sometimes can't keep up payments on their mortgage loans when they are facing financial problems. In many of these cases, the homeowners agree that they owe the money. What they need is a short-term strategy to prevent sale of the property and a long-term strategy for paying the back debt. Chapter Ten discusses ways to put in place a voluntary agreement to repay your mortgage company. This is called a workout. When you agree that you owe money and that you have no defenses to repayment, a workout is usually the first choice for addressing a foreclosure problem.

Chapter Eleven: The Legal Process of Foreclosure. Foreclosure is also a legal process with a variety of laws governing the rights of homeowners and lenders. Chapter Eleven discusses your rights in the legal process of foreclosure, including the right to use bankruptcy to force a lender to accept payments over time and in some case to reduce or restructure the amount you owe.

Chapter Twelve: Defenses to Foreclosures In Special Situations. Certain mortgages create special issues in the foreclosure process. Chapter Twelve provides an overview of special consumer issues in ten situations:

1. FHA and HUD guaranteed mortgages;
2. VA guaranteed mortgages;
3. Farmers Home (FmHA) mortgages;

4. Special state mortgage assistance programs and moratoriums on foreclosures;
5. Mortgages not used to purchase the home
6. Mortgages resulting from a home improvement contract (where the seller's misconduct can be raised as a defense on the loan);
7. Mortgages on terms that are unfair or oppressive;
8. Foreclosures involving condominiums;
9. Mobile home foreclosures; and
10. Where the loan was not secured by a mortgage, but where the creditor is foreclosing based on a court judgment or other lien.

If a home foreclosure involves one or more of those ten situations, there are specific rights and foreclosure prevention strategies which apply. The "special" strategies should be considered first, before considering the general strategies for dealing with straightforward foreclosures which are described in Chapters Ten and Eleven.

Using Multiple Strategies. You will often want to think about more than one strategy to prevent foreclosure of your home. Sometimes, several strategies can be used together at the same time. In other cases you may want to try one course of action and switch to another only if the first strategy does not work.

Foreclosure can be very complicated. It is usually a good idea to get some help from a lawyer or a non-profit counselor when deciding on the best foreclosure prevention strategy.

HOW FORECLOSURES WORK

When reviewing any of the next three chapters, it is useful to have a general understanding as to how the foreclosure process works and to know how imminent a foreclosure is for your home. For more information, see National Consumer Law Center, *Repossessions and Foreclosures* ch. 13 (3d ed. 1995).

Notice of Foreclosure. In every state, you will be entitled to some notice of a pending foreclosure on your home. However, the type, amount and timing of required notices varies considerably. You cannot necessarily rely on the lender to send notices, and, because of problems with mail delivery, you may not receive them. For this reason, if you know you are behind on your mortgage payments, you will need to stay on top of things by reading any notices you do receive carefully, by keeping track of deadlines and by contacting the lender or the lender's attorney at regular intervals, if necessary, to get information about what is going on.

In addition, since many foreclosure notices are sent by certified or registered mail, you should make sure to pick up these notices from the post office. Not knowing what is in a notice does *not* protect you. You can only be hurt by not knowing what is going on.

Some of the typical types of notices which may be received if foreclosure is pending are discussed here. However, remember that each state has different procedures.

Notice of Default. You will almost always get a notice from the lender which says that you have fallen behind on your payments. This is usually called "notice of default" or "notice of delinquency." It may look like any other collection letter.

This notice will usually tell you how many payments you are behind, and it will sometimes include the exact amount of money you need to catch up. This amount is often called "the arrears." In some states, if you offer to pay the total amount of the arrears at this stage, the lender must accept the payment. Even if the law does not require it, almost all lenders will be very happy to take your full payment at this point if you have it. Partial payments are often rejected.

You should treat the notice of default as an important warning that there is a problem. It will be easier to address the problem if you begin looking for a solution at this point, than if you wait until later in the process.

Notice of Acceleration. When your mortgage is behind, lenders in most states must take a legal step known as "acceleration" before they can foreclose on your home. Acceleration means that you are far enough behind on your mortgage that the law allows the lender to treat the whole loan balance as due now. In many states, and under some mortgage contracts, the lender must give you notice when this occurs. The notice will typically say that the whole balance (sometimes with the actual amount written into the notice) is due and payable immediately.

Receipt of a notice of acceleration is a good indication that the foreclosure process is moving quickly. This letter, if you receive it, should therefore serve as an important warning that you must put a strategy in place to prevent foreclosure or give up your home.

Court Notices. As discussed below, not every state requires a court action to foreclose a mortgage. However, if you are in a state which requires a court action, you will receive a summons or a similar notice (usually brought to the house by a sheriff, constable, marshal or process server).

This notice gives you a certain period of time to respond to the foreclosure lawsuit and to raise your defenses if you have any. You should take this deadline seriously. If you do not respond, the court will enter a foreclosure judgment against you. Although this is not the end of the process, you lose important legal protections once a court judgment is entered. Most importantly, you lose the right to raise defenses in most cases. For this reason, receipt of a summons or other court papers is always a good time to review your legal options and to see a lawyer if possible.

Notice of sale is generally sent *very late* in the foreclosure process. It usually represents your last chance to get help or to do something about foreclosure.

Notice of Sale. In all states, lenders are required to give you a notice of the date and time intended for sale of your property. The sale date is the most important deadline in the foreclosure process because the sale will cut off all of your rights as owner. Sale of the property will also generally cut off your opportunity to use the bankruptcy process to help prevent foreclosure.

Notices After Foreclosure. Once a foreclosure sale is completed, you may receive a variety of different types of notices. These may include notice of the outcome of sale (who bought the property and for how much), eviction notices and court papers related to eviction.

If the property was sold for more than the lender was owed, you maybe entitled to receive some money back. In this situation, when you move, you should let the mortgage company know your new address, since they will need to find you to pay you your share of the foreclosure sale receipts.

On the other hand, if the property was sold for less than the lender was owed, you may remain responsible for the balance. This is usually called the "deficiency." You may receive a variety of notices about the deficiency including collection letters and court papers. If you are in a deficiency situation, you may be less concerned about making certain that the lender knows your whereabouts.

It is important to remember that after a foreclosure sale, it is rare that you can do much to recover your home. However, in a few states you retain the right to redeem the property from foreclosure (discussed below). In addition, occasionally you can challenge the procedures under which the sale was held and, in extreme circumstances, have the sale set aside. Finally, you can protect your right to your fair share of the sale proceeds, if the sale was for more than the amount owed on any liens on the property.

How Long Does Foreclosure Take? The length of time you have before your property is sold varies a great deal from state to state. The amount of time also varies because some lenders move more quickly than others. Depending on these factors, together with any response you put in place, foreclosure can be as quick as three months from the time you default to as long as a full year or more. You should check local practice and stay on top of any information you receive in foreclosure-related notices, as discussed above.

Whatever the length of time for foreclosure in your situation, your rule for action should always be the same. That is —*it is always better to act sooner rather than later.*

Delays can lead to a serious loss of legal rights. This will reduce your options for preventing foreclosure. Although delaying a sale will always help you, delay in taking action to prevent the sale will not. You will need both a short-term strategy to evaluate your options and a long-term strategy to prevent the foreclosure.

How a Lender Gets Permission to Foreclose. Foreclosure procedures vary from state to state. The procedures are established by state laws and by local practice. In some states, foreclosures involve court proceedings. First the lender files suit in a court — usually in the county where the property is located. Unless you successfully contest the foreclosure in court, a judgment is entered for the lender. This gives the lender permission to foreclose unless you can work out an agreement or you take some other action (such as bankruptcy) to prevent it.

Other states have "non-judicial foreclosures." In those states, lenders foreclose without a court action and without official permission to go forward. They advertise the home for sale, using a legal notice in a newspaper. If you want to contest this type of foreclosure, you must file a lawsuit and ask the court to stop the sale. You may have to file a bond to protect the lender. Some states allow both types of foreclosure. Practicality and local custom usually dictate a lender's choice of one type over the other.

The Right to Cure and the Right to Redeem. Many states allow you a second chance. In these states you can avoid foreclosure by "curing" the default. This gives you an opportunity to undo whatever led to the default in the first place. Usually this means getting caught up on the arrears (missed payments together with foreclosure fees and costs). Occasionally, lenders claim that you breached your obligations in some other way, such as failing to keep the property insured. These defaults can also be "cured" by taking care of the problem.

Most states also allow you to "redeem" the home up to the time of a foreclosure sale. To redeem, you must pay off the full amount of the loan in one payment plus the lender's foreclosure fees and costs. That is, instead of just paying off the delinquent payments, you have to pay the whole remainder of the mortgage.

In states which allow you to redeem the mortgage after default, you can stop the foreclosure by paying the entire balance owed. Since most people don't have enough cash, common methods of redemption include taking out a new loan or privately selling the house so that you have cash. In a few states, the right of redemption continues for a certain time *after* the foreclosure sale.

Some states have both a right to redeem and a right to cure. Many states place conditions on using these rights. You will need to check the law in your state. However, even in states which do not allow you to redeem or cure, many lenders will agree to accept redemptions or cures voluntarily.

Additionally, you have bankruptcy rights under federal (national) law, rather than state law. You have a right to redeem and a right to cure in bank-ruptcy which trumps any limitation on those rights under the law in your state. In fact, as discussed in Chapters Eleven and Eighteen, the bankruptcy right to cure in a chapter 13 case includes a right to pay the arrears in installments over a period of time which can be as long as three to five years. This means that if you are behind, you can use a chapter 13 bankruptcy to get caught up over a period of time even if your state's law would not allow it. As you can see, these issues can be complicated. Consider seeking out a lawyer or non-profit foreclosure counselor to help you.

The Foreclosure Sale. Generally, a foreclosure sale is usually a poorly advertised and poorly attended auction. In many cases, no one attends except the foreclosing lender, who bids no more than the balance of the debt, and maybe significantly less. Depending on state law, the auctioneer might be a sheriff or other court official. In other states, usually where there is "non-judicial foreclosure," the auction is conducted by a lawyer or an auc-tioneer hired by the lender. Although you can attend the auction and bid on the property, every state has rules about making a down payment at the auc-tion and paying any balance in a limited period of time.

The Mortgage Deficiency. If the sale does not bring in enough to pay off the lender, in many states the lender can seek a "deficiency." A deficiency is the remainder due on the loan plus costs, less the amount the lender was paid from the sale proceeds. Some state laws prevent lenders from seeking this deficiency or place certain conditions on lenders before they can seek the deficiency. If lenders can collect a deficiency under your state's law, the deficiency will be an unsecured debt. You may be sued in court and you will have the right to defend against the lawsuit. For a discussion of dealing with collection lawsuits, see Chapter Seven.

10

Mortgage Workouts

• When You Should and Should Not Negotiate a Workout Agreement
• How to Prepare for the Negotiation, How to Start the Process,
What to Ask For, And What It Will Cost You
• What to Do If the Workout Negotiation Is Not Going Well

MORTGAGE LENDERS
NOW WILLING TO NEGOTIATE

In the past several years it has become much easier for you to negotiate pre-foreclosure "workout" agreements. A workout is any agreement between you and the lender which changes how you pay your mortgage off or otherwise prevents foreclosure.

Many lenders now realize it is better for them to accept what you can afford to pay rather than foreclose on your home.

In the past consumers were often frustrated in any attempt to work out a deal with a mortgage lender when they fell behind in their payments. It might have been impossible to determine who in the lender's office to contact to discuss a workout. When a consumer did find the appropriate person, that person generally had little flexibility to consider postponing a foreclosure or arranging reasonable workout terms. While borrowers with huge debts, such as Donald Trump, were getting significant concessions, individual homeowners with small mortgages were generally told that immediate full payment with fees and costs was necessary.

More recently, however, the potential for reasonable agreements with reputable lenders, while still imperfect, has begun to improve. To a large extent, this improvement is because lenders are realizing that large numbers of foreclosures on small properties is not in their self-interest.

After a glut of foreclosures in the late 1980's and early 1990's, lenders were left with the problem of managing large numbers of deteriorating properties. Although some foreclosures were very profitable because of the potential for the lender to resell property bought cheaply at foreclosure at full fair market value, large portfolios of foreclosed property generally lost money. For these reasons, most lenders will now talk to anyone, including owners of small properties, about agreements to avoid foreclosure.

THE IMPORTANCE OF
GETTING HELP

In most cases (as long as the potential pitfalls discussed below are avoided), it can't hurt to try to arrange a workout on your own. If you have a good idea of what you want, an ability to work with numbers, and an aggressive approach, good results are possible.

However, arranging workouts is a tricky business. Too often, the lender will have far more information than you about available options. They may push you to choose an option which is not what you want or which is really too expensive for your family to afford in the long term. For this reason, it is a good idea to try to find a non-profit counselor or a lawyer who has experience with mortgage workouts to help you through the process. Having an advocate will help you get a fair deal by balancing the bargaining power between you and the lender. If you do try to arrange a workout on your own, you should read the rest of this chapter to get some tips on how to prepare, on what to ask for, and on how to negotiate with a lender.

SHOULD YOU CONSIDER
A WORKOUT, AND, IF SO,
WHEN SHOULD YOU SEEK IT?

For many homeowners facing foreclosure, negotiating a workout is the best strategy for saving their home. But it is not always the best approach for all homeowners, and, even when it is, care must be taken to initiate negotations with the lender at the optimal time. This section provides guidelines to help you decide whether and when to initiate discussions about a workout agreement.

You Should Determine if You Have Defenses to Repayment. As discussed in Chapter Eleven, there are some situations in which you have defenses to repayment of a mortgage. You should never agree to repay money which you do not owe, unless you can work out a compromise on the amount in dispute or you obtain an agreement to eliminate the inappropriate charges.

In some cases, you may have potential consumer defenses to collection, such as Truth-in-Lending violations, usury, fraud or unfair and deceptive practices. When appropriate, legal claims can be used as bargaining chips for workouts either before or after legal action is commenced. You should remember, however, that a lender who took advantage of you in making the original loan also may look for ways to take advantage of you in arranging for a workout. If you are going to try to obtain a workout on a high rate mortgage, you should try to seek help from a lawyer.

Do Not Initiate a Workout When There Are Other Financial Problems Which Are Equally Pressing. A workout does not make sense if you will lose the home anyway because of another mortgage problem which cannot be worked out. You do not want to throw away money on a mortgage workout if you are going to lose your home anyway.

Sometimes, if you have a large number of pressing financial problems, bankruptcy will be a better option than a workout because the bankruptcy process will allow you to deal with all of your financial problems together.

Do Not Initiate a Workout When It Is Too Late to Finish the Process Before the Sale. If your foreclosure sale is very soon, a workout process can be risky. Workout negotiations almost always take at least 30 days to complete. If you are close to a scheduled sale date, always obtain a *written* agreement to postpone the sale. Absent such an agreement, you will be better off exercising your bankruptcy rights since you will get the benefit of an automatic stay of the foreclosure sale by filing bankruptcy.

When to Start Workout Discussions, If Appropriate. In situations other than those described above, a workout discussion with the lender is usually a good first approach if you have defaulted on a home mortgage. Always begin a workout discussion as early as possible after the default. There are five reasons to do so.

1. It is easier to negotiate a workout before you get too far behind in payments.
2. Starting early avoids the difficulty of negotiating at the last minute with a potential foreclosure sale date pending.
3. You will appear more responsible if you try to prevent the problem from getting out of hand.
4. Beginning early avoids potential foreclosure fees and costs, which can be substantial.
5. It is better to begin negotiations before the lender has turned the matter over to a foreclosure lawyer.

As discussed above, when a foreclosure is pending, careful attention must be given to preventing the sale. A foreclosure sale will cut off your right to own the property, the ability in most cases to cure the default in bankruptcy, and the right to raise most defenses to the validity of the mortgage.

If you are thinking about bankruptcy, workouts should generally be considered prior to the filing. Once bankruptcy is filed, most lenders will not negotiate an agreement which goes beyond the best potential result under the bankruptcy law.

TIPS FOR PREPARING
FOR A WORKOUT

Gather Information Before You Contact the Lender. An important key to success is extensive preparation. This begins with understanding your own financial situation, how much you can afford to pay on the mortgage, and what you will need to make things work in the long and short term.

Throughout the process, remember that no proposed solution makes sense if you cannot really afford it, because you will only fall behind again.

Prepare a Reasonable Budget for the Future. You will need to provide detailed information about your debts, assets, income and expenses. Realistic income and expense projections are particularly important. You will need to provide documents which support your financial information as well.

After gathering this information, you and your family should agree on a strategy before you contact the lender. You should base your strategy on a budget for the future which is as realistic as possible. This budget should detail both your income and expenses. More information about budgeting and sample forms are contained in Chapter Two and in the Appendix.

Reexamine the Budget to Determine If You Have Any Way to Increase Your Income or Reduce Your Expenses. Ways to reevaluate your budget in times of financial stress are discussed in more detail in Chapter Two. Careful budgeting is important to the workout process for two reasons. First, you may find that you have more (or less) money than you thought to devote to the mortgage. An accurate forecast is essential to make everything work in the long term. Second, if you are living a too expensive lifestyle, the lender is likely to reject your proposal. Since workout agreements are voluntary, lenders want to see that the homeowners they work with are doing as much as they can to cut expenses in other areas.

In setting up your budget, remember your priorities. You should not spend any money, for example, to pay unsecured debts, such as credit cards and medical bills, at the expense of making your mortgage payments. Although you will need to tell the lender about your credit card bills and other debts, you should inform the lender that these creditors will not be paid in any month before the mortgage payment is made. Only food, utilities, necessary current medical expenses (not past due debts), property insurance and essential transportation costs should come ahead of the mortgage. Non-essential costs such as private school expenses, charitable contributions, costs of eating out and entertainment are likely to cause a problem when you are seeking a negotiated agreement from a lender.

At the same time, you should look at all your expenses, even those for necessities, to see if there are ways to reduce them. You should also evaluate your income to see if there are options for increasing it.

Develop a Plan to Deal With Other Significant Debt Problems.
Workouts on one mortgage will have little benefit, for example, when there is no plan in place to deal with other mortgages on the same property or to keep utility services flowing for the residence. Similarly, if you need a car to get to work, you will need a plan to pay those bills as well, to prevent repossession. On the other hand, if a creditor can do little to hurt you, (such as credit card debts when you have not been sued), you can plan to pay nothing on those debts until your situation improves.

Prepare a "Hardship" Letter Which Explains Why You Defaulted.
One of the things the lender will want is a short letter which explains the reasons why you fell behind in your payments. Sympathetic aspects of your situation should be thoroughly explained. The lender may also want documentation on issues which can be verified. For example, the lender may want proof that you have been laid off and have applied for unemployment compensation. Lender representatives are human beings and they will often go farther to assist you if they feel some sympathy for you based on the reasons you fell behind.

Gather Certain Information About The Property and Its Value. It is also important to obtain information about your property, particularly its condition and its value. You might consider having a broker evaluate it for the purposes of sale. Other potential sources of information about value include what you know about sales of neighboring homes and tax assessments. The lender's willingness to discuss a deal may depend in large part on the real value of the property in the event of a foreclosure. Physical problems with the property, including deterioration or liability associated with ownership (such as lead paint liability), make foreclosure a less desirable option for the lender. As discussed below, such information may be an important bargaining chip.

Decide Before You Contact the Lender What You Want and Why You Should Get It. You should know before you contact the lender what type of workout you need to resolve your situation. A variety of options are discussed below. Think about what you realistically need to make things work.

For example, if you are experiencing a temporary lay-off, you may need only a period of temporary help on mortgage payments. However, if you have a permanent income reduction (because of retirement, for example), you may require a complete loan restructuring. You also may see from the beginning that you have little choice other than to sell your home, but need time to arrange a full value sale to obtain the benefit of your accumulated equity.

In general, the rule is to ask for what you need to make things work out, but not for more than what you need. Lenders will be turned off by your being too greedy. Where your needs are so unrealistic as to be out of the question for any reasonable lender (if for example, you cannot afford to pay any interest at all), consider the possibility that you will need to sell your home, because you cannot afford to pay for its mortgage and related expenses.

Understand the Details of Your Loan and the Amount of the Default. An understanding of your existing loan terms and the amount of your default is essential to a workout negotiation. A high existing interest rate, for example, might be negotiated down to market rates.

Obtaining a breakdown of the default from the lender between principal, interest, late charges, insurance escrow, tax escrow, and foreclosure fees will also help. It is easier to negotiate reduction of late charges than reduction of actual costs — like insurance charges paid by the lender.

Additionally, in some cases, a breakdown of the default will reveal that some charges claimed are not proper. For example, the lender may not have credited a payment you know you have made. Foreclosure fees and costs, for example, may be paid out to a lawyer on retainer, but not expended. The lender should recover unexpended fees and costs and deduct them from the arrears if a workout is achieved.

HOW TO START THE WORKOUT PROCESS

You will always need to begin the process of arranging a workout as early as possible in the foreclosure process. For you to understand whom you should contact, and that individual's role in the foreclosure process, will take some explanation of the various parties involved with your mortgage. There may be a mortgage holder, the mortgage servicer, the foreclosure attorney, and a mortgage insurer. In some cases the mortgage holder hires a separate servicer for foreclosure.

Usually You Do Not Contact the Mortgage Holder. The mortgage holder is the lender which actually holds your mortgage. The mortgage holder is the party that has the right to foreclose. Since many mortgages are transferred after you borrow the money, the mortgage holder is not likely to be the bank or mortgage company which made the loan to you originally.

A high percentage of mortgages are now held by investors, including Fannie Mae (The Federal National Mortgage Association) or Freddie Mac (The Federal Home Loan Mortgage Corporation). Other mortgages are pooled and sold pursuant to a trust agreement so that the mortgage holder is a trustee for a larger group of investors. As described below, you generally do *not* initially contact the mortgage holder.

> ## You should determine who holds your mortgage, who is servicing the mortgage, and if there is mortgage insurance.

Usually, You Initially Contact the Mortgage Servicer. Although the mortgage holder has final authority to decide whether to accept a workout, very often some or all of this authority is transferred to one or more companies who are responsible for dealing directly with customers. These companies are called "servicers." The servicer may or may not be the same company as the lender you borrowed from. For example, you may have taken out a mortgage from the Third National Bank, who sold your loan to Fannie Mae. The Third National Bank may continue to service the loan for Fannie Mae, or the loan servicing may have been sold separately to the Sixth National Bank.

Sometimes a loan is transferred to a special servicer for the purpose of foreclosure. Substantial confusion frequently results when a loan is transferred, although the law now requires that you get notice of who is servicing the mortgage.

In some cases, the servicer will be an out-of-state entity which processes thousands or hundreds of thousands of mortgages. Fannie Mae, Freddie Mac and a variety of mortgage holders give their servicers differing amounts of authority to act on their behalf. This authority is spelled out in writing in servicing guides.*

Frequently, the servicer will be the only party with whom you have any contact. Only on investigation will it become apparent that the servicer is acting on another company's behalf. If you request it, the servicer must tell you the name, address and telephone of the mortgage owner or master servicer. In addition, servicers are required by Freddie Mac to tell you on their own initiative if Freddie Mac is your mortgage holder.

It is almost always appropriate to begin the workout process with the servicer. The servicer should have workout specialists who will tell you what you need to provide, take your application, and provide information on the normal standards for a workout. Contact the servicer, explain that you are interested in a loan workout and ask to get any available information packages as well as the documents the lender will want you to submit.

You may want to keep a record of contacts with the servicer, including keeping names and phone numbers of the people you speak with, as well as a record of what you are told. Significant communications should be confirmed in writing.

In this chapter, we use the term "lender" to apply both to the "servicer" and the "mortgage holder." That is because you will rarely have any contact with the mortgage holder. The mortgage holder will rely on the servicer to deal with you directly.

---

*These guidebooks are available for purchase, but can be expensive. The Fannie Mae *"Servicing Guide"* costs $300 and can be obtained from a Fannie Mae regional office. Phone numbers for the regional offices can be found later in this chapter or you can call Fannie Mae's main office at (202) 752-7000. Upkeep is free after the initial investment.

If you cannot afford to order the whole guide, Fannie Mae publishes two similar, but not identical, inexpensive booklets which are relevant to understanding its workout policies: *Delinquency Prevention and Management* and *Foreclosure Prevention.* These can be ordered for $4 each by contacting Fannie Mae, Customer Education Group, 3900 Wisconsin Avenue, NW, Washington, DC 20077-4984. The latter is the one to order if you can only order one. It covers the different types of alternatives to foreclosure available from Fannie Mae. It states: "Fannie Mae does not want to foreclose any mortgage if there is a reasonable chance of saving it."

Freddie Mac has its own multi-volume Seller/Servicer guide and no booklets to short circuit the expense. The guide may not be available directly to the general public It is not unreasonable to use the Fannie Mae booklet as background for making workout proposals to Freddie Mac and its servicers. Freddie Mac's articulated policy is to consider all proposals.

If You Are Referred to the Lender's Attorney. The lender's attorney also works for the mortgage holder, although sometimes the attorney is hired by the servicer. Some servicers will ask you to speak only to their attorney once the legal process of foreclosure has begun. When the servicer tells you to do so, you have little practical alternative.

Although some attorneys will readily participate in workout discussions or give permission for you to speak with the lender directly, others will need to be pushed. Unresponsive attorneys should be reported to the servicer or to the mortgage holder if necessary.

You Should Also Immediately Contact Any Mortgage Insurer.

Mortgage insurance is increasingly common in residential mortgage transactions. If your downpayment was less than twenty percent of the purchase price, private mortgage insurance was probably required. In other cases, mortgages are insured by the Federal government (FHA, FmHA or the Veterans Administration) or by a state housing finance agency.

If you default and your property is sold, the mortgage insurer generally will pay the lender any monies not recouped in the foreclosure process. The good news is that mortgage insurers realize they have an interest in preventing foreclosure in many cases. They will sometimes step in to insist on acceptance of proposed workout terms. Alternatively, they may agree to pay a small arrearage or part of it or provide other limited relief in order to help you keep your home. They do so in order to prevent a potential larger loss in the event of foreclosure.

If you are paying for private mortgage insurance, it is a good idea to find out the name of the insurer and to send them copies of anything you send to the lender to keep them informed of the progress of workout negotiations. The name of the mortgage insurer should not be kept secret from you; you are the one paying for the mortgage insurance. Check your original mortgage documents or ask the lender. Even if the mortgage insurer is not willing to participate in the workout discussions, keeping it informed will keep the mortgage holder and servicer on their best behavior.

If the mortgage is insured by a federal or state funded entity, special servicing requirements may apply. HUD (FHA insured mortgages), the Veterans Administration (VA) and the Farmers Home Administration (FmHA) have substantial programs to avoid foreclosures. These are discussed more fully in Chapter Twelve. In some cases, these programs may be better than a workout.

Make Partial Payments on Your Mortgage. If you can afford to make partial payments on your mortgage and want to try to arrange a workout, you should start submitting partial payments to the lender. You can then try to formalize partial payments through the workout.

If the Lender Refuses Partial Payment. The lender has no obligation to accept partial payments and your payments may be returned to you. If payments are returned to you, it is crucial to save this money (as well as to continue to put aside as much as possible) while you are attempting to arrange a workout agreement.

If possible, any funds saved should be placed in escrow. At a minimum, they should be placed in a savings account which earns interest. You should resist the temptation to dip into these funds as other financial problems come up. Once the money is put aside, consider it as if the money has already been spent on the mortgage.

Many lenders will provide much more favorable workout terms if you have a lump sum saved toward curing the default. Over a period of time, the lender's incentive to agree to a workout may increase based on a lump sum, even if you are actually further behind.

If a workout is arranged, the money will be used to reduce your future obligations on the mortgage. If a workout is not possible, you can use the money to move and start again.

The Workout Application Process. Different lenders have different workout application processes and forms. Every lender will require you to provide financial information about your debts, assets, income, and expenses with appropriate verification. You will also need to submit a hardship letter explaining your reasons for default. Many lenders require, additionally, a property appraisal and/or a credit report. It is usually a good idea to get any necessary forms from the lender and an understanding what kind of supporting information will be required prior to submitting a workout application. Otherwise you may have to submit an application twice.

Your income is usually verified by pay stubs, unemployment compensation award letters, back tax forms, and the like. You may have to submit verification of your expenses as well, such as utility bills, tax payments and other fixed costs of homeownership. Since a workout involves giving you a second chance on a defaulted loan, it is not unreasonable for the lender to expect information similar to that required for qualifying for a mortgage.

Additionally, it is not unfair for a lender whose collateral is at risk to want an appraisal or, at minimum, a property inspection.

The application form may not have a space to describe what workout terms you are seeking. If it does not, you should include your request in the hardship letter or in a cover letter to the application. You should also explain the reasons you have for making your proposal.

Once the application is made, you may have to follow up with the lender. It is not uncommon for applications to be swallowed up as if by a black hole. It is a good idea to find out who has the application at any given time (as well as the name of that person's supervisor) and to make polite but regular follow-up phone calls. Some give-and-take may be required. Remember that proposals are subject to a negotiation process.

WHAT TO ASK FOR IN A WORKOUT

General Considerations. The most important part of a workout negotiation may be deciding what terms to request from the lender. There are a variety of workout terms available and lenders use an infinite number of labels to name those terms. Try using the names for workouts used here. You may need to offer a further explanation if the lender does not understand the names you have used.

You should always propose workout terms which are sufficient to address the problem which caused your default. There is little value to you or the lender in negotiating terms which, if accepted, will not resolve your problems for both the long and short term. For negotiating purposes, you might consider asking for a little more than you need at the outset in order to get to an agreement you can live with.

The following list includes a variety of different potential workout terms. Some lenders may not offer each of these terms, while others may offer terms which are not listed here. The rule of thumb is to ask for what you want. Do not assume a particular option is not available.

It may also be necessary to use more than one option in combination. For example, if you are currently unemployed, but you have found a lower paying job which will not start for three months, you may need a temporary moratorium on payments, recasting of the missed payments to the end of the loan term, and a permanent interest rate reduction. (All of these options are discussed in more detail below.)

Request a Delay of Any Impending Foreclosure Sale. At the outset, the most important request may be for a delay of the foreclosure sale process long enough to make a workout application. A completed foreclosure sale will generally cut off all workout possibilities (although there are some exceptions).

You should always request a delay when a scheduled sale is less than 60 days away. If the sale is not yet scheduled or if it is more than 60 days away, you usually have time to complete a workout negotiation before the sale is held.

A request for delay is more likely to be granted when preliminary information is provided about your circumstances and your ability to make a reasonable workout proposal. For example, if you have recently returned to work, documentation of employment would usually justify postponing a sale. Similarly, an offer of partial payment may help obtain several months' delay.

Lenders have different approaches to handling requests for delay. Some may not agree to a delay until the sale date is fairly close. One pitfall to avoid is leaving the decision to grant a delay in the lender's hands to the very last minute. The risk is that you will assume that the application is being acted upon even if it is not, and you will lose the opportunity to pursue other strategies prior to sale. When you request a delay well before the foreclosure, the delay should be granted at least seven days before the foreclosure sale date. If not, this is a good indication that the lender is not really serious about negotiating a workout.

> **Be careful that your home
> is not foreclosed while you
> are waiting to finalize
> your workout agreement.**

When you receive an agreement to delay a sale, you must get it in writing. In most cases, it is sufficient if the lender puts the agreement in a letter to you. But, if the foreclosure sale is a court-supervised process, you should make sure that you meet applicable procedural requirements to delay the sale. These will vary from state to state. Whatever the process, it is a good idea to verify that the sale is actually canceled.

If there is no sale date or if that date is a good way off when workout negotiations are commenced, it is still important to keep an eye on the sale process. It is not unheard of for a property to be sold while a workout application is pending.

Traditional Payment Agreements. A payment agreement (or "forbearance agreement," "reinstatement agreement," or "deferral agreement") involves curing a default by making regular monthly mortgage payments as they are due, together with partial monthly payment on the arrears. For example, a typical agreement might call for making one-and-a-quarter monthly payments until the default is resolved. Until recently, most lenders limited payment agreements to no more than one year. Agreements up to 36 months are now becoming common. This type of agreement is most similar to a cure of arrears in the context of a chapter 13 bankruptcy.

You are most likely to benefit from this traditional payment agreement if you have experienced temporary financial difficulties which are now resolved. You need to have some excess income in your budget to commit to the mortgage beyond the regular monthly payment.

One pitfall to this type of arrangement is that you may fail to account for the extra initial expenses associated with recovery from temporary financial difficulties. Homeowners often have substantial budgetary pressures for several months after dealing with a temporary financial problem. Other bills, including utilities, may have fallen into arrears and expenses, such as urgent clothing needs for children, may have been deferred. The agreement must realistically take these expenses into account — perhaps by proposing graduated payments on the arrears.

Temporary Interest Rate Reduction. You may want to seek a temporary interest rate reduction if your financial problems are likely to last only for a certain period of time, but you cannot presently meet your mortgage payments. You generally must have a reasonable plan for increasing your income so that you can make full payments by a certain date.

The theory behind a temporary rate reduction is that if you get help by lowering payments in the short term, you will be able to keep from falling further behind while waiting, for example, for a recall from a lay-off. Some lenders want assurance that if you can't return to paying the full rate within a reasonable time, foreclosure will go forward unopposed.

Typically, rates can be reduced fairly easily to the market rate of interest or, with a good reason, below market. Fannie Mae may be willing in appropriate cases to lower rates to as low as 3%. You should make certain that any temporary interest rate reduction agreement does not just lower your payments, but actually lowers the interest rate used to compute the outstanding principal. Otherwise, the lender may add the interest you have been forgiven back into the loan amount you have to eventually repay.

Recasting of Missed Payments. Another form of temporary mortgage relief is known as "recasting" or "deferral". Recasting involves canceling your present obligation to catch up on missed payments, and instead delaying your obligation to make those payments until the end of the loan term. That way you can start making your regular monthly payments again, without having to immediately address the problem of your back due payments. It is ideal for those whose financial situation has improved enough to start making regular mortgage payments, but not enough to allow them to get caught up on their mortgage default.

Lenders are much more willing to recast payments you have already missed than to recast payments due in the future. In addition, most lenders are unwilling to recast more than six past due monthly payments.

Permanent Modification of Loan Terms. In some cases lenders will agree to permanent changes in loan terms, such as permanent interest rate reduction, extension of the loan's payment period, reamortization, capitalization of arrears, cancellation of principal, or some combination of these. An agreement of this type occurs most frequently when you can no longer afford the original loan terms due to a permanent change in your circumstances (for example, your retirement), and it is not in the lender's financial interest to foreclose.

The lender generally does not have a financial interest to foreclose when a forced sale of your home will bring in significantly less than what you owe. This might occur where your property's value has gone down since taking out the mortgage, where lead paint or other hazards may create liabilities for someone foreclosing on the property, where you have a large, senior mortgage with another lender, or where the property is unmarketable for some reason.

A permanent modification may also be available if you have counterclaims or other leverage to exchange for the change in loan terms. As discussed briefly below, you also may achieve the same change in loan terms by a complete refinancing with a new lender. There are at least five ways to permanently change the loan terms:

1. *Interest Rate Reductions.* The most common scenario for a permanent interest rate reduction is when the existing rate is above market, and is unaffordable. In some cases, this may involve converting your variable to a fixed rate loan or vice versa. The lender may recognize that if it forecloses on the property and then makes a loan on the property to sell it to someone else, it can obtain no more than the market rate of interest. Some lenders will combine a temporary interest rate reduction below market interest rates with a permanent reduction, at some point in the future, to a market interest rate. This is sometimes called a "step-up" plan.

2. *Extension of the Loan Payment Period* is a change in loan terms which helps some homeowners by allowing them to repay the principal over a longer term, thereby reducing the monthly payment. For example, an older homeowner who borrowed $100,000 in 1970 on a thirty year mortgage might owe only $20,000 today. Payments might be $750 monthly based on the original note. By extending the term back to 360 months on the $20,000 balance, monthly payments can be reduced to $175 dollars (even if the interest rate is increased from the market rate in 1970 to the market rate today.) The lender does not lose out as long as the rate is at least as high as the market rate, because the entire current principal will be repaid with the applicable interest.

3. *Reamortization/Capitalization of Arrears.* If a loan is reamortized, the existing interest rate is applied to the existing principal balance over the remaining loan term as if there is no default. That is, the lender recalculates fixed monthly payments based on the current principal amount.

    In most cases in which there has been a default, "capitalization of arrears" will also be necessary in connection with reamortization. When arrears are "capitalized," the amount of the arrears is included in the principal before the interest rate is applied and the payment is recalculated. The theory under which this makes sense is that the arrears are owed anyway. It is easier to repay them over the remaining length of the loan, rather than in a lump sum (or even in monthly payments of a few years.)

Capitalizing the arrears and reamortizing the loan, even without extending the period or changing the interest rate, may help you because it lets you spread out whatever payments you have missed over the remaining term of the loan while canceling your arrears. If the lender does not agree to adjust the loan rate, period or principal, your monthly payments will go up slightly. If reamortization is combined with an interest rate reduction, an extension of the period of the loan, or a cancellation of principal, your monthly payments can go down significantly, even though your total outstanding balance is higher.

4. *Reduction of Principal Balance* may be available in some cases where the loan amount is more than the value of your home because reasons beyond your control have lowered the value of your home. (You may also be able to reduce your principal balance if you have legal claims against your lender.) The lender recognizes that it is better to receive mortgage payments on a lower principal than to foreclose on property worth far less than the amount of the mortgage. Most lenders will require an appraisal of your home before considering an agreement to modify the principal. Once your principal is reduced, if the loan is reamortized, your payments will be lower.

5. *Deferred Junior Mortgages.* Some lenders will only reduce their principal if they are allowed to keep a "deferred junior mortgage" in the amount that the principal is reduced. This protects the lender in the event that the property value later goes up. Deferred junior mortgages typically require you to pay the principal on that mortgage only if you transfer your home to someone else. Your granting the lender such a junior mortgage may be a bargaining chip to obtain a modification agreement.

Other Creative Workout Terms. Some lenders will consider other offers of workouts involving temporary or permanent relief, even if they are highly creative. Some examples are making a home equity loan for emergency home repairs (particularly if your failure to make the repairs will reduce the value of your home and thus the lender's collateral), cancellation of arrears, or substitution or surrender of other property in exchange for a modification. However, some lenders may be uninterested if the proposal is too complicated.

Pre-Sales For Fair Market Value. A "pre-sale" is a sale or transfer of your home in lieu of a foreclosure. Some lenders also refer to deeds in lieu of foreclosure and refinancings by third party lenders (discussed below), as pre-sales.

In many cases it is in your interest to sell the property rather than to have it foreclosed, since the property is likely to sell for a higher price through a realtor than in the foreclosure process. This is especially true if you have substantial equity and little likelihood of being able to afford reinstatement or modification of your loan.

When substantial equity is present, the lender is not hurt by a short delay in the foreclosure, because the equity in the property means that the mortgage will be paid in full with interest from the sale price, even if the property takes a short while to sell. On your side, you get any other money from the sale above the amount of any liens on the property. You will have to pay off not only the first mortgage, but also the second and any other junior mortgage, or your sale will not go through.

Most pre-sale agreements require you to list your home with a realtor immediately. The lender reserves the right to approve the sale, but will always do so if the sale price is sufficient to cover the amount due on the mortgage. The lender will generally require you to use good faith efforts to market and sell your home and you will be required to sell the home within a fixed period of time, usually no more than six months.

Other lenders will not consider this type of sale until a buyer is found and a "purchase and sale" agreement is signed. It is in your interest to move the process along quickly since you do not want your private market sale to be trumped by a foreclosure sale. Once you have a signed "purchase and sale" agreement, you should push the lender, if necessary, to agree to postpone a pending foreclosure sale until your private sale is completed.

Short Sales. Some lenders, particularly in a depressed real estate market, will agree to let you sell your home through a realtor rather than a foreclosure sale, even if the sale proceeds will not cover the amount due on the mortgage. This is called a "short" sale. A short sale may help the lender avoid foreclosure costs. It also avoids a foreclosure notation on your credit report. At the time of an agreement for a short sale, make sure you get an agreement in writing that the lender will forgo payment on the balance of the debt. Realtors, particularly those who have experience dealing with that particular lender, may be able to help you convince the lender to agree to the short sale agreement. The realtor's incentive is the commission on the sale.

Mortgage Assumptions and Other Transfers. Some mortgages can be assumed (taken over) by a third party. When a mortgage is assumable, the property can be transferred, and the person to whom it is transferred can pick up the payments on the mortgage. If payments were behind when the mortgage was assumed, absent a workout agreement, the person assuming the mortgage will be in default and subject to foreclosure. The advantage may be that the assuming party is in a better position to deal with the default than you.

A mortgage is always assumable if the contract documents say it is, or, in most states, if the documents are silent on this issue. Other mortgages contain a "due on sale" provision, a clause specifying that transfer of the property creates a default. There are a number of situations in which assumption can take place despite attempts by the lender to enforce a due on sale provision. For example, lenders generally cannot block a transfer from parent to child.

Your lender may let another consumer assume your mortgage even if your loan documents say otherwise.

Even if a mortgage is not assumable, lenders will sometimes agree to what are usually called "delinquent assumptions" so that they can start getting payments from someone. If you want to transfer the property to someone who can better afford the mortgage payments, it does not hurt to ask the mortgage company for permission.

MODIFICATION FEES, FORECLOSURE FEES AND LATE CHARGES

Many lenders charge a modification fee for handling workout applications. Some want this fee at the beginning of the workout process regardless of the application's outcome. Fees can run as high as $600 or more plus costs. There are a number of approaches you can take in dealing with this request. One approach is simply agreeing to pay the fee, which may be a small price to pay for an agreement to lower the interest rate or to make serious modifications to your mortgage.

Where possible, however, you should try to minimize your modification fees. Request a waiver or a fee reduction to make the modification affordable. Remember that a modification can in some cases save the lender thousands of dollars in foreclosure fees, loss of principal, and resale costs after foreclosure. In some cases, a mortgage insurer will agree to step in and pay the fee or to pressure the lender to waive it.

The lender's out-of-pocket costs to modify your mortgage, such as appraisal fees and credit report charges, probably will not be waived. However, these fees should be scrutinized to make certain they are reasonable. If the fees exceed $200-300, they should be reduced. Where legitimate, however, it is difficult to argue that you should not pay these. You can request an agreement to pay some or all of the modification fees in installments or to have the fee lumped together with the loan balance if the modification involves capitalization.

Related problems arise when the lender has already begun to incur foreclosure fees and costs when you request a workout. These should be scrutinized to make sure that they are legitimate and reasonable. They should be minimized whenever possible. A typical problem is an attorney's retainer for foreclosure which is not expended, due to your workout agreement preventing the foreclosure. These fees should then be credited back to your account. To the extent foreclosure fees and costs are valid, they need to be paid or otherwise accounted for in the modification process.

Late charges will often be waived if you ask, especially if it is necessary to make a workout agreement possible. You should push for waiver of late charges whenever possible.

DOCUMENTING A WORKOUT AGREEMENT

The lender generally has forms which it requires for finalizing a workout agreement. These should be reviewed carefully to make sure they are consistent with the agreement.

If there is a delay in signing the forms for the workout, you should nevertheless make sure that the basic terms of the agreement are spelled out in writing in the meanwhile. If a sale needs to be postponed while you are finalizing the agreement, make sure this happens and make sure that you have a record in writing. A trained professional can be very helpful in this part of the process.

Many workout forms include an agreement under which you give up all legal claims which you may have against the lender. You should never sign that type of agreement (which may be labeled "release") until the actual workout agreement is finalized, because if you do not complete a workout agreement, you may want to pursue other legal remedies. Once a workout agreement is reached, it may make sense to give up your legal claims as part of the final agreement, but you should do so knowingly. To complete an agreement, you should make sure all the forms are properly signed by the lender and recorded, if necessary, with the mortgage in the property registry.

IF YOUR WORKOUT NEGOTIATION IS NOT GOING WELL

Appeals to Higher Ups. If you feel you aren't receiving sufficient cooperation in negotiating a workout agreement, ask to speak to a supervisor. It is also appropriate to go over the head of the loan servicer and complain directly to the mortgage holder or mortgage insurer. Fannie Mae, Freddie Mac and some institutional investors have loss-mitigation departments which will intervene, if pushed, to address a proposed workout. The applicable Fannie Mae offices are regional. Freddie Mac's loss mitigation is done on a national basis. If you are having a problem with the servicer, it is a good idea to learn the location of the mortgage holder's office and to find a person in that office to call or write with specific complaints about the servicer's conduct. (It is best to ask to speak with someone in "loss mitigation" or "workouts.")

Who to Contact at Fannie Mae and Freddie Mac. Fannie Mae's home office can be reached at (202) 752-7000. Usually, though you should try to contact the regional office where the mortgage servicer is located (not the regional office near where you live):

FANNIE MAE REGIONAL OFFICES

OFFICE	TELEPHONE	SERVES
The Midwestern Regional Office	(312) 368-6200	Illinois, Indiana, Iowa, Michigan, Minnesota, Nebraska, North Dakota, Ohio, South Dakota, and Wisconsin
The Northeastern Regional Office	(215) 575-1400	Connecticut, Delaware, Maine, Massachusetts, New Hampshire, New Jersey, New York, Pennsylvania, Puerto Rico, Rhode Island, Vermont, and the Virgin Islands
The Southeastern Regional Office	(404) 398-6000	Alabama, D.C., Florida, Georgia, Kentucky, Maryland, Mississippi, North Carolina, South Carolina, Tennessee, Virginia, and West Virginia
The Southwestern Regional Office	214) 773-HOME	Arizona, Arkansas, Colorado, Kansas, Louisiana, Missouri, New Mexico, Oklahoma, Texas, and Utah)
The Western Regional Office	(818) 396-5100	Alaska, California, Guam, Hawaii, Idaho, Montana, Nevada Oregon, Washington, and Wyoming

To lodge a complaint about a Freddie Mac servicer, it is necessary to call 1-800-FREDDIE and access the customer service representative by pressing 8 at the initial menu and 1 at the second menu.

Refinancing With Another Lender. If your existing home mortgage lender or lenders will not agree to a reasonable workout, you can consider refinancing your existing mortgages with a new lender. If your existing mortgages are at high interest rates or if there is just a short term left on your existing mortgages, refinancing at a lower interest rate and/or with a longer payment period can greatly reduce your monthly payments and bring the payments within reach. Moreover, refinancing a low interest first mortgage and high interest second mortgage into a single low interest first mortgage can also reduce payments.

For example, a family with a 25-year, $10,000 first mortgage at eight percent interest and a 15-year, $30,000 second mortgage at 18 percent interest has combined monthly payments of $560.31. Refinancing what is left owing on those two mortgages with a 25-year, $30,000 first mortgage at 10 percent will result in new monthly payments of $272.61. This is $287.70 per month less.

On the other hand, many refinancing schemes are frauds. Even legitimate refinancing options that look like an improvement may, on closer inspection, be far more costly than the existing mortgage. Whatever choice you make about refinancing, it is never a good idea to pay-off other presently unsecured debts with a debt secured by a mortgage. It is essential that you carefully review Chapter Four to decide whether refinancing makes sense.

If you decide in favor of refinancing, you should make every effort to obtain a loan at a reasonable rate, usually from a savings bank, a commercial bank, a credit union, or a legitimate mortgage company. Many finance companies and certain mortgage companies do not make residential loans at reasonable rates and terms.

You should *not* assume that legitimate lenders with low interest rates will turn you down because you are in financial distress. Only by applying can you determine the availability of a loan from a particular lender. Chapter Six sets out guidelines that mortgage lenders may utilize in reviewing your credit rating in conjunction with a mortgage application.

When applying for a residential loan, you should present your financial problems in the best possible light. The presentation should show how the problems are being solved, and how refinancing will provide substantially lower payments. You should stress your past financial, residential, and employment stability, and indicate your plans for the future. People often refinance high interest rate loans when rates drop; you should not feel that your application will be considered unusual.

If your application is rejected, you should obtain the reasons for the rejection and determine whether the reasons are legitimate. You should try to cure any problems so that the next application will be successful. Your rights under federal law to be notified as to the reasons for your rejection are detailed in National Consumer Law Center, *Credit Discrimination* (1993).

Some lenders solicit financially distressed families for refinancing loans. Usually the terms of their loans are not just unfavorable, but disastrous for those who subscribe to them. In general, avoid such offers unless approved by a counselor, lawyer, or accountant you can trust.

Refinancing With a Reverse Mortgage. If you are an older home-owner, and workout negotiations do not seem to be working, another possibility is to consider refinancing with a reverse mortgage. Although a reverse mortgage is not always a good idea because it uses up the equity in your property which might otherwise be a financial resource, in certain situations reverse mortgages make sense. In most reverse mortgage transactions, you do not have to make payments, because the lender will recover the amount you borrow and accrued interest from the property when you no longer live there. Anyone interested in this option should find a qualified reverse mortgage counselor to go over the pros and cons. See also the discussion in Chapter Four

Deeds in Lieu of Foreclosure. If a lender will not agree to a workout, it may offer that you turn over your deed "in lieu of foreclosure." That is, you voluntarily turn over your home to the lender as an alternative to foreclosure. (Lenders will not be interested in deeds in lieu if there are junior mortgages or other junior liens on your home, because in that case foreclosure is necessary for the lender to obtain clear title to your home.)

Deeds in lieu are usually, but not always, a bad idea. A deed in lieu of foreclosure will voluntarily terminate your ownership. You should not offer a deed in lieu unless the lender agrees to something in exchange for the agreement, such as waiver of deficiency claims (if you live in one of those states where you are still personally liable for any deficiency after the foreclosure sale), elimination of a negative credit reference, or an extra period of time for you to remain in the property before eviction. Some lenders will even agree to pay a small amount of cash (under $2,000) in exchange for a deed in lieu. This may help you move. The lender may agree to these terms in order to save the time and expense of foreclosure. If you do decide to give a lender a deed in lieu of foreclosure, be sure to get the agreement in writing, including anything the lender agrees to give you in exchange for the deed.

Deeds in lieu are almost always a poor choice if you have significant equity in the property. That equity can only be realized by a sale, even, perhaps, a foreclosure sale.

Foreclosure Defense

• *Giving Yourself Time to Find a Solution*
• *Nailing Down Exactly How Much You Owe*
• *Curing Your Delinquency and Keeping Your Home*

If your home is being foreclosed, you are not powerless, as long as you are realistic in defining your objectives relating to the foreclosure. You often have a good chance of achieving the following three objectives in the legal process of defending a foreclosure:

1. Delaying a sale to give you enough time to find a permanent solution to the foreclosure problem.
2. Finding out the valid amount you owe on the debt so that you are not repaying more than you should.
3. Using legal rights at various stages in the process to cure your default or to redeem your home. You can usually also exercise those rights by filing a chapter 13 bankruptcy.

This chapter focuses on the steps you can take to meet these three objectives, no matter what type of foreclosure is involved. The next chapter sets out additional rights you have to accomplish more extensive objectives for certain special types of mortgages, such as loans insured by the FHA or VA, or where fraud or unfairness is involved. In those specific situations you may be able to keep your home even though you defer payments for a while, or you may even be able to wipe out your mortgage in whole or in part.

The previous chapter discussed saving your home with a workout agreement. Often you are better off first trying to enter a workout agreement than defending a foreclosure. A workout may accomplish your goals without resorting to a legal process, when a foreclosure defense may not even result in your saving your home. Nevertheless, a foreclosure sale may be so imminent that a workout agreement is not possible, or the lender may not agree to an acceptable arrangement. In such situations, your only option may be to defend the foreclosure.

GET LEGAL ADVICE

Because foreclosure is a harsh legal process, when threatened with foreclosure you should immediately try to obtain legal help. Possible sources of low cost legal help are the neighborhood legal services office and a bar association panel of pro bono attorneys. A small number of other community lawyers may handle foreclosure defense cases for a fee, and many lawyers will handle bankruptcies. You should exercise care in hiring a lawyer to help you with foreclosure defense, just as you would in hiring any professional. Find someone you trust to do what you need them to do, if possible by referral from a friend or relative.

The size of the fee should not be the only consideration. A free legal services lawyer may be the best in town. A costly lawyer may rip you off. The important thing is to find someone you feel comfortable with retaining.

One thing to avoid is "quick fix" attorneys who may advertise or solicit through the mail from published foreclosure lists. Many times these practitioners will push you to file a bankruptcy prematurely. A bankruptcy may be necessary at some point, but, as with many things, proper timing may be critical.

Another source of help in some cases is non-profit foreclosure prevention counseling (sometimes called "default counseling"). Contact a local non-profit housing organization to find out where this service is offered in your community.

Too often, people postpone getting help until after the time to assert their legal rights has passed. Others prematurely walk away from their homes in frustration, leaving themselves without any equity and vulnerable to deficiency claims. For each foreclosure situation, a counselor or lawyer must carefully evaluate your objectives and interests. It is better to get this help too soon rather than too late.

DELAYING THE
FORECLOSURE PROCESS

Foreclosure can move very quickly. One advantage of exercising your legal rights is that you can create delay. In the short term, delay can be helpful because it will give you more time to put a long term solution to the problem into place.

If you succeed in delaying the foreclosure, you should do everything possible during that delay to put money aside toward your mortgage to avoid falling further behind. You should also act diligently to try to deal with your underlying financial problems.

While delay can be helpful to you, you cannot properly delay foreclosure for its own sake. The actions you take must be based on some underlying legal claim which is raised in good faith.

Procedural Defenses May Delay the Process. In most areas of the country, foreclosures are seldom contested, and lenders' attorneys tend to assume that there is no defense to foreclosure. Consequently, lenders may be sloppy in their procedures and sometimes do not comply with pre-foreclosure requirements. Lender noncompliance can be to your benefit when you are contesting foreclosure, forcing the lender to start over, or, at the very least, to comply with required procedural requirements. This will provide you with additional time to refinance, sell privately, or work out a forbearance agreement.

Foreclosure procedures and defenses to foreclosure vary significantly from state to state. Therefore, a lawyer or some other professional will have to determine whether the lender has complied with all the required procedures and whether defenses to foreclosure are available. This will require scrutiny of state laws establishing foreclosure procedures and judicial decisions interpreting those laws.

Examples of possible defenses include the failure to give you the proper notice, failure to give you a fair chance to correct the default, failure to properly advertise the sale, failure of a lender to introduce the original documents in the foreclosure proceeding, failure to sue all of the proper parties, failure to sue in the name of the real mortgage holder, or discouraging bids at the foreclosure sale.

In states where foreclosure cases are resolved by court action, you can raise defenses in that action. If the creditor can foreclose without a court case, because your state allows non-judicial foreclosure, then you will have to bring a legal case of your own, and ask the court to stop the foreclosure. Many of the legal remedies discussed here are covered in more detail in National Consumer Law Center, *Repossessions and Foreclosures* (3d ed. 1995).

The Lender's Acceptance of Partial Payments May Be Grounds to Delay a Foreclosure. Late or partial payment on a mortgage generally triggers the lender's right to "accelerate" the loan — to call in the full amount of the mortgage due immediately. Failure to pay the full amount then leads to foreclosure.

Nevertheless, many courts refuse to allow foreclosure if the lender surprises you by suddenly calling a loan due when the lender has been lenient in accepting late or partial payments in the past. If a lender habitually accepts late or partial payments, it must warn you that it will no longer continue to accept those payments, before it calls the whole loan due and attempts a foreclosure. Failure to do so may provide you with grounds to stop a foreclosure and give you another opportunity to catch up. The delay can be substantial.

Similarly, if the lender accepts a payment after foreclosure has started, you can argue that the default claimed is no longer in existence. In some states, this will require the lender to restart the foreclosure process from the beginning.

Asking the Court for More Time. In some states, courts have the power to delay foreclosures for other reasons. Two situations where delays may be granted are serious hardship and if there is substantial amount of equity in the home which protects the lender against losses on its claims.

Serious hardship claims must be documented and they must involve more than the unfortunate circumstance of homelessness. If a family member has a serious illness, for example, a temporary delay may sometimes be granted. Usually the hardship must be temporary. If the hardship will last forever, the judge may feel that now is as good a time as any to allow the foreclosure.

If you have a great deal of equity in your home, a court may allow you a short period of time to sell the home without foreclosure. This will allow you to get the best possible price and to preserve your investment. The lender is not hurt because, even if its claim against the property goes up because you are unable to make payments, there is enough value in the property that the claim will be paid in full.

A Chapter 7 Bankruptcy May Create a Temporary Delay. As discussed in more detail in Chapter Eighteen, a chapter 7 bankruptcy case cannot address a foreclosure problem in the long term. That is because mortgages and other liens (with rare exceptions) survive chapter 7 bankruptcy without being affected.

However your filing a chapter 7 bankruptcy case will delay a foreclosure because the automatic stay in the bankruptcy case will temporarily prevent the foreclosure process from continuing. The lender cannot continue foreclosure without permission of the court (this usually takes at least 60 days) or until the case is over.

Filing for bankruptcy will
delay a foreclosure, but
only some bankruptcies will
permanently prevent foreclosure.

Two things are important to keep in mind. First, you cannot file a chapter 7 bankruptcy solely to delay foreclosure. You must have some other legitimate purpose to file bankruptcy. For most homeowners in financial distress, this is hardly a problem because there are a multitude of other debts outstanding. Second, if you want a more permanent solution to your mortgage problem, you will need to file under chapter 13. This is discussed in more detail below.

OBTAINING A DETERMINATION OF THE AMOUNT YOU OWE

One silver lining in the dark cloud of foreclosure is that a foreclosure proceeding gives you an opportunity to get a determination of the real amount you owe. It is quite common for a lender to claim more than you believe is owed and foreclosure provides an opportunity to have the balance due accurately determined. As a side benefit, if you have a real claim that the lender is seeking more than it is entitled to receive by foreclosing on the property, the process of deciding the accurate amount of the debt will delay the foreclosure process to some extent.

Some common disputes about the amount claimed due include:

1. failure to credit all your payments made;
2. crediting payments you made in a way which is inconsistent with the accounting principles required by the contract;
3. compounding interest when compound interest is not permitted;
4. failing to properly reduce interest rates as required in a variable rate mortgage;
5. crediting amounts paid by you in ways which are not permitted by the contract (for example, applying payments to credit insurance which you did not authorize);
6. failure to properly manage escrow balances, (for example, failing to make timely tax payments and thereby incurring late charges);
7. charging the mortgage account for things not permitted by the loan contract or for amounts which are not reasonable under the circumstances (for example, excessive inspection fees);
8. charging excessive attorneys fees or costs for foreclosure (only real costs can be charged to your account — the lender should not be able to profit by padding foreclosure fees);
9. double counting foreclosure fees and costs by including them in the escrow balance and then also separately breaking them out as individual charges;
10. charging late charges in amounts which are not permitted by the contract.

Occasionally a lender will cause the default entirely by one or more errors in accounting or by otherwise mishandling your money. Problems commonly arise when servicing is transferred from one lender to the other. Payments get lost and accounting can be mishandled. In rare cases you may be able to prove that you don't owe anything at all.

Using the foreclosure process to determine the real amount of the debt can be very important. It can reduce what you have to pay in order to get caught up. Even if you don't have the financial resources necessary to get caught up, you will want to minimize the amount collected from the proceeds of the foreclosure sale (or any voluntary presale) by the lender. This will increase your potential to recover some of your equity if you cannot get back on track with your payments.

The ability to raise and win any of these issues will often require complicated legal work. You will need to review the lender's records in a process known as "discovery." You will also need to present evidence which supports your own position. More often then not, a lawyer will be required to effectively raise these issues. One helpful resource on many of these issues is National Consumer Law Center, *The Cost of Credit: Regulation and Legal Challenges* (1995).

In some foreclosures, there will be other significant defenses and counterclaims, usually because the lender has done something seriously wrong. Those issues can also be raised in the foreclosure process. Some of those defenses are discussed in more detail in the following chapter.

Setting Up a "Tender" Defense. If you have a real dispute with your lender about the amount owed, you may want to set up the defense of "tender." To "tender" means to offer the lender the undisputed amount of the debt. The purpose of tendering is to prevent the lender from being able to argue that even if your defense is accepted, there will still be a default which gives rise to a right to foreclose. Although it is not required that you tender the balance in order to dispute the amount claimed due, your effort to tender will help prevent foreclosure and will make your case more sympathetic to a judge.

If you can afford to do so, tender is usually achieved by mailing the undisputed amount of the debt (by check or money order) to the lender with a letter explaining that you dispute the balance. The letter should also state that the amount you tender is offered in full satisfaction of the dispute.

Most often your tender will be returned. If it is returned, you have the defense that the money was offered and refused. Keep your letter and the lender's response as proof. Put the money into escrow while the dispute is being resolved. You can add the claim of tender to your defenses in the legal process.

If your tender is accepted, in some states you can then claim that acceptance by the lender settles the dispute in your favor. This defense is usually called "accord and satisfaction." One disadvantage of tendering is that if the money is kept, and later you cannot afford to keep the property or the dispute is resolved against you, you will not be able to get the money back. Sometimes in foreclosure this can mean that you are further investing in a home which will not belong to you in the long run.

Even if you cannot afford to tender, or choose not to do so for other reasons, it is a good idea to put money aside during a dispute. The money can be used to cover as much as possible of the mortgage payments if you lose the dispute or to cover any undisputed portion if you win. In the worst case scenario, if foreclosure goes forward, you can use this money to move.

LEGAL RIGHTS TO CURE AND REDEEM

Using the Foreclosure Process to Cure or Redeem. In many states you have a legal right to cure a default by paying all the back due payments plus certain fees and costs which the lender is permitted to charge you. In most states you also have the right to redeem before the sale by paying the total amount owed on the mortgage. In a few states, you can even redeem after the sale. These rights are usually limited in a variety of ways by state laws.

Although many lenders will accept cures or redemptions even when they have no legal obligation to do so, others will not. Some lenders prefer to foreclose, either because they think foreclosure will be profitable or because they no longer want to deal with a borrower who has had financial problems.

> You can usually stop a foreclosure if
> you are able to pay all back due mortgage
> payments plus certain costs.

If you have money to get caught up or to pay off the full balance owed on the mortgage, you can usually use the legal process to force the lender to accept it — even if at first glance it looks like your state's law permits the lender to refuse the money. That is because judges have discretion in most states to impose fair resolutions of disputes. This can include ordering things like cure or redemption.

Most judges will not want to be party to putting a family on the street when the family has money to pay the arrears or the full balance owed. Even in states where judges do not have this power, offering a cure or redemption to the lender in court in front of a judge will sometimes embarrass the lender into accepting.

Filing Bankruptcy Will Always Stop a Foreclosure. You should carefully consider filing a bankruptcy case if you are in financial distress and about to lose your home. This can stop the foreclosure process and allow you time to regroup and try to work out a plan to keep your home. Chapter 13 of the bankruptcy law always requires lenders to accept cures and redemptions even when state law says otherwise. In fact, in chapter 13 bankruptcy, you can usually cure or redeem in installment payments over time rather than have to come up with a lump sum.

Bankruptcy is covered in detail in this book's Chapter Eighteen and in even more depth in National Consumer Law Center, *Consumer Bankruptcy Law and Practice* (4th ed. 1992). Only some of the most important impacts of the bankruptcy process on foreclosure will be discussed here.

The bankruptcy option may not be effective unless carefully planned and timed. For example, a premature bankruptcy filing may cancel your right to receive special state assistance or may remove a good equitable defense case from a sympathetic state court. If you file too late, your ability to cure or redeem may have been lost. You will almost always have to file before the foreclosure sale in order to cure or redeem.

The Automatic Stay. The first reason why bankruptcy is a potent method of dealing with a foreclosure is the "automatic stay." The filing of your petition in bankruptcy automatically stops most creditor actions against you and your property, including foreclosure, foreclosure sales, and the filing of liens against your property.

The lender cannot proceed without first asking for the bankruptcy judge's permission to do so. The bankruptcy judge will often *not* give the lender permission to proceed — especially if you have proposed a plan in chapter 13 to cure or redeem the debt on the mortgage.

Curing Delinquent Payments and Reinstating the Mortgage. The automatic stay gives you time to take advantage of other aspects of the bankruptcy law. In a chapter 13 bankruptcy filing, called a "debt adjustment" case, you can "cure" the delinquent payments gradually over a period of years so long as you can also keep up on future mortgage payments as they come due each month. In a chapter 13 case, you normally have three years to pay back due mortgage payments, but that can be extended to five years if there is a good reason.

The following example of a cure in a five year chapter 13 case shows how helpful a bankruptcy filing can be. Assume you are six months behind on $500 monthly mortgage payments, so that your total arrears is $3,000. In a five year chapter 13 case, you can cure by making future $500 payments as they come due, and catching up on the past due $3000 in 60 monthly payments of $50 each.

You may also have to pay interest on the $3,000 while you cure the default and a commission to the bankruptcy trustee for handling your payments. This will add about $16 a month to your obligation. Although a few courts require that you get caught up in less than five years, most presently will allow a five year payment plan if it will take you that long to get caught up.

You can cure delinquent payments in a chapter 13 bankruptcy case even if a lender has already accelerated payments so that the full loan amount is due or even if the lender has obtained a foreclosure judgment. You can also pay a mortgage in bankruptcy even if the last payment has already become due or if it will be due during the bankruptcy case itself. However, you cannot cure a default after a foreclosure sale is completed.

Another important issue when using the bankruptcy law to cure a mortgage delinquency is the extent to which lenders can collect attorney's fees and costs as part of the amount needed to cure. The lender is only entitled to attorney's fees and costs if the credit agreement clearly provides for collection of such charges. Even then, many state laws either place significant limitations on fee arrangements or prohibit them entirely.

When fees are appropriate, they should be assessed only if they are reasonable, necessary, and actually paid. A lender whose litigation is unsuccessful or unnecessary should not be allowed to collect fees.

Redemption (keeping your home by paying off the full debt) is another option in a chapter 13 bankruptcy. If you redeem, you can do so over the full three or five year term of the chapter 13 plan, and, in some parts of the country, you can reduce the interest rate on your loan principal from the rate originally specified in the loan to interest rates prevailing in your community today for similar loans. This can be a big savings.

Sale of a Home in a Chapter 13 Bankruptcy. If you can no longer afford your mortgage payments, you will not benefit from the ability to cure past delinquencies. However, you can use the bankruptcy process to sell the home yourself in an orderly fashion, thereby keeping your equity and avoiding the problems of a foreclosure sale. This strategy is probably only available to you if you will realize enough from the sale of the property to pay both your secured and unsecured creditors in full from the sale proceeds.

If you want to sell your home after filing bankruptcy, you usually have to request that the court approve your realtor. When a sale is arranged, you will also have to file with the bankruptcy court a "Motion to Sell Property Free of Liens" and obtain an order from the bankruptcy court approving the sale and allowing the property to be sold free of liens. (Many title insurance companies require this order for the sale to go through.)

This section provided only a brief overview of your options in bankruptcy. If you want to use bankruptcy to help prevent a foreclosure, you should also read Chapter 18.

— 12 —

Foreclosures Which Create Special Consumer Rights

• *FHA, HUD, VA, and FmHA Mortgages and*
Special State Mortgage Programs
• *Mortgages Not Used to Buy Your Home, Rip Off Home Improvements,*
and Unfair or Deceptive Loan Terms
• *Condominiums, Mobile Homes, and Judicial Liens*

The prior chapter examined your rights in defending against a foreclosure of your home. That chapter is generally applicable to any foreclosure. In addition, you have special rights and concerns that you must know about if your mortgage falls within one or more of the following ten categories:

1. Your mortgage is insured by FHA or HUD;
2. Your mortgage is insured by the VA;
3. Your mortgage is insured by the Farmers Home Administration (FmHA);
4. Your state has a mortgage assistance program or a foreclosure moratorium;
5. The mortgage at issue is a second mortgage or a first mortgage not used to purchase the home (so that you may have Truth in Lending rescission rights);
6. The lien or mortgage at issue results from a home improvement scam;
7. The mortgage is based on an unfair or oppressive loan;
8. Where your home is a condominium;

9. Where your home is a mobile home;
10. Where the creditor has no mortgage, but is foreclosing based on a court judgment.

The discussion of each of these ten topics will reference other sources of information. For all of these topics, if you wish more information, you can see National Consumer Law Center, *Repossessions and Foreclosures* ch. 13 (3d ed. 1995).

FORECLOSURE OF FHA/HUD-INSURED MORTGAGES

For More Information. At present, families with mortgages insured by the Federal Housing Administration (FHA) and the United States Department of Housing and Urban Development (HUD) have many significant rights not available to families with conventional loans. Because Congress is presently considering changes for these type of mortgages, you will need to check with an expert about whether your rights have changed since when this book was published.

Information about your rights under a FHA or HUD mortgage also can be found by asking your HUD regional office for information on how you can obtain HUD Handbook Numbers 4330.1 and 4330.2. The National Consumer Law Center's *Consumer Law Pleadings Number Two* (1995) contains sample legal pleadings that may benefit homeowners faced with foreclosure who have HUD insured mortgages.

How to Tell If You Have a FHA or HUD Mortgage. To tell whether you have an FHA or HUD insured mortgage, look at your original mortgage or loan documents. Usually a special box on the form is checked. Since many lenders use the FHA form for all mortgages, you cannot assume that if the form says FHA or HUD anywhere on it, that you have an FHA or HUD insured mortgage. There must be an additional indication on the form of FHA or HUD insurance. If you have any doubt, you can call and ask your lender. Their records should be clear on this issue because the existence of the insurance is a benefit to them.

Your FHA and HUD Rights in a Nutshell. You should challenge any foreclosure where you have not been afforded certain basic rights available to all FHA/HUD borrowers:

1. Lenders must give you notice of your default no later than the end of the second month of your delinquency;
2. Lenders must make reasonable efforts to arrange face-to-face interviews with you before three full monthly installments are due and unpaid;
3. Lenders must accept partial payments in many circumstances;
4. Lenders cannot foreclose if your only default is an inability to pay an escrow shortage in a lump sum;
5. Lenders cannot foreclose on the mortgage until you are delinquent on three full monthly payments;
6. Lenders have authority to enter into special forbearance agreements which would reduce your monthly installment for a period of up to nine months and can consider other types of similar agreements with HUD approval;
7. Before the lender forecloses, you can ask HUD to accept "assignment" of the mortgage. If HUD accepts the assignment, it temporarily reduces or excuses mortgage payments.
   [Note: Congress may soon eliminate this special program.]
8. Lenders cannot foreclose while a request for such an assignment is pending.

A lender's failure to meet these obligations can be a defense to foreclosure.

You may be able to stop foreclosure on a FHA or HUD mortgage if the lender has refused to work with you.

The HUD Assignment Program. HUD's assignment program has been an important special protection for those with FHA/HUD mortgages. When HUD receives assignment of a mortgage, HUD reduces or suspends payments for a period of years, and then lets you catch up on delinquent payments slowly over a period of years. While assignment may not be a permanent solution (you will eventually have to repay all the mortgage payments temporarily excused), assignment brings immediate relief from foreclosure and allows you to modify your mortgage payments to make them affordable.

As this book was being prepared, Congress was considering canceling the HUD assignment program. For this reason, we recommend that you speak to a lawyer or counselor familiar with the program in order to obtain an updated review of how to apply for the program and what benefits it will provide. Unfortunately, it is likely that the program will be cancelled.

FORECLOSURE OF VA-GUARANTEED MORTGAGES

If your mortgage is insured by the Veterans' Administration (VA), you have rights that are not available to homeowners with private conventional mortgages. Additional information can be found in the VA Lender's Handbook, VA Pamphlet 26-7, and VA Circulars applicable to the servicing of single family mortgages, which should be available from your VA regional office.

To tell whether you have a VA mortgage, look for the VA logo on the top corner of the mortgage or other loan documents. If you are unsure, call and ask the lender.

Restrictions on Lender's Right to Foreclose on a VA Mortgage.

Families with VA mortgages have certain protections against foreclosure. The lender cannot foreclose unless you fail to make three full monthly payments. The lender must give the VA 30 days warning of its intent to foreclose, and must make all reasonable efforts at forbearance before actually foreclosing on the property.

The lender must consider temporary suspension of payments, extension of the loan, and acceptance of partial payments. If the lender still intends to foreclose, you can stop the foreclosure by paying all delinquent payments, late charges and any of the lender's foreclosure expenses to date.

The lender's failure to meet its obligations in this area can be a defense to foreclosure. If you hope to use this defense, it is a good idea to send a letter to the lender which asks the lender to consider one or more of these foreclosure avoidance strategies. The lender's failure to respond appropriately would then be evidence of its failure to meet its responsibilities.

You may have defenses in addition to those described here. Chapter 3 of National Consumer Law Center, *Consumer Law Pleadings Number Two* (1995), contains a letter that sets out various defenses to foreclosure on a VA mortgage and includes a request for a hearing before a neutral hearing officer.

The VA Assignment Program. Theoretically, the VA can stop a lender's foreclosure by accepting "assignment" of a VA mortgage from the lender. The VA would then hold the mortgage and could excuse or reduce mortgage payments for a period of time. When a family's financial crisis has abated, normal payments would resume. Meanwhile, a foreclosure would be averted.

Unfortunately, this is more of a theoretical option than a practical strategy. The VA has sole discretion whether to accept a mortgage assignment. Government studies show that the VA accepts assignment in less than 1% of mortgages subject to foreclosure.

FORECLOSURE OF FARMERS' HOME ADMINISTRATION MORTGAGES

Farmers Home Administration (FmHA) guaranteed or insured loans provide rural borrowers (even if they are not farmers) with significant rights unavailable to homeowners with private conventional loans. For more detailed information on your rights under a FmHA mortgage, see The National Housing Law Project, *FmHA Housing Programs: Tenants' and Purchasers' Rights* (2d ed. 1992), available from the project at 2201 Broadway, Suite 815, Oakland, CA 94612, (510) 251-9400. Another useful resource is the FmHA's Instructions, particularly 1951-G, and 1900-B, which you may be able to obtain by contacting your regional FmHA office.

To tell whether your mortgage is FmHA insured or guaranteed, look at the mortgage papers or loan documents or call the lender. The FmHA has a variety of excellent programs to help people avoid foreclosure.

Moratorium Relief from Foreclosure. If you have a FmHA mortgage, you may be able to stave off a foreclosure by successfully asking FmHA for a moratorium on payments for up to two years. The moratorium can also be retroactive for up to three months. This would mean that delinquencies over the last three months would no longer be delinquent until the moratorium period ends.

When the moratorium expires, FmHA has various options to restructure the loan, depending on your ability to pay at that time. FmHA will give you anywhere from two years to more than the remaining term of the loan to catch up the payments excused during the moratorium period. FmHA can even permanently excuse the interest incurred during the moratorium period.

How to Apply for a Moratorium. You are eligible for FmHA moratorium relief if, because of circumstances beyond your control, you cannot continue making scheduled payments without impairing your ability to pay for essential living expenses. If you qualify, you should apply at your local FmHA county office.

The initial decision to grant or deny moratorium relief is made by the county supervisor that administers the county office. Supervisors' decisions vary widely based on the individual supervisor's predispositions. For example, while some county supervisors do not require formal proof that you will be able to resume payments after the moratorium period, other supervisors only grant relief if you have a good payment record.

The county supervisor's decision can be appealed, but that appeal must be filed within 30 days of the supervisor's denial of the moratorium request. While the appeal is pending, there can be *no* foreclosure. Appeals involve an informal hearing where you will have to prove that you are entitled to moratorium relief.

Refinancing an FmHA Mortgage into a Low-Interest Mortgage. Federal law provides families experiencing difficulty paying their FmHA mortgages with another effective approach that can significantly lower their monthly mortgage payments. The FmHA provides low interest (as low as 1%) mortgages to low income homebuyers under its "interest credit" program. There is no reason why a homeowner with a regular FmHA mortgage should not be able to refinance that loan into a low interest loan under the interest credit program. Unfortunately, the FmHA to date appears not to offer this right that federal law provides to all eligible homeowners.

SPECIAL PROTECTIONS
AVAILABLE IN CERTAIN STATES

Homeowners in a few states have special protections from foreclosure. These protections may involve a state program to provide temporary payments to help pay mortgages or state laws that prohibit foreclosures in certain situations. These protections are relatively rare, but states are more likely to reinstitute such programs during hard times.

State Mortgage Assistance Programs. Pennsylvania presently has a special mortgage assistance program that provides loans from state funds to homeowners who are threatened with foreclosure, to help them get caught up on delinquent payments and make some future payments. Apparently, similar programs in Maryland, Connecticut and New Jersey are temporarily or permanently closed due to lack of funds.

If you receive a notice about the availability of special assistance with foreclosure, you should apply if you can arguably meet the program's criteria. Often these programs have short time periods and deadlines which you must meet. Failing to meet the deadlines will disqualify you.

Private Programs. There are also a variety of private programs for financial assistance with mortgage payments in different parts of the country. To find out about these programs, you should contact a local non-profit housing counselor or other specialist.

One pitfall, however, is that some scam artists have learned to design their rip-offs to look like assistance offered by a non-profit. Before getting into a deal too deeply, investigate to make sure the program is legitimate. Never sign away rights to your home in order to get help.

State Bans On Foreclosure. During the economic depression of the 1930s, many states enacted moratorium laws postponing foreclosure sales of homes and farms. Where still in effect, these laws sometimes prevent foreclosures by requiring lenders to accept smaller payments during moratorium periods. For example, the Iowa foreclosure law provides general relief in cases of natural disasters and both Iowa and Minnesota provide relief when the governor declares an economic emergency.

Occasionally, a state will declare a temporary local emergency and allow foreclosure relief in areas where plant closings have created widespread distress and depressed housing markets. This gives dislocated workers time to put their affairs in order. Similarly, during a plant closing crisis in the early 1980s in Pennsylvania, local judges and sheriffs postponed home foreclosures against dislocated workers without resorting to a moratorium law. Massachusetts had a temporary moratorium in 1991 on foreclosures. The legislature was responding to widespread instances of home improvement fraud and other second mortgage scams.

When there is a state ban on foreclosures, you will be temporarily protected for a period of time. This will give you an opportunity to get back on your feet.

MORTGAGES NOT USED TO PURCHASE YOUR HOME

Truth in Lending Rescission Provides Potent Relief in Certain Circumstances. Federal law provides you with an extraordinarily effective means of stopping a foreclosure in certain special situations. Instead of giving you more time to make reduced payments, this federal remedy allows you to permanently *cancel* your mortgage and significantly reduce the amount of the debt you owe the lender. Once the mortgage is canceled, there can be no foreclosure.

If you can legally rescind your loan under Truth in Lending, you, not the lender, will be in the driver's seat.

This remedy, called Truth in Lending rescission, is not available to cancel a mortgage used to purchase or build your home. But it may be available to cancel other types of mortgages, such as second mortgages, first mortgages not used to purchase your home, refinanced mortgages, home equity lines of credit, and even liens placed on your home by contractors or other workers.

Experience has shown that Truth in Lending rescission is most effective when dealing with onerous credit contracts imposed by home improvement contractors, finance companies, and mortgage companies that prey on families in financial distress. In fact, in 1994, Congress added to the law for just this purpose. High interest rate loans and loans with high up front costs now carry special rescission rights.

While Truth in Lending rescission sounds almost too good to be true, there are three catches. First, Truth in Lending rescission does not apply to certain types of loans. Second, the lender must have made one of a list of basic mistakes when signing you up for the mortgage. Third, you must usually go to court to convince the lender to honor your Truth in Lending rescission rights.

Obviously, a lawyer or other highly specialized professional will be necessary if you are to successfully utilize Truth in Lending rescission. Contact your local bar association referral service, your local legal services office, or seek a recommendation from a local non-profit. You may want to ask for a specialist in consumer law. If your case is successful, the home will be free from the mortgage, your indebtedness may be reduced by thousands of dollars, and the lender may have to pay for your attorney.

This section is not a detailed analysis of Truth in Lending rescission, which can be quite technical. This section does help you identify when Truth in Lending rescission is definitely not available and when it may be, thus telling you whether it is worth contacting an attorney to discuss your rescission rights. More detailed information is available in National Consumer Law Center, *Truth in Lending* (3d ed. 1995). Besides a detailed analysis of all aspects of the law, the volume reprints the key sources of Truth in Lending law — the Truth in Lending Act (TILA), the federal TILA regulations, and the official federal TILA interpretations, as well as sample letters and pleadings.

When Does Truth in Lending Rescission Apply? Truth in Lending applies to most home mortgages except the ones taken when you buy or build a home. It even applies to liens that contractors and other workers place on a home, such as artisans', mechanic's, or materialmen's liens. When more than one person has the right to rescind a transaction (such as husband and wife), any one of the individuals can exercise the right and cancel the transaction on behalf of all.

Nevertheless, TILA rescission does *not* apply if:

• The mortgage loan was used to purchase or build the home;
• The mortgage loan was not for consumer purposes, but was for business or agricultural purposes;
• The lender was only involved in a very few loans within the last year;
• The mortgage is on investment property, a vacation house, or other property *not* your principal residence at the time the loan was extended. (A mobile home, condominium, coopera-tive, two or three-family home, trailer, even a houseboat *can* be a principal residence);
• You no longer own the home that the mortgage relates to;
• The mortgage is a refinancing of an existing loan where no new money is borrowed and the same property stays mort-gaged;
• *Possibly* if the loan was extended more than three years ago (many courts allow you to defend foreclosures through TILA rescission even if a loan is more than three years old).

For the majority of people, the most important exceptions will be for mortgages used to purchase the home and the possible exception for loans more than three years old. Otherwise, TILA rescission is usually applicable, and the key question is whether the lender made a mistake which allows you to cancel the mortgage.

When Can You Rescind a Mortgage? There are three different situa-tions where you can use TILA rescission to cancel your mortgage. You can rescind for any reason within three days of first taking out a loan that uses your home as collateral. This obviously will have little relevance in most foreclosure situations, but is very useful when dealing with high pressure lenders and home improvement sellers.

You can also cancel a mortgage loan if you did not receive proper notice that you could rescind the loan. Lenders must deliver two copies of the notice of the right to rescind. The notice must be on a separate document that identifies the transaction, discloses that the lender has a mortgage on specified property of yours, and that you and joint owners have a right to rescind. The notice must also give directions on how to rescind, with a form for that purpose, with the appropriate addresses, the effects of rescission, and how long you have to rescind. Failure to include all this information or failure to give you this notice are grounds for you to cancel the loan.

The third basis for canceling the loan is if the lender makes a mistake in its disclosure of certain important terms of the loan. If the disclosure is improper, you can rescind the loan unless you are given a corrected disclosure. In practice, since lenders rarely correct mistakes, you can cancel even as late as just before the foreclosure at least for loans less than three years old. As mentioned above, some courts allow rescission even for loans older than three years if you are trying to prevent a foreclosure.

For many loans, the key issue will be whether the lender has made a mistake on the disclosure form sufficient to allow you to cancel. This issue can be quite complicated. However, errors are often made in important calculations, especially when there are a variety of costs and charges in connection with the loan. In 1995 Congress tried to make it harder for homeowners to rescind mortgages by increasing the limit for permissible errors; however, most of the changes do not apply when you are using the law to defend against a foreclosure.

Uncovering Truth in Lending Errors. Any decision to pursue Truth in Lending rescission should be made with the assistance of an attorney or other professional experienced with financial calculations and Truth in Lending issues. In fact, the analysis necessary to uncover lender mistakes may be intimidating for many. Nevertheless, there are several steps that you or your counselor can take to explore whether your home can be saved through Truth in Lending rescission:

- *Check the Numbers.* Based on the payment schedule, is the total of payments accurate? Is the annual percentage rate calculation correct? Does the amount financed and finance charge add up to the total of payments? The National Consumer Law Center's *Truth in Lending* manual explains what mathematical errors to look for and how to show that the lender made a mistake.
- *Review the Calculation of the Amount Financed.* See what happened to the "amount financed," that is the money you bor-

rowed, by reviewing the contract and any itemization you received. Be suspicious if large portions of the amount financed do not go to you or to your benefit. When a loan is loaded with broker's fees, points, insurance, assorted fees, and the like, it may pay to ask a lawyer familiar with Truth in Lending to scrutinize the contract. NCLC's *Truth in Lending* manual gives a step by step analysis as to whether the existence of these charges in the amount financed will allow a homeowner to rescind.

- *Prohibited Terms in Some Loans.* If you have a recent high interest rate loan or a loan with high fees and costs, the rules for lenders are more stringent. Many unfair terms are prohibited in those loans, including most balloon payments, negative amortization, and most prepayment penalties. Including a prohibited term in these loans is a ground for you to rescind.
- *Did You Receive Information About Your Right to Cancel?* If not, the loan is rescindable. For home improvement contracts, did the contractor begin working before the three day period elapsed?

How to Cancel. If you think you may have a right to cancel, you should check with an experienced consumer lawyer. You will need to send a notice of rescission to the lender, but the requirements for doing so after the three day period has expired may be somewhat technical. (If three days have not expired, return the cancellation form provided by the lender. Make sure to do this by the deadline, and be sure to keep a copy for yourself). Several sample forms related to cancellation are included in National Consumer Law Center, *Truth in Lending* (3d ed. 1995).

The Effect of Your Cancellation. Sending the rescission notice automatically voids the mortgage. As long as the rescission was proper, the lender no longer has the right to foreclose on your home. Within twenty calendar days after the lender receives the notice of rescission, the lender must cancel the mortgage and file that release on the public record. Although you may later have to return to the lender the amount borrowed (not including interest and other charges), you need not do so at the outset. The mortgage is still void and the home is out of danger.

Of course, a lender receiving a cancellation notice but no loan payments will not be happy. Typically, the lender will ignore the notice and pursue the mortgage foreclosure. What this means is that you will have to retain an attorney to fight for enforcement of the right to rescind. Your lawyer can raise the Truth in Lending rescission as a defense to the foreclosure.

There is much misunderstanding, even by lawyers, as to a consumer's financial responsibility after rescinding a loan. It is true that rescinding a loan does not mean that you necessarily get to keep all the loan proceeds. On the other hand, many people mistakenly believe that the consumer, when rescinding, must immediately tender the full amount of the loan. Obviously, this usually would be impossible.

The exact answer as to when and if you must pay the loan back after rescission will depend on many factors. The bottom line is that you should not have to pay anything back before the mortgage is voided, meaning that the home will be safe from foreclosure.

The amount you do pay back will often be significantly less than the amount borrowed. If your rescission is proper, you will not have to repay interest, most fees, closing costs, points, insurance payments and other charges. Any payments you have made will be credited to the principal.

For a home improvement contract, you may just have to return the value of the work done, which is often much less than what you paid for it. Furthermore, the lender's Truth in Lending violation will usually mean that you can knock off at least another $1000 from the amount owed, and perhaps significantly more.

You will probably need to go to court for a decision about whether your cancellation was proper. In such a case, you should also raise whatever other legal claims are available, such as breach of warranty, deception, and the like as additional reasons why the amount owed should be further reduced.

If you still have to return a sizeable amount to the lender, you may not be able to do so. But there may not be much the lender can do about that. The amount might become an unsecured debt, depending on the situation. Unlike the canceled debt, your home would no longer be collateral for the loan. Alternatively, you can seek to refinance the amount owed (which should be much less than the original loan amount) with a different lender and at lower interest rates. This may well result in affordable payments.

MORTGAGES RESULTING FROM
A HOME IMPROVEMENT SCAM

A widespread and vicious scam is to pressure you into a home improvement contract — aluminum siding, basement waterproofing, replacement windows, roofing, etc. — and then have you sign up for very unfavorable financing and a mortgage on your home. If the home improvement contractor never completes the work or the work is shoddy or wildly overpriced, you then have resulting legal claims against the home improvement contractor. A different company, often a finance company or a mortgage company, will nevertheless collect on the loan and foreclose when you refuse to pay or get behind.

In almost all such situations, you can fight the foreclosure based on the misconduct of the home improvement contractor. That is, even though the contractor and lender are not the same company, there is enough connection between the two so that you can raise the contractor's misconduct as a reason why you need not repay the loan. Remember that this is a defense to a loan related to the home improvement work, and is not a defense to a loan totally unrelated to the misbehaving merchant.

If a contractor ripped you off, you may not have to repay your construction loan.

While raising the conduct of a related seller is a very effective defense to a foreclosure, it is best to obtain legal representation to make sure that the defense is raised correctly. More detailed information (than what is presented below) about raising the contractor's misconduct as a defense to a foreclosure is found in another NCLC manual, *Unfair and Deceptive Acts and Practices* (3d ed. 1991). You also may wish to look at National Consumer Law Center, *Sales of Goods and Services* (2d ed. 1989) for a description of many defenses you have against the home improvement contractor in these sorts of transactions.

When Is Your Lender Responsible for Your Contractor's Misconduct? You can almost always defend a foreclosure based on the home improvement contractor's misconduct. In most cases the loan documents will say that any holder of the loan is subject to all claims and defenses that you have against the seller. In other words, the very loan the lender is trying to enforce will say that you can raise the contractor's misconduct as a defense.

Where this provision is not in the loan documents, you still may be able to raise the contractor's misconduct as a defense. First, distinguish between loans where the contractor was the original lender and loans where the contractor arranged for a different party to be the original lender.

In the first situation, the contractor's name will be on the loan as the lender, and the contractor will then have sold the loan to another lender. In that situation, the law allows you to raise against the second lender all defenses that you could have raised against the home improvement contractor.

The situation is not so clear-cut when another lender (not the contractor) was the original lender. About half the states have laws that say that the lender is responsible for what a closely related seller did. So, if the home improvement contractor referred the lender to you, the lender is responsible for what the contractor did. In the other half of the states, there are various arguments that a lawyer can make as to why you can still raise what the contractor did as a defense to the foreclosure.

Defending a Foreclosure Based on Contractor Misconduct. A contractor's leaving a scratch on a window is probably not enough to stop a foreclosure. It is important to understand what type of contractor misconduct can act as a defense to a foreclosure.

If the contractor never did any work or if the your claims against the contractor exceed the amount of the loan, that should be sufficient to stop a foreclosure. These create warranty or deceptive practices claims.

Similarly, door-to-door sellers (including contractors who go door to door) have to give you a three day cancellation right, either under Truth in Lending or under door-to-door sales laws. If this right to cancel was never given, or if work began before the three day period expired, you may be able to cancel the home improvement contract. A canceled sales contract would be a complete defense on the loan.

More troublesome is the situation where you have claims against the contractor, but the claims may be smaller in amount than the whole amount you owe on the loan. Then the loan may still be a binding obligation even though you will not have to pay all of it.

If you are in default, the lender may be able to foreclose even though you only have to pay part of the loan. Nevertheless, some courts will delay the foreclosure until the amount owed is established and then you need only keep current on the new loan payments. Alternatively, you can consider refinancing with a reputable company for the amount which is still owed.

MORTGAGES BASED ON UNFAIR AND OPPRESSIVE LOANS

Some lenders engage in outrageous loan conduct, and victimized borrowers should defend the foreclosure based on the lender's misconduct. Especially suspect are high interest loans from home improvement contractors, finance companies, and mortgage companies. There are many types of lender practices that may provide you with a defense on a foreclosure.

Conduct That May Void Your Loan. Look for the following, which may eliminate your obligation to repay the loan and thus stop the foreclosure:

- The lender misrepresented the nature of the document you signed, for example, saying — "this is just an application;"
- The lender misrepresented the basic loan terms;
- The interest rate exceeds the state maximum;
- The lender is not licensed to do business in your state;
- Illegal terms are included in the loan documents;
- The lender coerced you into signing the loan;
- The person who signed the mortgage was not the real owner of the mortgaged property (sometimes this involves forgery);
- The person who signed for the loan was not legally competent to do so (for example, children below a certain age or people who are mentally infirm).

Where these defenses are available, you can have the loan declared void. Often you will need the help of a lawyer to do so.

Other Types of Lender Misconduct. Other lender conduct may not nullify your loan, but may influence a court in a foreclosure proceeding to give you more time and lower the amount you owe. Generally speaking, anything that the lender does that is unfair, unconscionable or deceptive can be the basis for a claim.

Similarly, the lender's failure to accurately disclose important information, such as the disadvantageous nature of a consumer loan, creates a legal claim. If the lender's misrepresentation was intentional and knowing, the lender may even be liable for punitive damages in addition to your actual injury from the misrepresentation.

You may have a defense if the lender knew you could not afford the loan payments, or arranged a variable rate loan knowing that your income was fixed. You should also consider challenging consolidation loans if the monthly payments are higher than the total payments of the loans being consolidated.

Lenders also should not refinance low or no interest debts, such as medical or utility bills or low rate first mortgages, into a high interest loan. Continually re-obligating consumers with new refinanced loans may be unfair if prepayment or rebate penalties apply with each new loan.

A loan may also violate one of a number of credit laws, such as a state usury law or the federal Truth in Lending law. Usually it takes a professional well versed in these areas to identify such violations. Substantial additional information on identifying these types of claims and how to pursue them is contained in National Consumer Law Center, *Unfair and Deceptive Acts and Practices* (3d ed. 1991).

CONDOMINIUM FEES

If you are having trouble paying the mortgage on your condominium, you are probably also behind on your condominium fees. It is important for you to understand the implications to you of your delinquent condo fees.

Condominium owners own their unit, but the building, the land on which it sits, and the other "common areas" are owned by the association of unit owners. Each unit owner has a percentage interest in the common areas, and the condominium association collects a fee (usually monthly) from each unit owner to pay for upkeep of the common areas and for certain other services (e.g. landscaping, snow and trash removal, etc.).

The condominium association will have collection remedies for your failure to pay your condominium fees, and may pursue them aggressively. State laws vary in terms of how associations may go about collecting the debt.

A recent trend in some states has been to give condominium associations a priority lien for the payment of fees. A priority lien means that the condominium association may foreclose and collect a certain amount of its fees through the foreclosure of your unit. This means that you can lose your condominium unless you pay your fees or reach some type of agreement to get caught up over time.

When condominium association liens are put on your property records, they may complicate the process of arranging a workout with your other mortgage lenders. That is because the mortgage may be at risk if there is a foreclosure on the condominium liens. For this reason, when pursuing a workout agreement in a state that allows associations a lien, you will need to pay off your fees or negotiate with the condominium association at the same time as you deal with your other lenders.

Another common way for an association to get its fees is through legal action. The association's trustees may file suit and then seek to enforce the court's judgment if they win. If your unit is rented, they may also seek to collect rent from your tenants until the arrears are paid. If your condo association pursues a remedy in court, the lawsuit will be just like any other lawsuit to collect a debt. Your options for dealing with debt collection lawsuits in general are discussed in Chapter Seven.

It is important to communicate with the association's trustees or property manager if you are unable to pay your condominium fees. Let them know the reason you fell behind and try to arrange an agreement which will address the problem based on your financial circumstances. Remind them that you have to make your mortgage, food, and utility payments first, and then you can apply funds toward the condominium fees. Since the other owners are your neighbors, they may be willing to work out an agreement with you that will help you through difficult times.

MOBILE HOMES

Is a Mobile Home Realty or Personal Property? Mobile home owners face some unique issues when dealing with a threatened foreclosure. The first question is whether the mobile home is real estate (similar to a home) or personal property (similar to a vehicle). In states that treat mobile homes as realty, the lender who wants to foreclose will have to use real estate foreclosure procedures. If your state treats mobile homes as personal property, the lender may be able to repossess the mobile home through a judicial procedure, commonly known as replevin or through self-help repossession.

Whether a mobile home will be treated as real property or personal property depends on your state's laws. You will need to get information about your state's approach to this question. In some states there is no clear answer, because the treatment of a mobile home depends on a variety of factors, including where the mobile home was when the mortgage was signed. Was it on the dealer's lot or attached semi-permanently to land? If it was attached to land, was it your own land or was it in a mobile home park?

It is important to know that the law in some states may treat your mobile home as personal property in some circumstances and as real property in others. You may need legal help to answer this important question.

You should consider discussing the possibility of a workout agreement with the lender if you are behind on payments whether your mobile home is real estate or personal property. A variety of options for workouts are discussed at Chapter Ten.

If a workout is not possible and your mobile home is treated as real estate under your state's law, then your legal rights will be consistent with the legal rights of other homeowners, as discussed in this and the previous chapter. If your state treats your mobile home as personal property, then your legal rights will conform more closely to the rights of automobile owners facing repossession. These rights are discussed in Chapter Fifteen.

Special Rights for Mobile Home Owners. Mobile home owners may have certain rights not available to other homeowners. Federal protections apply to certain mobile home first mortgages. You have thirty days to get caught up on a default after notice of the default is provided.

A lender does not have to provide this federal protection, but the federal government offers certain incentives for lenders to do so, and many choose to do so. If so, the lender must send you a notice of default by certified mail, return receipt requested. The notice must state the nature of the default, what you must do to cure the default, the lender's intended actions if you fail to cure, and your right to redeem the property under state law. The lender may not repossess your mobile home or call the rest of the note due until thirty days after the notice is mailed. To cure, you must pay the delinquent amounts due plus any late or deferral charges.

Since issues related to mobile home foreclosures and repossession vary significantly from state to state, it is recommended that you also consult with someone who is knowledgeable about the laws in your state. Pamphlets may also be available from your state's attorney general or at a local counseling agency or legal services office.

Mobile Home Lot Rent. If you rent your mobile home site, failure to make your lot payments can result in eviction. Typically, the mobile home park or other landowner that owns the lot will have to bring a legal action to evict you. In some states this legal action will be similar to other landlord and tenant actions, as discussed in Chapter Thirteen. About half the states have special legislation dealing with mobile home park evictions, and that procedure will apply instead.

If the owner of the lot evicts you after a court action for failing to pay rent, at a minimum you will have to move the mobile home. Sometimes this presents practical problems because the home is not really movable, is expensive to move, and because you may have nowhere else to put it.

It is just as important to pay your lot rent as your mobile home mortgage.

Equally importantly, the lot owner may have special remedies allowing it to take action to repossess the mobile home in the event you fail to pay your lot rent. In many states, this process is the same as for any other creditor with a claim against you. The lot owner can seek a money judgment and then use that judgment as a lien on your mobile home. These issues are discussed in Chapter Seven. In other states, however, special laws give the lot owner the right to an automatic lien and special repossession rights ahead of other creditors.

You will need to check with a specialist who is knowledgeable about these issues in your state. You can also ask a mobile home park tenant's association or mobile homeowner's association for advice. But it is important to deal with your lot rent as a priority debt just as high as your mobile home mortgage payment.

Consumer Issues Associated With Mobile Homes. Mobile homes are the source of a variety of abuses. It is not uncommon for mobile homes to be defective, for loans used to purchase mobile homes to be made on unfair terms, or for mobile home park owners to exercise abusive collection tactics. These practices may give rise to defenses against foreclosure or eviction. They may also create legal claims for which you have the right to recover money.

If you think you have a defense to foreclosure or eviction or an affirmative claim for damages, it is a good idea to check with a lawyer or mobile home park association sooner rather than later. Delay can cost you your legal rights. In some locations, local legal service organizations will advise you about your rights or represent you for free.

Mobile home-related debts raise unique issues which can be very complicated. Further information can be found in National Consumer Law Center, *Repossessions and Foreclosures* (3d ed. 1995). Other useful publications include National Consumer Law Center, *Unfair and Deceptive Acts and Practices* (3rd ed. 1991) and *Manufactured Housing Park Tenants: Shifting the Balance of Power* (AARP 1991).

FORECLOSURES BASED ON A JUDGMENT LIEN

Most foreclosures are based on your non-payment of a mortgage, a tax lien, or a workman's lien. Creditors without a mortgage or lien can also try to seize your home, but you have important protections. First of all, the creditor has to go to court to sue on the debt. (See Chapter Seven for tips on defending such lawsuits to collect a debt.)

After a hearing, if the judge rules for the creditor, a lien, called a "judgment lien," may be placed on your home. The creditor can later "execute" that judgment by asking a court to sell your home and use the proceeds to satisfy the amount of the judgment lien.

Even then, state homestead laws usually prevent such a sale. Additionally, bankruptcy is likely to give you the opportunity to remove the lien if you do not have substantial equity in your home. Further discussion of these and other protections available against judgment liens is contained in Chapter Seven.

— 13 —

Evictions
and Other Disputes
With Landlords

• Advice on Getting Out of Your Lease
• Preventing Eviction
• Coping With Problems at a New Rental Unit

If you cannot afford your rent payments, you are likely to be facing one of three significant problems: 1) you want to stay in the residence, but your landlord is seeking to evict you; 2) you want to move out, but the landlord wants significant damages because you will be breaking the lease; or 3) you do move, and then experience problems with the new, less expensive rental unit. This chapter will provide advice on the best way to deal with each of these problems.

GETTING OUT OF A LEASE

Getting Out of Your Lease as an Alternative to Eviction. Affordable rents quickly can become unaffordable when you lose your job or when, for some other reason, your financial situation worsens. Moving to a less costly apartment or house may be your best option, at least until your situation improves. This is usually better than being evicted and then being forced to find another residence under severe time pressure.

If you break a lease, you may owe your landlord rent not just for those months you are in the apartment, but for some number of months after you leave. Nevertheless, switching apartments on your own time schedule, even with this penalty, may still be a better choice than waiting to be evicted.

Eviction can be a devastating and disruptive experience. It compounds the financial hardships you are already experiencing because the eviction will entail extra costs and pressures on you. The speed of the eviction process may force you into unwanted choices, extra expenses, and acceptance of far from satisfactory alternative living arrangements. Frequently, the only other housing available is more expensive than that from which your family was evicted.

So moving out on your own, on your own terms, is usually better than an eviction. While you may owe your landlord a penalty for breaking the lease, there are steps you can take to lessen this amount, as set out below.

Read the Lease. The first step in terminating a lease is to read the rental agreement carefully. If the agreement provides that either party can terminate the lease by giving advance notice, you need only give the notice specified in the lease. Then you may move without responsibility for additional payments.

Many tenants have formal or informal month-to-month rental agreements with their landlords, and state landlord-tenant law will establish the rules for terminating those agreements. In most states you must give 30 days notice before moving, unless something is seriously wrong with the property, making it unsafe to remain there.

Landlords will often forgive back rent
payments or reduce the penalty for your
terminating the lease early in exchange
for your agreement to move.

Negotiate With Your Landlord to Reduce What You Owe. If the lease requires you to pay for all rent due until the end of your lease, try to get a better deal from the landlord. Start by asking for a rent reduction, explaining why the rent is no longer affordable. Lowering the rent may be less costly for the landlord than going to the expense of evicting you and finding a new tenant. If the landlord will not reduce the rent permanently, ask him to do so for a few months until you get back on your feet.

Landlords may also allow you to break the lease without penalty so that they can rent to others who are better able to pay. You can even try to get the landlord to forgive your back rent if you move out by a certain date (which will help the landlord avoid eviction costs). Be sure to get in writing any deal you make with the landlord! This will protect you if the landlord breaks his or her word.

Find Someone Else to Take Over the Apartment. There are two different ways that someone else can take over your apartment and the rent payments for you. One way is a sublease, where someone else takes over your apartment and pays the rent. In a sublease, you are still obligated to pay the landlord for any rent your subtenant fails to pay. The other way is for someone else to take over not only the apartment, but the whole lease, called assuming the lease. Then you can wash your hands of the lease forever even if the new tenant does not pay the rent.

Look at the language in your lease to see if subleasing or lease assumption are allowed, and whether the landlord must approve the new tenant. Whatever the wording of the lease, the landlord may let you move out early with no penalty, if you have arranged for responsible tenants to sublet or assume the lease. Even when a lease permits subletting or assumption, landlords should be consulted before you begin looking for new occupants. Landlords are more likely to cooperate with a sublease or an assumption if you let them know what you are trying to do.

Breaking the Lease. If it is impossible to negotiate a friendly early termination, assumption, or sublease, you should evaluate the financial cost of breaking the lease. Although there may be financial consequences of breaking a lease, the alternative of eviction, or of continuing to bear an expensive lease, is usually worse.

When a lease is broken, the amount you will owe the landlord is limited in most states. The landlord must try to find a new tenant for the unit right away. If the landlord does not try, this may provide you a defense to the landlord trying to collect additional rent from you.

If state law does not limit how much you owe or if the landlord cannot find a new tenant, you may then owe the monthly rent for the remainder of the lease and any costs associated with finding a new tenant. You can only be forced to pay, however, if the landlord goes to court. Landlords who take their cases to court may sometimes also be awarded court costs or attorneys' fees, if such fees are allowed by the lease agreement and state law. If a new tenant is found who will pay rent in an amount lower than you would have paid, you may be responsible for the difference.

One helpful thing is any amount you owe your old landlord need not be paid right away if you cannot afford it. (If the landlord does sue you for rent owed, see Chapter Seven.) Because you have not put up your car or other property as collateral for this debt, the debt to the landlord is an unsecured debt. It can only be collected by a lawsuit. Even after the landlord obtains a judgment against you, it must find non-exempt property to satisfy the judgment. A bankruptcy may also eliminate the landlord's right to collect on the judgement.

If the landlord does not sue, your loss will be limited to the security deposit, last month's rent, or other money held by the landlord (together with anything you agree to pay voluntarily). Many landlords will not even report the debt to a credit bureau.

An unsecured obligation to a landlord is normally preferable to continuing to throw your limited resources at an unaffordable apartment.If you are having financial trouble, you should concentrate your resources on purchasing food, clothing and other necessities. You should also consider saving something for the various security deposits that a new landlord and new utility service will require.

Other Things to Do If You Decide to Break the Lease. If you decide to break the lease, here are some steps to take to minimize your liability for damages:

- You should give the landlord plenty of notice, preferably thirty to sixty days, so the landlord will have time to advertise for new tenants. Payments by new tenants will minimize what the landlord can seek from you.
- You should consider advertising the apartment yourself, either by word of mouth or through newspaper classified advertisements. Even if a sublease or lease assumption is not permitted, offering a suitable substitute tenant will make it hard for the landlord to argue that no other tenants were available.
- The premises should be cleaned thoroughly and left in good condition when you move so that there are no claims of dam-

ages against your security deposit. You should request that the landlord go over the property after you clean it to prevent any dispute over damages. You may also want to have a neutral party review the condition of the property before you move in case you need a witness later. Alternatively, you can take pictures of the clean apartment to use in the event of a dispute.

• Check newspaper ads to verify that the landlord is making an effort to find new renters.

• After you move, you may also want to observe the rental unit from time to time for signs of new occupants.

The bottom line is that if you break a lease, you will probably lose your security deposit. However, if you plan carefully, making sure that the landlord suffers no loss of rent and has no unplanned expenses, you may minimize your liability for additional damages.

State landlord-tenant laws provide specific procedures for recovering your security deposit if the landlord does not return it voluntarily. In most states, you can recover damages in a court case if the deposit is wrongfully withheld.

RESPONDING TO A LANDLORD'S EVICTION ATTEMPTS

Sadly, if you are unable to pay your full rent on a regular, ongoing basis, you almost inevitably will have to move. Although some defenses to eviction are available, landlords can nearly always remove you eventually for nonpayment of rent.

The best potential outcome to an eviction proceeding is generally to ensure that your family has enough time to find alternative housing that is both affordable and adequate, with minimal disruption to your lives. You should move when it is best for you, not when the sheriff pulls up with a van to put you out. You can also seek to ensure that proper and fair eviction procedures are used, that payments to the old landlord upon moving are kept to a minimum, and that conditions in your new apartment are adequate.

The legal steps for an eviction vary from state to state, so you must become familiar with local rules. Most eviction proceedings take place very quickly. The entire process may be completed in as little as two weeks. In some states, the process can take considerably longer, particularly if you have reasons to argue that you should not be evicted. Appeals are also possible if you lose.

If you lose an eviction case, the court will usually order that you move out immediately. If you do not move out, court officials or the sheriff will come to put you out. How long that takes depends on your state. It may be days, weeks, or even months. The local legal services office or the court clerk should be able to tell you how long you usually have.

Here are some general rules about the eviction process:

The Notice to Quit Is a Warning. In most states, the first step in an eviction is a notice telling you that you must move within a short time. This is usually called a "notice to quit" or a "notice to vacate." If you have not paid your rent, the notice usually instructs you either to pay rent or to get out.

A "Notice to Quit" does *not* mean you have to leave — it is just a warning.

This notice does not, by itself, require that you move — no one shows up on the date contained in the notice to evict you. Instead, landlords that want to put legal teeth behind the notice must first go to court after the time allowed in the notice has expired. A notice to quit should be seen as a warning, not a final notice. (In a few states this notice is not required and the landlord may go directly to court.)

Generally, the notice will give you a specified number of days in which to vacate the premises. In many states, the notice must also give you the right to stay in the apartment by "curing," that is, paying a specified dollar amount of back rent within a specified number of days. Sometimes the landlord will also claim other violations of the lease, such as damage to the premises or keeping a pet forbidden by the lease. These violations may also be cured by taking care of the underlying problem.

Negotiating With the Landlord. Even after receiving a notice to move out, you should consider talking to the landlord about a mutual agreement which would resolve the problem. For example, if you are having trouble paying your monthly rent in a lump sum, some landlords agree to accept weekly or biweekly installments. Landlords sometimes also agree to lower the rent, at least temporarily. Whether a landlord will agree to work something out depends upon the landlord and your own relationship with the landlord in the past.

At the very least, you can suggest that the landlord exchange lower rent for your agreeing to move in a certain number of months. This would let you leave on your terms without the threat of an immediate eviction. Landlords who know that their tenants will definitely move, usually allow them some extra time. This saves the landlord the expense of eviction.

Temporary and Permanent Rent Assistance. You may also want to look into various sources of temporary rent assistance that can buy you some time. Emergency rental assistance is available in some states, usually through the local welfare office. In other places, you may want to call local community action agencies.

General Relief programs also can benefit tenants. Often operated by individual counties under their own guidelines, most of these programs provide housing payments to needy individuals, at least for short periods. In addition, church groups and private charitable organizations are potential sources of financial assistance.

Tenants who do not already receive a government housing subsidy can also apply for various kinds of government housing assistance, including special rental assistance, state or nonprofit housing programs, and traditional public housing. Waiting lists are quite long. Urgent circumstances, such as homelessness, illness, or small children, sometimes move applicants higher on waiting lists.

Priorities for assistance and the length of waiting time vary from program to program and from community to community. Needy individuals should promptly apply for any assistance for which they may be eligible. The best place to start is to contact your local or regional housing authority for more information.

Responding to the Eviction Case. If you have not paid the full back rent nor moved out by the time specified in the notice to vacate, the landlord can file an eviction action in court. This is sometimes called a forcible entry, detainer or ejectment action. (We refer here to all these actions as "eviction actions.")

Eviction actions are usually scheduled for a hearing right away. State laws require that you be given the landlord's complaint and a summons to appear in court — generally by a process server or a local official. State law also specifies a minimum number of days, often as few as five, between when you are served and when the hearing takes place. Therefore, you should promptly take steps to respond, or consult a lawyer.

If you disagree with a landlord's complaint, or if you have any defenses, you should immediately contact the court and file an answer or counterclaim. Some common defenses and counterclaims are discussed briefly below.

Many landlord-tenant cases are held in less-formal housing courts or justice courts. You should be able to file your own answers or counterclaims without using sophisticated legal terminology. Some courts charge a fee for filing papers — but the fee should be waivable if you can show inability to pay.

Attending the Eviction Hearing. If you have been served with notice of an eviction proceeding, you should always attend — whether or not you have already moved out. Even if you believe you have no defenses, you should attend the eviction hearing to make sure you know what is going on. You want to be certain, for example, that the landlord does not misstate the amount of rent you owe or ask that you be put out by a quicker than normal process.

Even if you have no defense, you can request that the judge give you additional time before moving if there are special circumstances. Some examples might be illness of a family member, a lease for a new apartment which is not yet ready to move into, or unavailability of emergency shelter. The judge will be more likely to grant additional time if you are able to offer at least partial rent, or if other housing has been arranged. For compelling circumstances, such as illness, or for families with many small children, judges are also more inclined to grant delays.

At the hearing, if you have a defense, you will need to be prepared to present your side of the story. This should include relevant documents and witnesses, if any. Preparing a case for court is discussed in Chapter Seven. Some defenses which may be available in an eviction case are discussed below.

Raising Defenses. Tenants with defenses to an eviction must raise those defenses at the eviction hearing (or in some states earlier by filing required papers — usually called an "answer" or an "appearance"). Defenses will always be lost if you do not appear at the hearing.

Most courts require that an evicting landlord strictly comply with all the technical requirements of the eviction law, including the content, timing, and service of all required notices and court documents. Any mistake in complying with these requirements, if it is pointed out to the court, may cause a landlord's petition to be dismissed. The landlord will then be required to begin the procedure anew.

State law sometimes allows other defenses or claims that might defeat or delay an eviction. For example, some states recognize a defense called "peaceable possession." This defense states that if a landlord neglects to file an eviction action promptly after the expiration of a notice to vacate time period, the landlord has consented to continued occupancy. Peaceable possession may result in dismissal of the eviction, although the landlord can send a new notice to vacate.

Another possible defense is that the landlord habitually accepted late or partial payments, and then suddenly, without warning, started eviction proceedings based on late payment or nonpayment of rent. The eviction is then improper, because it was started even though the tenant was no later in payments than usual.

Yet another defense is based on the requirement in many states that landlords give tenants a notice to pay the specified amount of rent owed. If the notice misstates the rent owed, for example, indicating that three months payments are delinquent when only two and a half months rent is delinquent, the notice is probably defective.

Other issues may be present when a landlord is subject to federal housing laws, such as HUD or FmHA regulations. In addition to state laws, these laws provide specific requirements for a landlord's eviction case.

Legal advice may be necessary to understand specific procedural requirements for the landlord's action and your potential responses. In many communities eviction clinics or legal pamphlets on tenants' rights are offered by the local legal services office, the bar association, or the court clerk.

Substandard Housing Conditions as a Defense; Retaliatory Evictions.

In most states, courts will recognize defenses or counterclaims based upon the property not being "habitable" (in livable condition) or if the property is not properly maintained. These claims are based on the landlord breaching the rental agreement by not keeping the property in good repair. Another defense is available in many states if you can show that an eviction action is in retaliation for your exercise of legal rights.

The availability of defenses and counterclaims based on the condition of the apartment varies widely from state to state. Almost everywhere, you will have a defense if the apartment has been cited for housing code violations. If there are serious problems with the apartment, you may want to call the housing inspector to have the conditions reviewed. If a citation is issued, you should make sure to get a copy to take with you to court. A "certified" copy may be required in some courts. Ask the housing inspector how to get a certified copy of the report.

Even if there are no housing code violations, problems with the apartment can still partially or fully offset your obligation to pay rent because you have not gotten what you bargained for. Take pictures of any problems, if possible. In the alternative, for problems like lack of adequate heat, a disinterested witness may testify.

Many states require prior notice to the landlord of the bad conditions before the conditions can be used as a defense to eviction. The notice requirement is designed to give the landlord an opportunity to correct the problem. It is always a good idea to provide the landlord with notice in writing with a copy for your records. This notice should be sent by certified mail if you have a history of disputes with your landlord. You should bring several copies with you to court in order to prove that you have complied with the law.

Some evictions are brought by landlords in order to punish tenants for enforcing their rights. The classic example is an eviction case which is brought because one tenant has organized other tenants in the building. Similarly, some landlords routinely evict tenants who contact housing inspectors because of problems with the property. Retaliatory eviction cases are hard to prove — especially when there is also a back rent issue. Among the important questions will be the time of the eviction and its relation to your actions, any statements or threats made by the landlord, and whether the underlying problems about the property had merit. If a retaliatory eviction has occurred, it is a good idea to consult a lawyer.

Appeals. If you lose an eviction case and the court orders an eviction, one possibility is to appeal the case to a higher court. This may buy you more time to move in a more orderly fashion. In fact, the threat of an appeal may allow you to negotiate more time with the landlord.

An appeal may require that you pay certain filing fees or other charges.

Sometimes these fees can be waived if you can show you cannot afford to pay. In addition, frivolous appeals should not be taken. Fines or other sanctions may result.

Other Responses to a Court's Eviction Order. You should respond to an eviction order by making arrangements to move before you are forced out into the street. It is always a mistake to just ignore the eviction order.

In some states, but not all, you will get notice of an actual eviction date. You may want to consult the sheriff, a court clerk, or your local legal services office about how long you are likely to have. Often, you will have only a very short opportunity to move before you are put out.

In some cases, arrangements to move by a certain date can be made directly with the landlord or by the court with a judge's approval. Sometimes, you can get assistance with moving costs from the welfare department in your community or from a charity.

If you have not vacated by the time specified in a court eviction order, a sheriff or a similar official may move your belongings onto the sidewalk, or place them in storage. You will then have to pay moving and storage costs.

In some states, landlords can place a lien on your furniture and other possessions to cover moving and storage charges. Until you pay those charges, you cannot get your property back. It is better to avoid this problem entirely by moving voluntarily.

Lockouts and Seizures of Personal Property. Seizures of your personal property as part of a court-ordered eviction process may be legal. On the other hand, in most states, it is illegal for a landlord to seize your personal property without court permission.

There are a few states that do give landlords the right, if you are behind in paying rent, to seize all or part of your belongings on the property without first obtaining court permission. You may then be forced to go to court to seek return of the property, and you may have to post a bond to obtain its release.

A tenant whose property has been seized should seek legal advice. Even in those states that allow such seizures, certain property will be listed as exempt from seizure. There may even be grounds for a constitutional challenge to the procedure itself.

Lockouts, utility shut-offs and eviction-related harassment are illegal in all states. When landlords take these actions, they are generally known as "self-help evictions." If you are locked out, or if your landlord is harassing you to get you to move out (including the common practice of shutting down utility service to your property), you are likely to be entitled to get back into the property and to have the harassment ended by a court. You also may be entitled to damages. Legal assistance for a case of this type is a good idea.

Without permission from a court, landlords cannot padlock your apartment, shut off your utilities or otherwise force you to leave.

When you are locked out, or if your utilities are shut off, your landlord may claim that you have abandoned the apartment. You may want to let the landlord know in writing that this is not the case. If the landlord does not let you back in or turn on the utilities, a copy of the letter will serve as proof that the landlord knew that you had not moved out.

The Landlord's Suit for Back Rent. Landlords sometimes sue for back rent or property damage after a tenant moves or is evicted. As part of that suit, a landlord may also ask that the tenant be required to pay the landlord's attorney fees.

A case for back rent may or may not be included with the eviction. If you are sued for back rent, it should be treated just like a suit for money by any other creditor. A discussion of ways to address lawsuits generally is included in Chapters Seven and Eight. In addition, some special considerations apply.

Some of the claims that you may raise in evictions are also potential defenses or counterclaims in suits for back rent. Common defenses include: substandard housing conditions; miscalculation of the amount owed; illegal attempts by landlords to seize your property; a landlord's attempt to lock you out; or a shut-off of utility service. Landlords, collection agencies, management companies and their lawyers are also potentially responsible for debt collection harassment. For any of these claims, you should consider consulting a lawyer.

DEALING WITH PROBLEMS
IN A NEW RENTAL UNIT

There are two common problems faced by those moving into new residences: the condition of the property and problems hooking up utility service. Tips on hooking up utility service at a new address are found at Chapter Fourteen. This section explains your rights if the new apartment has substandard conditions.

To protect against substandard conditions, the law in most states requires that a dwelling meet minimum standards of habitability. Rental property must meet local housing, health, fire, and building ordinances. Heat and hot water must be available. Appliances must be safe and in working order. When housing is not habitable, you can take several steps.

Written Requests that the Landlord Make Repairs. When substandard conditions are present, the first step toward correcting them is to request that the landlord make the desired repairs. Because repair disputes tend to arise frequently, the request should be made in writing. Any oral request should be confirmed in writing.

Reporting Code Violations to a Housing Inspector. If a direct request to the landlord does not bring results, then city or county ordinances, available at a city hall or public library, should be checked for possible housing code violations. Or you can call the housing inspector's office directly to ask about the applicable regulations. If violations of the housing code are present, you can complain to the local housing inspector. Again, this complaint should be in writing and copies retained. The resulting enforcement action against the landlord should be designed to get the problem fixed.

Resist Retaliatory Evictions. Some landlords react badly to tenants' complaints and to inspectors' reports, and attempt to evict complaining tenants. However, many state landlord-tenant laws protect tenants from retaliatory evictions. It is important to get legal advice from a neighborhood legal services office, pro bono attorney, or other source when a retaliatory eviction is threatened, so that you can properly mount a legal defense consistent with the state law.

Forcing the Landlord to Make Repairs; Rent Withholding. If tenant requests and inspector reports bring no results, you may decide to go to court. Courts can order landlords to make repairs, to refund your rent, or to pay for your damages. A landlord's refusal to make necessary repairs also gives you the right to terminate your rental agreement and move elsewhere. Sometimes, if conditions become so bad that you are forced to move, a landlord may be required to reimburse you for the cost of temporary substitute housing.

Depending upon the circumstances, some state laws permit you to withhold rent to pay for necessary repairs. Sometimes these laws require you to follow specific steps in withholding your rent, and it will be important to follow these rules.

None of these strategies should be considered without first consulting a lawyer, a tenant counselor, or a clerk at a local housing court. Legal education pamphlets published by bar associations, community legal services programs, and public interest groups explain the rules for withholding rent, for court injunctions, and for lease terminations. These laws should be carefully followed, or your rights may be affected.

14

Utility Terminations

- *Ways to Reduce Your Utility Bills*
- *Your Rights When a Utility Threatens Termination of Service*
- *Getting Your Utility Service Turned Back On*

We all know how important it is to maintain our utility service — we need the electricity to light our homes and run the furnace; we need the water to drink and bathe and clean with; we need the gas or other fuel to heat our home; and we need the telephone to make and receive essential calls. Unfortunately, we do not generally have a choice of utility providers — we must use the only telephone company and electric company and water provider that serves our area.

Also, unlike other creditors, utility providers are generally allowed by law the drastic remedy of cutting off service to force payment of back bills. So, when faced with a large utility bill, you may feel that you are between a rock and a hard place — pay an unaffordable bill or lose essential service. This chapter explains that there are other things you can do.

WAYS TO REDUCE YOUR UTILITY BILLS

Even if your most pressing concern at the moment is getting *past-due* utility bills paid to maintain service, you should still be interested in reducing your *future* bills, to avoid repeating the problems of this moment. This section will provide specific ideas on how to reduce the bills, by:

- reducing the amount you are charged for the utility service you do use;
- changing the type of service you receive;
- changing the way you are billed to make the bills easier to pay;
- reducing *usage* of the utility service through a number of weatherization methods; and
- obtaining cash assistance in paying your bills.

You May Be Eligible for a Discount Utility Service Plan. Often utilities have special programs which will allow you to reduce the charges for the utility service that you receive. It only takes some investigation to see what the different utilities have to offer and whether you are eligible for the program.

Discounted Rates for Financially Distressed Households. Many utilities around the nation have special programs for low-income households to help them pay their utility bills. Some of these programs reduce the bills by a set amount each month; others provide discounts based on the amount of the bill. Check with your utility to see what is available.

PIPS or Energy Assurance Programs. Additionally, a growing number of utilities have plans by which families pay only a certain percentage of their income instead of the amount called for by their normal utility bills. This results in lower bills. Typically, your consistent payment of the lower amount is rewarded by gradual forgiveness of old unpaid bills. So you get two benefits in one.

These plans are sometimes called Percentage of Income Plans (PIPs) or Energy Assurance Plans (EAPs), but each utility seems to have its own unique name for the program. The best way to determine if a utility has such a program is to contact that particular utility or the public utility commission in your state capitol.

Telephone Discounts. There are special programs for discounts of telephone rates for low-income households. In most states, households in financial distress can obtain a significant discount on telephone monthly charges under the "Lifeline" program run by your local phone company. Contact the public utility commission or the local telephone company for details.

Eligibility. Eligibility for each of these programs varies considerably. Some simply look at household income, others look for receipt of, or eligibility for, governmental benefits, such as Social Security, SSI, Aid to Families with Dependent Children (AFDC), Food Stamps, or the Low Income Home Energy Assistance Program (LIHEAP). Check with your utility company to see if you are eligible.

Changing the Type of Service Can Reduce Your Bill. You may be receiving some utility services which you can fairly easily do without. While the charges for each of these individual services may not seem a lot, together they can add up to quite a few dollars each month. A careful review of your bills and a discussion with each utility company may yield some real savings.

Electric Service. Sometimes you can save considerably by going to a "time of use" type of service with your electric supplier. Whether you actually save money is entirely dependent on the type of program that your electric supplier has and your household's actual electric use patterns. A "time of use" type of service means that you are charged less for using electricity at some times of the day — generally during the evening and night hours and the weekend, and more for electricity used during the daytime. These programs often work well for households where no one is home during most of the work day. Check with your electric company to see if this program is available and would be of benefit to your family.

Cable TV Service. Are there cable TV services that you can drop? During your period of financial difficulty, can you return to using an antenna for your television, and eliminate the entire bill?

Local Telephone Service. Examine your telephone bill. Are you paying for call waiting, call forwarding, call answer and other high tech services? Would you do without these services to save $6 to $15 a month? Are you paying for extended area service (local rates for calls to an area which otherwise would be long distance)? How much is this costing you, and do you really call to the extended area enough to justify the extra cost each month? Another question is whether you are you paying a lot for local measured service — which is when you are billed separately for each local call. Contact the telephone company and see if they have different programs which might save you money.

Long Distance Telephone Calls. How much does your long distance service cost? Shop around with the different long distance carriers. Their various deals are often complicated, but can result in significant savings depending upon your calling patterns. Some programs have less expensive calls during the day, others at night. Look for the long distance service which best fits your actual calling patterns.

Sometimes, your long distance bill includes calls you did not make. If you are billed for calls that you did not make, or do not feel you owe the full long distance bill, ask the carrier to delete these charges from your bill.

To prevent bills for unauthorized calls from occurring in the future, you may want to investigate a blocking service. Every local telephone company must provide a service to its customers which will block long distance calls from being made unless a password or some other device is used. The local telephone company can charge for these blocking services. Keep in mind that blocking is not foolproof. A creative and sneaky relative or friend can figure out a way around the long distance blocking, and you will still be charged for the calls. So be careful who you let use your telephone.

Other Telephone Charges. Are you being billed high amounts for 900 calls or other "audio text services" that you didn't make or didn't authorize? Every local telephone company is prohibited from terminating your *local* telephone service for nonpayment of these "pay per call" services. Further, you can put a block on your telephone so that these calls can no longer be billed to your telephone. Unlike the block for long distance service, this block should be free, and should be foolproof.

REDUCING YOUR BILL BY CHANGING YOUR BILLING PATTERNS

Level Payment Plans. If you are able to pay your *average* utility bill, but have difficulty meeting your heating bills in the coldest months of winter or your electric bills in the hottest months of summer, a level payment plan might make sense for you. A level payment plan allows you to avoid running up debts during high usage months by averaging your expected bills so that you can pay the same amount each month. Many states require their regulated utilities to provide these plans.

In a level payment plan, your projected yearly bill is divided into equal monthly installments; monthly bills reflect this amount rather than each month's actual use. For example, a customer whose total gas bill for a year is $1200, would pay $100 each month instead of $200 to $300 a month in the winter, and $30 to $40 a month in the summer. At some point during the year, the average bill and the actual usage are reconciled.

Just changing your payment schedule may make your utility bills more affordable.

Dealing with Quarterly or Bi-Monthly Bills. Some utilities do not normally bill on a monthly basis. If financial problems cause you temporarily to live month to month, you may find it difficult to deal with quarterly or bi-monthly bills, particularly when those bills represent significant portions of your monthly income. Contact your local utility company and explain the difficulty and see if they will bill you on a monthly basis. In the alternative, ask them to accept monthly payments from you, even if they won't send you a separate bill each month.

If you make this choice, ask about "service charges" or "finance charges." This is the cost of paying over time. If the cost is too high, this type of payment plan is a bad idea.

Avoiding Late Payment Charges by Changing the Date Your Bill Is Due. If your main source of income arrives in the mail on the 5th of the month, but your utility bill is due to be paid on the 4th, it is obviously going to be very difficult for you to pay your utility bill on time. The result can be that you not only have the high utility bill to contend with, but you also have the additional charges added to your bill because payment is late. Generally, utility companies will help you deal with this, if you explain the situation. Although they may insist that you pay the late charges that have already been billed to your account, the utility company should agree to change the date your bill is due each month so that late charges don't keep accruing. By avoiding the late charges, you may reduce your bill by $5 to $15 each month.

REDUCING YOUR BILL BY
REDUCING YOUR UTILITY USAGE

Utility Sponsored Weatherization or Conservation Programs.
Many utilities have programs that provide free, or low cost weatherization
or conservation services. Sometimes these programs are available to all
households, sometimes they are limited to the elderly, or homes with disabled persons and/or children. Sometimes the eligibility for the program
may be based on the household's income or eligibility for a government
program, such as Energy Assistance (also called Low Income Home
Energy Assistance Program or LIHEAP) or the Weatherization Assistance
Program.

These programs run the gamut. In the best programs, the utility sends
someone who conducts a full energy audit of your home and provides
extensive weatherization services. Other programs simply provide hints on
how you can reduce usage, or they supply conservation products such as
special energy efficient light bulbs, insulating hot water tanks, "low flow"
efficient faucets, or other conservation products. Even the less ambitious
programs which provide only some conservation advice should be helpful
to you. Investigate by calling your local energy and water providers and
finding out what programs they have available.

Other conservation measures may be expensive. You should be very cau-
tious before investing more than a few dollars in any weatherization or
conservation efforts with a contractor. While it might make sense in the
long run for households with extra cash, it is often not the wisest use of
funds for households which are strapped to pay for rent and food. To know
whether an energy conservation investment is a good use of money, you
must analyze the cost of the investment against how long you expect to live
in this residence and your anticipated energy savings. This type of analysis
is beyond the ability of all but the experts.

Government Sponsored Weatherization Programs. Several programs
are designed to provide weatherization assistance for owner-occupied housing as well as rental units. The primary program is the Weatherization
Assistance Program. Households that qualify generally receive over $1000 in
actual weatherization benefits which are provided at no cost. Although there
may be a long waiting list, it is worthwhile looking into these programs.

Additionally, many states have weatherization programs. Cities also have

Community Development Block Grant money which may be used to help low-income households weatherize their homes.

Self-Help Weatherization. If you are unable to find or qualify for any of programs through your utility or the government, there are still a number of practices which may help reduce your usage. (Note, these procedures are unlikely to reduce your bills significantly, but even a 3 or 5% reduction means some added dollars for you.)

Check for air or water leaks. If you are a tenant, try to get the landlord to fix these leaks. If you own your own home, and it is possible, try a number of homespun fix ups. For example, for air leaks around windows use heavy tape. For leaks around doors, leave a rolled up towel next to the bottom of the door. If necessary to stop leaks around the top and sides of doors, tack up a blanket or large towel. You will be surprised how much warmer a house or apartment can be without the heat loss from cracks between openings and walls. As the home warms up, you can consider turning down the heat.

Remember that your sewer bill is generally determined by how much water you consume. So that by saving water you are saving twice — on your water and your sewer bill. Putting a brick in your toilet tank may seem silly, but it will actually cut down on the amount of water consumed each time you flush. Turn off lights and heat or cooling when not at home. Also close the door for any rooms you are not using, and don't try to heat or cool them.

REDUCING YOUR BILL
THROUGH GOVERNMENT ASSISTANCE

If you have a low income and high utility bills, you are probably eligible for one or more of several sources of assistance with your utility bills. These programs vary a great deal. Some types of aid are available only certain times of the year, others are available only if you have a certain type of fuel. Some programs only help you if you are facing a termination of utility service; other programs only help you if you are not facing a termination. All programs have eligibility requirements, but they differ considerably in their specific terms.

The Federal Low Income Home Energy Assistance Program (LIHEAP), which is run by the states, helps low-income families pay their utility bills. Most states provide this assistance for winter heating bills; although some states also use LIHEAP funds to assist families with summer cooling expenses. LIHEAP benefits can even go to some renters and public and sub-sidized housing tenants, with the energy assistance payments going directly to the landlord's fuel supplier and the amount being credited against the family's rent.

Guidelines for LIHEAP eligibility vary by state, but most states require that family income over the past three or twelve months be below 150% of the federal poverty guidelines. (In some states, income must be even less.) The size of a family's LIHEAP benefits generally depends on the family's income and the number of household members, and may also depend on housing type, fuel type, fuel prices, weather conditions, or actual energy consumption.

To apply for LIHEAP benefits, a household should contact the local agency in the community administering the program. This is usually a non-profit agency, such as the local community action program (CAP), or a county department or social services office. Benefits are sometimes paid directly to the utility company or fuel vendor, and the family's utility or fuel obligation is reduced accordingly. Other times, joint checks are made out to the customer and the utility. In a few states fuel assistance checks are pro-vided solely to the customer.

YOUR RIGHTS WHEN
THE UTILITY THREATENS TO
TERMINATE YOUR SERVICE

Utilities Must Follow Rules Before Terminating Your Service. In most states there are laws which provide a variety of significant protections when utility companies threaten termination of your utility service. Many of the larger utilities are regulated by commissions called public utility com-missions, or public service commissions. Utility companies can only shut off your service if they have followed the requirements set out by these commissions.

Utility termination rules generally have the following basic requirements:

- notice of the proposed termination;
- a right to a hearing;
- a limit on circumstances permitting termination;

- the right to a deferred payment plan;
- protection from terminations during the winter months;
- no terminations if there is serious illness in the household;
- information provided about places to go for assistance with paying the utility bill;
- protections for tenants from termination of service by landlords;
- prohibitions on termination of local telephone service for bills for other services;
- in some states, a temporary limit on termination of utility service when there is a plant closing.

The utility's failure to follow these termination rules typically provides grounds to demand that the termination process start all over, and utility service must be maintained throughout the process. Wrongful termination of utility service generally will give you a claim for damages. An attorney can often get a special court order (an injunction) to stop termination or to have service restored when the utility has failed to follow the rules on termination procedures.

You can use a utility's violation of shut-off rules to prevent termination of your service.

Often utility representatives refuse to negotiate a payment plan, or fail to give notice of all your important rights, such as the opportunity for appeal or the right to participate in a payment plan. Because your only information provider is generally a company representative, you should not hesitate to contact a local legal services or other attorney or the consumer services division of the state public utilities commission to find out whether the utility has complied with the termination rules. Public utility commissions generally have dispute resolution authority, and a call to the appropriate person can often stall or prevent a termination altogether.

In addition, you have certain rights to stop a termination when you file for bankruptcy. Finally, you may be eligible for certain emergency funds you can use to stop the shut-off. Here is a more detailed explanation of your rights concerning a threatened utility termination:

Notice. Prior to termination of your utility service, you must be given notice that the service is subject to termination, and of the various rights that you have to prevent termination. Often this requirement includes a repeat written notice. Face-to-face notice may also be required in certain parts of the country.

Limit on Circumstances Warranting Termination. Regulations typically permit disconnection for non-payment, but often prohibit disconnections for very small amounts, or for bills which have been owed for less than a certain number of months. Further, if you dispute that you owe the bill which the utility says must be paid, the utility is generally prohibited from terminating service until the dispute is resolved. If you dispute part of the bill, you must pay the undisputed amount to preserve your rights.

Right to a Hearing. Before or after termination, you have a right to appeal to both the utility and to an independent third party such as the Public Utility Commission. In many states, informal appeals can be made by telephone prior to termination and often utility service will be maintained or reconnected during the appeals process.

A utility commission's consumer division responds to phone calls, letters, and visits by residential customers. Many of these complaints are resolved informally, by consultation between the consumer division and the utility. Consumer divisions also hold hearings on complaints that cannot be resolved informally. In large states, several hundred of these hearings are held each year.

Consumers generally have a legal right to a hearing whenever they have grounds to contest a utility termination. Simply request the utility commission to provide a hearing before service is terminated. (If you dispute only part of a back bill, you will usually have to pay the undisputed part to keep your service on while the dispute is being decided). While city owned utilities are generally not regulated by the utility commission, customers of municipal utilities have a constitutional right to a hearing before termination.

You do not need the services of a lawyer at the hearing. However, it may be helpful to have a paralegal or experienced utility counselor assist with the hearing. To support the claim, it is important for you to bring all relevant documents, such as a physician's affidavit or old bills. It may also be helpful to have witnesses such as friends and neighbors present.

Right to a Deferred Payment Plan. Before utility service is shut off, most states require that a customer be informed about the option to pay all overdue bills over a period of some months through a reasonable installment plan. Often this payment plan has a six month or a one year limit for bringing the account up-to-date.

The plan may be designed so that you pay current usage, and slowly catch up on the amount you are behind. However, if your financial circumstances require, sometimes you can negotiate a better plan whereby the monthly payments do not even completely cover current bills, and do nothing to catch up on arrears.

To make a successful payment plan, develop a simple budget that you can reasonably meet, and be assertive with the utility company employee who negotiates the agreement. Payment plans need not be level. For example, seasonal workers may want to pay less toward arrears in the winter and more in the summer, or vice versa.

The utility company may want a payment plan that requires larger payments than you can afford. Large payments are in the company's short-term interest, because they recover past debts more quickly. Too many customers, believing they have no choice, agree to these payments.

It is usually a bad idea to agree to a payment plan which you know you cannot afford. This will only make things worse in the long run. It is better to explain your financial circumstances and push for an affordable agreement from the beginning.

Unrealistic plans harm both you and the utility company in the long term. You may not be able to make the payments, and may lose the service, and the company does not collect its debt. In some states, utilities are not required to enter into a second payment plan with consumers who have defaulted on a first payment plan. If a company refuses to agree to a reasonable payment plan, help can be obtained from the consumer division of the local utility commission.

Winter Moratorium on Terminations. In most northern states, heat-related utilities are prohibited from terminating any residential customer between November 1 and March 31st. In other states, there is usually a limited moratorium to prevent utility terminations for households with elderly or disabled residents, and occasionally for households with infants. Generally, financial hardship must be shown. Some of these rules require that, before a household be considered for the moratorium, all efforts to obtain state energy assistance must have been pursued.

Note that a moratorium only prevents disconnection of service. Your bill will still be charged and you will be responsible to pay for service used during the moratorium period. For this reason you should pay, if you can, even if your service is not subject to being disconnected.

No Termination If There Is Serious Illness. State law or public utility commission regulations often restrict termination of service for households whose members face a serious illness, are threatened with serious illness, or depend upon life support systems. Often, the illness must be certified by a doctor. A family with very young children may also be able to use the health risk to the children as grounds to stop utility termination.

Information About Sources of Assistance. Utility companies often must provide consumers, before a disconnection, with information about the existence of energy assistance programs, such as LIHEAP or local crisis intervention programs. (See the discussion below concerning these sources of emergency assistance.)

Tenants Protected from Termination of Service for Landlord's Failure to Pay. When a landlord is responsible for providing utility service, it is all too common, particularly in difficult economic times, for a landlord to fail to pay for that service, putting tenants at risk of losing the utility service. Tenants in this situation sometimes have special protections. In some states, tenants must receive a special shut-off notice if the landlord is delinquent. Then, tenants make utility payments directly to the utility, and deduct those payments from their rent.

Tenants Protected from Landlord Initiated Shut Off. It is illegal in almost every state for a landlord to cut off your utility service as a way of making you move. Landlords must go through the courts to evict tenants; they cannot make the place uninhabitable by terminating the heat or water service so that the tenant moves. Generally, you not only can stop a "self-help" eviction when the landlord tries this, but also you are entitled to recover damages for the landlord's wrongful actions.

No Termination of Local Telephone Service for Bills for Other Services. Some states prohibit the local telephone company from terminating your service for non-payment of long distance service, but the majority of states do not yet have these protections. Also, every local telephone company is prohibited from terminating your local telephone service for nonpayment of 900 calls or "audio text" services.

A Moratorium Linked to a Plant Closing. Sometimes a utility or utility commission will impose a temporary prohibition against termination of utility service for customers or neighborhoods particularly hard hit by a recent plant closing. If such a moratorium is not in effect, it may be possible for families affected by a plant closing or their unions to negotiate one. A moratorium does not erase financial liability for utility service used before or during the moratorium period. The moratorium only prevents the utility company from terminating service if bills incurred during the moratorium period are not paid. When the moratorium period expires, the utility can then start the termination process for amounts not paid during the moratorium. Most utilities encourage their customers to pay what they can afford during a moratorium.

Bankruptcy Protections. The filing of a bankruptcy petition automatically requires the utility to restore service or stop a threatened termination. The bankruptcy filing starts a twenty day period during which you are entitled to service from all applicable utilities. The utility can only terminate service after that twenty day period if you fail to pay bills arising *after* the bankruptcy is filed. Then, if you successfully complete your bankruptcy case, you never have to pay the past due arrears. The utility, though, can also require that you provide adequate assurance that *future* bills will be paid, most often by requesting a new security deposit. Bankruptcy is explained in more detail in Chapter Eighteen. The process can be complicated. Professional advice is a good idea.

Sources of Emergency Assistance. There are several sources of emergency assistance that may provide you with funds to prevent a utility termination. The following sources should be pursued:

- *LIHEAP Crisis Assistance.* Contact your local CAP agency (community action program) or the county department of social services to find out who provides these funds in your area.
- *AFDC Emergency Assistance.* If you have children and you are about to lose essential utility services (water, heat in the winter months, etc.) contact your county department of social services to see if special emergency funds are available to help you.
- *State Emergency Assistance.* Some states have special funds to help prevent utility terminations. Also many counties have "homeless prevention" funds which can be used to prevent utility terminations. Contact your local CAP agency or the county department of social services.
- *Utility Fuel Funds.* Many utilities collect money from their customers or their shareholders to go into a special fund to help people pay their utility bills. Contact the utility which is threatening to shut off the service to see if they have a fund which might be of some assistance to you. You should not assume that, because they haven't told you about it, that they don't have such a fund, or that you are not eligible.
- *Salvation Army, Local Churches.* The Salvation Army and other local religious and charitable organizations often have money that is available to help needy people in the community with emergency bills such as utilities. Check around, ask the utility company, the public utility commission, or the department of social services. Some churches that have these funds do not limit them to their own members.

WAYS TO GET YOUR
UTILITY SERVICE TURNED BACK ON

Establishing new service after a move or after previous service has been terminated can be difficult and expensive. However, utilities are prohibited from discriminating in service, and required to establish reasonable rules for customers to follow.

If you have had your prior utility service terminated for non-payment, it may be difficult establishing renewed service. You will generally have to pay the old bill plus late charges, a reconnection fee, and often a deposit. However, there are a number of things you can try to reduce the amount of money you have to come up with to establish new utility service.

Dealing With an Old Bill. If the bill is *very* old, such as more than three or four years, it is possible that the utility can not legally require you to pay it before providing you with new service. Check with a local attorney if you have a very old bill. However, generally, the bill will be more recent.

The best method to deal with old bills which must be paid may be to request the utility to allow you to pay the old bill off in installments over a period of six to twelve months or longer. So long as you maintain your payments on the new service you will be receiving, there is no reason for the utility to refuse to provide you service under this arrangement. After all, a utility provider is generally permitted to terminate utility service only as a way of avoiding future losses. If you are ready and willing to pay for future service as it is provided, and to pay for the old service, over time, the utility does not have reasonable grounds to deny you this new service.

Late Charges. Generally a utility will charge late fees for paying a utility bill after it is due. There should be specific rules on how much these late charges are, and state law and regulations generally limit the late charges to reasonable amounts. The purposes of the late charges are to compensate the utility for its extra costs in collecting the overdue bill, and to discourage you from missing payments by imposing an extra charge when you fall behind.

If the late charges are so high as to be unreasonable, try contacting the consumer services division of your state public utility commission to challenge the amount. Otherwise, try to negotiate with the local utility about the amount. If you lost your job, went through a separation or divorce, or suffered an illness in the family which caused you to be late on your payments before, you can show that this was a temporary difficulty which has now passed — so you do not need the *lesson* that late charges are meant to provide. Bargain with the utility; in many cases they will reduce all or part of the late charges, especially if you had a good reason for missing payments.

Reconnection Fee. This is a fee which may be imposed on a household after it has its service terminated for non-payment. The purpose of this fee is similar to late charges. Try the same type of arguments and negotiation to get the utility to reduce or waive this fee.

Deposits. Before establishing new or renewed service, many utility companies ask households with poor payment histories to pay a deposit, usually equal to an average monthly bill. Utilities are prohibited from discriminating against certain types of customers in setting the deposit requirements. Customers who believe that a deposit is being requested unreasonably, or that a requested deposit is too large, should not hesitate to complain to the public utility commission's consumer division.

If the issue is not reasonableness, but affordability, some of the sources of assistance listed earlier in this chapter may be available to help pay deposits. Later, when you have established a good payment record, or when you decide to terminate service, request that the utility return the deposit, with interest. This should always happen if you did not fall behind again after the deposit was made.

Instead of a deposit, some utilities accept the signature of a cosigner or guarantor, who agrees to be responsible for payments you fail to make. In some states, the cosigner is responsible for all payments you fail to make. In other states, the cosigner's responsibility is limited to several months' worth of unpaid bills.

Failure to Pay Bills from a Prior Address as Grounds for Denying Service. Utility companies often require customers to pay outstanding bills from a previous address before connecting service at a new address. An unpaid bill is the most common reason for refusing new service. But in many states it is not always legal for a utility to do this. Check with a local legal services or other attorney or the public service commission. If you are given no choice, and you must pay the bill from the previous address in order to obtain new service, you should be able to pay for the old service under an installment agreement.

Even in those states where the utility is permitted to require customers to pay for their outstanding bills from other addresses, it is generally prohibited for a utility to insist upon one customer's payment of another customer's bill. For example, you are not obligated to pay the delinquent bills of the prior tenant of your new residence, or bills that your old landlord was obligated to pay. Similarly, you may not have to pay an old bill where the old service was in someone else's name (for example, an old roommate or former spouse). You may be entitled to service in your name, even if one of your current roommates has an old delinquent bill.

When you are obligated to pay an old bill before service will be connected, one option is to file for bankruptcy. The old obligation will likely be discharged in the bankruptcy. The utility will have to provide new service as long as you provide a reasonable assurance, such as a deposit, of the ability to make *future* payment. The filing of the bankruptcy will immediately entitle you to service at the new address.

Failure to Provide Information as Grounds for Denying Service. Sometimes companies refuse to hook up service because you have not provided requested forms of identification or proof of residence. The company will use this information for various reasons, including to make sure that you do not owe money for service received at a previous address. This is generally not an unreasonable request unless the company carries it to extremes, such as demanding a birth certificate, or information about all previous residences.

> Where a utility refuses to provide
> service in your name, look for a rental that
> includes utility service in the rent.

Avoiding Utility Company Restrictions on New Service. When you cannot pay a prior bill with the utility or afford the security deposit, there are still ways to obtain utility service. Look for a house or apartment that includes utilities in the rent. Another option is to establish utility service in the name of someone else with a good payment history. However, since that individual becomes responsible for any unpaid bills, this approach must be considered carefully, with full disclosure of the risks to the individual assuming responsibility for the bills.

Special Telephone Link Up Program. In most states, households in financial distress can obtain steep discounts on new telephone service installation charges under the link-up program run by the local phone company. You may also be eligible for a significant discount on telephone monthly charges under the "Lifeline" program. Contact the public utility commission or telephone company for details.

15

Automobile Repossessions

- *When Your Car Can Be Repossessed and How Repossession Works*
- *Strategies to Prevent Repossession*
- *What to Do If a Repossession Has Just Occurred*
- *Creditor's Collection of the Balance Due After the Repossession*

WHEN TO WORRY ABOUT THE REPO MAN

When you buy a car on credit, you are almost always required to put up the car as collateral on the loan. Some consumers also put up their car as collateral on a loan unrelated to the purchase of the car. When you lease a car or when you put up a car as collateral on a loan, and then get behind on your payments, you risk the immediate loss of your car. The car may simply disappear some night because a repossessor can legally break into the car and drive it away.

The car may be seized only by a leasing company or by a lender that has specifically taken the car as collateral. The car cannot be immediately seized by some other creditor if you are behind on payments, if the car is not collateral for that debt.

For example, if you do not pay a credit card bill, the credit card company cannot repossess the car. All the credit card company can do is sue you, obtain a court judgment, and ask the sheriff to seize the car, if the car is not otherwise exempt under state law. This rarely happens in practice, and, if it does, it might occur a year of more after default. The situation is very different for car loans and car leases. Miss one or two payments and the car may be gone.

For anyone recently laid-off from work, car repossession is disastrous because the loss of transportation makes it much harder to look for and get a new job. But that is only the beginning of your problems after a car repossession. The creditor will sell the car for much less than it is worth, and your equity in the car will be wiped out. On top of all that, you may find yourself being sued for thousands of dollars that the creditor claims is the difference between the amount owed on your loan and the price for which the car was sold.

This chapter provides advice on how to avoid repossession and what to do if a car is repossessed — how to get the car back or avoid the worst consequences after repossession. While repossession law varies somewhat from state to state, this advice is generally applicable nationwide. Most of the advice here is also applicable to motorcycles and trucks, including trucks that you use for business purposes.

HOW TO TELL IF A CAR CAN BE REPOSSESSED

A car can be repossessed only if you have put up the car as collateral on a loan or if you have leased the car. Usually this is easy to check. Look at the loan documents used to purchase the car. Examine the front page of the loan or the separate one-page disclosure statement and see if the car is listed under "security." Sometimes this loan will in fact state that it is a lease, in which case the car is also subject to repossession.

Next, examine the car's certificate of title. Creditors that have rights to the car will usually indicate this right on the title. If the title is not in your name, but in the name of a company, you are probably leasing the car.

It is possible, but not likely, that a creditor will take a car as collateral and not indicate this on the certificate of title. The only way to discover this is to look at all the loans you have taken out and examine the "security" provisions to see if the car is listed.

HOW SELF-HELP REPOSSESSION WORKS

Self-help repossession is a very real and dangerous threat whenever you fall behind on even one car payment. Creditors in most states have the right to seize the car even when you are only a few weeks late in making payments, and in some cases even if the creditor just thinks you will not make payments when due.

The creditor need not obtain court permission to repossess the car. The creditor can have one of its own employees or a hired "repo man" seize the car. In most states, the creditor does not even have to notify you that a repossession is about to take place. As long as the seizure does not "breach the peace," it is perfectly legal.

There are important exceptions to a creditor's right to seize a car on its own (these exceptions prevent a creditor from seizing a car you own, but may not prevent a lessor from repossessing a leased car):

- The creditor must have taken the car as collateral.
- In some states, the creditor must first give you notice of the right to catch up on delinquent payments. See "Right to Cure" below.
- Self-help repossession is generally illegal in Louisiana and Wisconsin and on certain Indian reservations. Self-help repossession is allowed in Maryland only if the credit agreement allows it.
- A creditor cannot repossess a car owned by military personnel or their dependents if the debt was incurred *before* the individual entered the military.

STRATEGIES TO PREVENT YOUR CAR FROM BEING REPOSSESSED

Keeping Current on Car Payments. Do not pay credit card debts, doctor bills or other low priority debts ahead of car payments. You will not lose any property if you skip payments on low priority debts for several months. Skip one or two car payments, and you risk losing the car. (Keep your car's damage insurance payments current as well, or the creditor will buy insurance for you that is *much* more expensive than your own for *much* less protection for you.)

Curing a Default. In Colorado, the District of Columbia, Iowa, Kansas, Maine, Massachusetts, Missouri, Nebraska, New Hampshire, South Carolina, Virgin Islands, West Virginia, and Wisconsin, creditors (but generally not leasing companies) must give consumers a second chance to make up late payments before repossession. This is called a right to cure. The creditor sends you a notice of how many months payments are past due; you can prevent repossession by paying just these back payments and some late charges. (Rights to cure auto *leases* are available in Iowa, Kansas, Maine, New York, New Jersey and Wisconsin.)

In other states making all back payments may *not* prevent a repossession. Creditors generally insert into their agreements the right to call the whole loan due if you miss a payment. This is called "accelerating" a loan — the entire amount borrowed must be repaid immediately. When the creditor accelerates a loan, then you are only secure from repossession if you pay off the whole loan — which may be thousands of dollars.

In these states, paying just the delinquent payments at that point will not stop a repossession unless the creditor agrees to accept the back due payments and reinstate the loan.

That agreement should be in writing and specify that the lender will not repossess the car unless you fail to make future payments. Otherwise, the creditor may pocket the back-due payments and still repossess the car.

Negotiate a Work-Out. Many creditors are willing to negotiate a work-out arrangement, where your monthly payments are lowered, and where the lender agrees not to seize the car. Particularly where the loan amount is higher than the car's worth, a work-out may ultimately be less expensive for the lender. The work-out can be a good deal for you as well if you want to keep the car.

Carefully evaluate any work-out proposal before making it to a creditor. The importance to you of keeping your car should be balanced against the cost of doing so. Consider how much you have already paid, the risk of a deficiency if the car is repossessed (see below), and the importance of retaining the car. For example, a well-running car worth $3,500, with only $1300 still owed on the car loan, is worth trying to save. The same may not be true of a $17,000 car with $18,000 still owed and where car and insurance payments are beyond what you can hope to afford.

Work-out arrangements should also take into consideration whether you have any claims or defenses relating to the car loan or to the car purchase. Was the car a lemon? Were promised repairs made? Did the seller misrepresent features of the car or the financing arrangement? Were illegal debt collection contacts pursued? See Chapter Eight for more information on raising your car complaints as a defense to loan repayment.

An attorney may be able to raise these claims and defenses more effectively than you acting alone, and thus should be able to negotiate a more favorable work out agreement. Nevertheless, your clear and factual documentation of illegal conduct by the dealer, creditor, or collector should assist your work-out negotiations, even if you are not represented by an attorney.

Sell the Car. It may be that you simply cannot afford car and insurance payments and maintenance costs necessary to keep a car, or you cannot afford a car as expensive as the car you own. One option is to sell the car yourself, rather than wait for the lender to repossess the car and sell it at a repossession sale at a fraction of its real worth. When you sell the car yourself, you will get a *much* higher price. Just as important, you avoid repossession, storage, selling, and other expenses which the creditor would otherwise eventually charge. You also get a rebate on car insurance when the coverage is canceled early.

Before trying to sell your car, make certain that you own it rather than lease it. Since you do not own a leased car, you cannot sell it. If you do own the car, you must still obtain the creditor's permission to sell it. If you do not, you might even get into trouble for an illegal transfer of the creditor's collateral. In any event, the new purchaser will not have good title because the creditor's lien on the car will still be valid.

Consequently, it is essential that you coordinate the car's sale with the creditor. The creditor is unlikely to allow a new purchaser to assume the car loan. As a result, you will have to pay off the car loan in full to give the new purchaser clear title. You will have to get a pay-off figure from the creditor and work out with the creditor the mechanics of canceling the lien when the debt is paid.

If you cannot sell the car for as much as is owed on the loan, the lender is unlikely to cancel the lien. It will hold out for payment in full. Point out to the creditor that this is not in its own self-interest, that it will not net as much if the lender repossesses the car and sells the car itself. The creditor's self-interest is to release its lien on the car in return for the purchase price you have arranged.

If a creditor proves obstinate, make sure you have a written record of the amount offered for the car. If the creditor eventually seizes the car, the creditor may have difficulty justifying a sale price significantly lower than the bid you received.

Avoid anyone who offers to broker a sale or lease. In many states car brokerage is illegal. A widespread scam is for con artists to take money from both you and the new "purchaser," but not complete the paperwork for a real transfer in ownership. Instead, you will still owe the creditor or lessor the full amount. These brokers do not get the lessor's permission or release a creditor's lien on the car. The broker may not even forward monthly payments to the lessor or creditor.

Turn the Car in to the Creditor, But Make Sure You Get a Fair Deal. This strategy is similar to selling the car, only you let the lender sell the car. Although generally not a good idea (because the lender will do such a bad job selling the car), the strategy is acceptable if you get a *written agreement* from the lender that you do not owe anything else on the loan.

Make sure the agreement is in writing because one of the lender's employees may agree orally to certain terms while another employee may disregard the terms entirely. You can also try to negotiate an agreement that the lender will not report the default to a credit reporting agency.

Your agreement to turn the car in voluntarily is attractive to the lender because then it does not need to go to the expense of seizing the car or need to fear a legal battle to justify the repossession. The creditor will particularly not mind giving up the right to collect additional money if you have no other significant assets.

Too often consumers surrender the collateral voluntarily without trying to negotiate fair terms. Passive, voluntary surrender of collateral requires less effort, sometimes creates good will with the creditor, and generates fewer expenses (for towing, attorney's fees, and the like) than self-help repossession. However, voluntary surrender has serious disadvantages.

Voluntary surrender will not automatically prevent the creditor from seeking a deficiency claim (the amount of the debt less the re-sale price of the car). The creditor will normally sell the car for a low price and then come after you for the difference. In addition, a surrender can unwittingly waive some of your claims or defenses, such as a claim that the creditor did not have a valid security interest, you were not in default, or that the creditor had no right to accelerate the debt.

The situation is similar when you turn in a leased car. It is a common mistake to believe that you will have no further obligation on the loan agreement after you return the car. You will have no further obligation only if you turn the car in at *scheduled* termination of the lease. Your liability at *early* termination may be thousands of dollars, or even as high as $10,000 in some cases. Before turning in a leased car, negotiate with the lessor to reduce or eliminate your early termination liability.

Resisting the Repossession. You can try to frustrate the creditor's efforts to seize your car, although this approach has risks and may be only a temporary solution. The major leverage you have is that the repossessor in seizing the car cannot "breach the peace." You can make it difficult for repossessors to seize your car without breaching the peace.

Breach of the peace is a technical term, and the laws set out strict rules as to when repossessor conduct breaches the peace:

- The repossessor cannot use bodily force or threats. Physical contact is prohibited.
- The repossessor can seize the car from the street or even a driveway, but cannot break open a locked garage door to get at a car.
- The repossessor cannot take the car over your oral objections.
- The repossessor cannot be accompanied by a government official, such as the police, unless the official has a court order.
- Courts are divided over whether a repossessor can use trickery to seize the car, such as agreeing to make free repairs as a pretext for seizing the car.

In practice, this means that the repossessor cannot take a car if you or your family is present at the repossession and objects to the seizure just *before* the seizure takes place. Your objection should *not* involve force. You do not even have to scream. Just politely and firmly tell the repossessor not to take the car. Obviously, you should decline to turn over the keys when requested to do so. Do not be swayed by any legal advice offered by the repossessor or by any "legal documents" the repossessor may waive in front of you. You have an absolute right to object to the repossession, and you do not have to assent to the seizure.

Never resort to force. Never meet force with force. Never use force to object. Never use force to impede a government official. If the repossessor uses force or threats, or otherwise breaches the peace, call the police. Do not take matters into your own hands. After the fact, consult an attorney. There are significant legal remedies available to challenge an illegal repossession.

To avoid consumers objecting to the seizure, repossessors tend to take cars away in the middle of the night. This is perfectly legal, even if the car is parked in your driveway or in a company parking lot. On the other hand, repossessors cannot break open a garage door lock and force themselves into your garage.

You can stop a repossession by politely objecting — as long as you are there when the car is seized — or by storing the car in a locked garage.

Never resist government officials in the performance of their duties. But it is appropriate to verify the identity of any alleged government official appearing at a repossession and the basis for the official's presence. Government officials should only operate pursuant to written court orders and should not assist self-help repossessions.

Remember that people in uniforms are not necessarily government officials. If the "official" does not provide proper identity, politely object to the seizure — but do so orally, not physically.

Obviously, repossessors cannot seize a car they cannot find. They will have your address and place of employment, but will not know the address of every friend and relative. However, you should know that some state statutes makes it a criminal offense to conceal collateral or to move it out of state.

If you do not want your car repossessed, you should never turn it over for repairs to the dealer or anyone else the creditor would know. Do not drive the car to the creditor's place of business to discuss a work-out agreement. You may have to walk home after failing to come to a satisfactory arrangement.

Minimize the Loss of Personal Property Inside the Car. If repossession is imminent, leave as little personal property as possible in the car. Property left in a car has a way of disappearing after the car is seized. For example, tools, tapes and tape deck, clothes, and sporting equipment should be removed. Some items like child seats or even spare tires can be removed when the car is not being used, and returned when you use the car.

Before the repossession, ask friends to verify the items left in the car and their condition. You should also make a written inventory or take pictures of the car's interior. The creditor has no right to keep your personal property if you can prove what was in the car at the time of repossession. You can ask the creditor to pay for items not returned, and, if the items are valuable enough to justify the costs, you can file a lawsuit.

File for Bankruptcy Protection. It may not make sense to file for bankruptcy solely to stop a car repossession, but you may have other reasons to file for bankruptcy. In that case, you should know how bankruptcy can deal with the threatened repossession.

Filing several simple forms with a bankruptcy court (with the rest of the forms to be filed later) initiates the bankruptcy case and automatically triggers what is known as "the automatic stay." Under the automatic stay, no one, including car repossessors, can take any action against your property. Although a lender can later ask the bankruptcy court for permission to take the car, any attempt to repossess before such court permission is illegal. The repossessor could be held in contempt of court and may have to pay you both actual and punitive damages as well as your attorney fees. In practice, most creditors are careful not to seize cars after you file bankruptcy, particularly after you let them know about the bankruptcy filing. If your car has already been repossessed but not yet resold, bankruptcy can help you get it back. This is discussed in more detail below.

Once the automatic stay freezes everything, you can take several steps to try to permanently prevent the loss of your car (discussed below). See also Chapter Eighteen for a more detailed discussion of your bankruptcy rights.

WHAT TO DO AFTER THE CAR IS REPOSSESSED

Get Back Personal Property Left in the Car. Creditors cannot keep property left in your car when it is repossessed. The lender can only keep the car itself. As soon as possible, demand any property left in the car-- tapes, clothes, car seats, sporting goods, etc.

A lender's failure to return the property promptly is illegal. (A grey area is whether certain improvements to a car have become so much a part of the car that you do not have a right to their return, such as a tape deck or radio semi-permanently installed.)

Put the request in writing and specify everything left in the car and do so *quickly.* The longer the delay in doing so, the more likely your property will be "missing." Moreover, some credit contracts require (probably illegally) that you request return of your property within a certain number of days.

You Can Reinstate the Contract in California, Connecticut, the District of Columbia, Illinois, Maryland, Mississippi, New York, Ohio, Pennsylvania, and Wisconsin. Reinstating the contract allows you to recover the repossessed car and pay only the back due payments, not the full amount of the note. (In Illinois, you can reinstate only if you have paid at least 30% of the loan. Reinstatement applies to car leases only in Maryland.) You must act quickly. In most of these states, you only have a few weeks to reinstate after repossession.

You Can Redeem the Car. In every state, after a repossession, you can redeem the car (assuming you owned the car and did not lease it). The creditor must send you written notice of the date of the car's sale or a date after which the car will be sold. You can redeem the car up until the very moment before the car is sold.

To redeem the car, you must pay off the whole note in one lump sum, plus reasonable repossession and storage charges. Be sure to get a breakdown from the lender of how much you owe. The breakdown should include a refund for unearned interest and insurance charges that are not owed because the note has been paid off early.

Redeeming the car will rarely be a practical solution. Most owners of repossessed cars could not afford the monthly payments, never mind paying off the whole note in one lump sum. But, where the car is important to you and worth more than the loan, consider whether you can borrow from another source, including friends or relatives. It is rarely a good idea to mortgage the house to get the car back because defaulting on that loan may result in your losing your home.

Try to Negotiate With the Creditor. If a repossession has just occurred, it is often possible to negotiate for the return of collateral and for a reinstatement of the original payment schedule or even for a new schedule. The same considerations apply as when negotiating a work-out arrangement prior to repossession.

You are in a particularly strong position if you have significant claims or defenses relating to the car, its credit terms, or its repossession. If a car has minimal resale value, the creditor should also prefer a work-out agreement to a worthless asset.

If you do not want the car back, it is still worthwhile trying to get the creditor to permit you to sell the property privately. In the alternative, learn whether the creditor intends to sell the car at wholesale or retail, and encourage retail sale, which can produce a price at least 40 percent higher than wholesale.

Get the Car Back by Filing Bankruptcy. Even after a car is "lost" through repossession, you can get it back by filing bankruptcy. If the loss of the car is your only problem, a bankruptcy filing may not be justified. But if you have other financial problems, a bankruptcy may be justified and you should know how bankruptcy can help to get your car back.

You will have to file for bankruptcy before the lender resells the car. Then you may be able to obtain a court order directing the creditor to "turn over" or return repossessed property. In some cases, the car is not returned to you directly, but is instead given to the bankruptcy trustee to decide who should keep the car — you or the creditor. There are several reasons why the court could decide to give the car back to you instead of the creditor.

If you file a straight bankruptcy (known as a chapter 7 bankruptcy), you can keep the car by "redeeming" it. Redeeming a car in bankruptcy is different than redeeming a car outside of bankruptcy. Outside of bankruptcy, you would have to pay the full balance of the loan plus all the lender's costs. In bankruptcy, you merely pay the car's value.

Although this value often is less than the amount of the loan, most consumers will not be able to come up with the cash. Some creditors will let you redeem in installments. Additionally, since other debts are wiped out by the bankruptcy filing, you can redirect your financial resources and apply them to redeem the car. Of course, you may have more pressing needs for your cash, such as to pay rent or utilities.

Another way to keep a car is to file a chapter 13 bankruptcy, sometimes known as a "reorganization." In a chapter 13, you have several ways of keeping the car. Probably the best one is to set up a plan to pay off the car loan in monthly installments over a period as long as 5 years.

The interest rate charged in this plan can in some instances be far lower than what you are paying on the car loan. You may even reduce the amount owed to only the value of the car. The bottom line is you get to keep the car and significantly lower the car payments. See Chapter Eighteen for a more detailed discussion of your bankruptcy rights.

Where the Repossession Was Wrongful. Sometimes cars are seized even though the creditor has no right to seize the car or no right to take the car at that time. Other times, the repossession company will not follow proper procedure in seizing the car.

In each of these situations, you have a right to get the car back and to be paid money damages. As a practical matter, enforcement of your rights will usually require a lawyer or someone who understands repossession law. The next section provides an overview of this law in items one through four. (Items five and six deal with situations where the creditor or lessor has already sold the car.)

CREDITORS' COLLECTION EFFORTS AFTER THE REPOSSESSION SALE

After repossession, the creditor will sell your car and apply the sale price (after deducting all repossession and sale expenses) against the amount you owe. Creditors then sometimes come after you for any remaining amount due on the debt. This is called a deficiency action. (When a lessor repossesses a leased vehicle, the result is the same. The car is sold and the lessor seeks a further amount under the lease, called an early termination charge.)

Many consumers feel especially victimized in that they lose their car and the creditor still comes after them for more money. You should realize two things about the creditor's claim for a deficiency. First, the obligation is no longer backed up by any collateral, but is just an unsecured debt. The creditor can take no immediate steps if you do not pay. The deficiency debt is just like a hospital bill or a credit card debt. You should not pay this unsecured debt ahead of more pressing obligations, such as rent or utility bills. (For more on collection of "unsecured debts," see Chapter Five.)

Second, many defenses are available to you where a creditor attempts to collect this deficiency amount. Because the repossession and subsequent sale of the car occurred without court supervision, the creditor was required to comply with many technical requirements.

If the creditor trips up on even one technical requirement, the deficiency action may be thrown out or the creditor may even end up owing *you* money! Because creditors frequently trip up on these requirements, it is always a good idea to get legal advice before agreeing to pay any deficiency. This section provides an overview of six types of defenses you may have when the creditor seeks a deficiency.

A creditor tripping up on even one small repossession requirement is enough to wipe out your balance due and may even get you cash from the creditor.

---

1. Claims Concerning the Car or the Credit Terms. In many cases you can fight a deficiency claim by showing the car was a lemon, the dealer misrepresented the quality of a used car, the credit terms were illegal or not disclosed accurately, or the creditor engaged in debt collection harassment. These type of defenses are summarized in Chapter Seven.

The mere threat that you will raise these claims is helpful in negotiating a work-out agreement. Depending upon the value of your claim, a work-out can even lead to a "wash-out," so called because both parties agree to call the debt even, or a "wash," and release each other from liability for further payments.

2. Is the Car Collateral on the Loan? Sometimes the creditor trips up on a technical requirement to make the car collateral for a loan. If the creditor has not taken the car as collateral, it cannot repossess the car, even if you defaulted on a loan used to purchase the car.

Your agreement to put up the car as collateral must be in writing and signed by you. The agreement must also correctly identify your car, and the car's title must be in your own name. Otherwise, the lender has no right to seize the car.

For example, if a wife alone signs a loan and security agreement, but puts the car in the husband's name, the creditor may not have a valid security interest in the car. A repossession may also be illegal if the lender explicitly took the car as collateral only on an earlier loan, but not on the loan at issue. For more analysis as to whether a creditor has properly taken a car as collateral, see NCLC's *Repossessions and Foreclosures* Ch. 3 (3d ed. 1995).

3. Were You in "Default" When the Car Was Seized? Creditors can repossess your car only if you are in default on the car loan. Being late on payments does not necessarily place you "in default."

For example, if a creditor routinely accepts your late payments, the creditor cannot surprise you and seize the car just because a payment is late. You sometimes can also avoid a default by giving the lender notice that you are withholding payments because the car is a lemon.

Moreover, if state law gives you the right to cure the default, the creditor cannot repossess the car before the right to cure has expired. More detail on when a consumer is actually in default can be found in NCLC's *Repossessions and Foreclosures* Ch. 4 (3d ed. 1995).

4. Did the Car's Repossession Breach the Peace? Whether a seizure breaches the peace has already been discussed earlier in this chapter at "Resisting Repossession." See also "How Self-Help Repossession Works," above, for situations where self-help repossession is not permitted at all. When a seizure is wrongful, the creditor generally should not keep the car or collect a deficiency. The creditor may owe you money instead.

5. Improper Repossession Sale or Miscalculation of the Deficiency. Creditors must either keep the cars they repossess or sell them. If it keeps a car, which is rare, the creditor cannot seek any more money from you. A creditor can keep the car only if you have paid less than 60% of the debt, and the creditor has given you notice that it intends to keep the car. You can then object and ask that the car be sold instead.

After repossessing a car, creditors usually sell it. The law is very strict on the exact procedure the creditor must utilize in selling a repossessed car. You can defeat the creditor's attempt at a deficiency simply by showing that the creditor did not take the correct steps in selling the car. Tripping up on one technical requirement is usually enough to stop a deficiency. While these technical requirements are very briefly summarized below, see NCLC's *Repossessions and Foreclosures* Ch. 10 (3d ed. 1995) for more details.

If received in court, the creditors failure to meet these sale requirements may prevent collection of a deficiency:

- After a repossession or if you turned the car in voluntarily, you must be sent advance notice of the creditor's intention to sell the repossessed car. The notice must include the time and place of a public auction or the date after which the car will be sold privately. The creditor must make reasonable efforts to assure that you receive a fair warning of the sale date. This notice is very important, and many consumers have prevented a deficiency merely by showing errors in the notice of sale.
- The sale cannot be too rushed and it cannot be overly delayed. On the one hand, there must be time for you to receive the notice of sale and for others to read advertising about the sale. On the other hand, the creditor cannot wait too long to sell the car, or the car's value will depreciate.
- *Every* aspect of the sale, including the manner, the time, the place, and the terms must make business sense, and must be "commercially reasonable." Particularly if the sale price was unreasonably low, look at every aspect of the sale, including the decisions whether to sell at retail or wholesale, and whether to use an auction or to sell the car off a lot. Advertising for the sale must be sufficient, an auction must use competitive bidding, and the car should be available for advance inspection. At a private sale, usually neither the creditor nor the original dealer can purchase the car. This helps prevent hidden agreements to dispose of the car at a below market price.
- Check to see if the creditor correctly calculated the amount of its claimed deficiency. Were you given proper credit for all payments? Were the late charges correctly calculated and unearned finance charges and insurance premiums properly rebated? Were you credited with the car's actual sale price and not the car's "estimated" cash value? Were the creditor's expenses (repossession, reconditioning, sale, attorney's fees) reasonable and accurate?

6. Auto leases. Special laws and rules apply where you leased the repossessed car instead of buying the car on credit. The lease will specify the formula used to calculate how much you owe upon default or early termination. The formula is usually quite complex and difficult to understand, and may be unreasonable or not properly applied by the lessor.

Federal and state law provide you with powerful remedies when lessors apply unreasonable formulas or do not clearly disclose the formulas they use.

Aggressive attorneys can usually force lessors to settle for a "wash." That is, although it is not uncommon for a lessor to demand $5,000 to $10,000 at early termination of a car lease, proper legal advocacy may get car leasing companies to drop the whole claim. For more detail on challenging auto lease early termination penalties, see NCLC's *Truth in Lending* Ch. 9 (3d ed. 1995).

YOUR RIGHTS WHEN THE CREDITOR TRIPS UP

If the creditor trips up in its efforts to repossess and sell the car, the penalties are severe. In many states, any mistake will lead to the creditor being barred from seeking any deficiency. In other states, the creditor will have a difficult time proving how much it is owed because the sale price of the car is not considered by the court. The creditor will have a difficult time showing how much a car is worth since it is no longer in its possession.

Moreover, if the creditor trips up on one of the requirements, it may have to pay you as a penalty 10% of the car's original purchase price plus the whole finance charge on the car loan. This penalty can run into many thousands of dollars.

If repossessor conduct is seriously improper, you may also be able to recover punitive damages running into many thousands of dollars. Sometimes, the creditor will even have to pay your attorney fees. Usually to recover any of these penalties, legal representation is essential.

FOR MORE INFORMATION

To learn more about consumer repossession rights, the best legal practice manual is the National Consumer Law Center's *Repossessions and Foreclosures* (3d ed. 1995), which is the source of much of the information in this chapter. The manual covers all the federal and state laws governing consumer repossessions. *Repossessions and Foreclosures* includes step-by-step checklists for different types of repossession situations, and samples of different documents a lawyer will have to prepare in a repossession case. The manual covers both car loans and leases.

16

Threats to Seize Household Goods

• *Limited Situations Where Creditor Can Seize Your Household Goods*
• *Eight Strategies to Stop Household Goods Seizures*

UNDERSTANDING CREDITOR THREATS TO SEIZE HOUSEHOLD GOODS

One of the most frightening creditor practices is the threat to seize your household goods, such as your photo album, wedding rings, bedroom furniture and the like. These threats can be effective because of these items' special personal significance, even if they have minimal resale value.

In most cases, you should not take such threats seriously. The goods' limited economic value means the creditor has no financial incentive to follow through with the threat. Additionally, federal and state laws limit which household goods a creditor can take, and how it can seize those goods.

This chapter explains the limited situations in which a creditor can legally seize your household goods, how it must conduct the seizure, and what steps you can take to prevent such seizures. There are only four limited situations where a creditor can try to seize your household goods:

1. When you take out a loan specifically to purchase certain household goods, and agree to have those goods serve as collateral for the loan, the creditor has a "purchase money security interest" in those household goods. If you default on that loan, the creditor can seize those goods if it wants to go to the expense of a court

procedure or if you make the mistake of letting repossessors into your home.

2. When a loan is *not* used to purchase household goods, but the creditor insists that you put up household goods as collateral for the loan, the creditor has a "non-purchase money security interest." Federal law gives you special protections from the seizure of such goods.

3. When you do not put household goods up as collateral for a loan, creditors can ask a sheriff or other official to seize these goods only *after* obtaining a court judgment on the debt. The creditor uses that judgment to try to "execute" on the household goods. Even then, state law generally protects most of your household goods from such executions.

Unless the good is listed as collateral for the debt or rented, creditors can only seize goods *after* they have sued you and *after* they obtain a final court judgment. Even then, state exemption law usually protects those goods from seizure.

---

4. When you rent goods with the option to purchase them after all payments are made, this is called a "rent-to-own" or RTO transaction. Although the RTO merchant has the right to take the goods back if you get behind on payments, the merchant does not have the right to enter your home without your permission to take the goods.

These are the *only* four situations where creditors have *any* legal right to follow through on their threat to seize household goods. Outside these four situations, the creditor has *no* right to seize the goods.

Unless the good is listed as collateral for the debt or rented, creditors can only seize goods after they have sued you and after they obtain a final court judgment. Even then, state exemption law usually protects those goods from seizure.

You can usually determine if one of these four situations apply simply by looking at the loan documents. The credit agreement indicates if household goods are taken as collateral, and if the loan was used to purchase those goods. Sales agreements will also indicate if they are rent-to-own transactions.

EIGHT STRATEGIES TO PROTECT YOUR HOUSEHOLD GOODS

This section lists eight strategies that can help you keep your household goods when a creditor threatens to seize them. For more details, see the National Consumer Law Center's Repossessions and Foreclosures *(3d ed. 1995).*

1. Do Not Panic; Determine If the Threat Is False. The first thing to realize is that the creditor usually is bluffing. The value of most household goods sold at auction, after deducting repossession, storage, and selling expenses, is negligible. The creditor has no economic interest in the goods, and therefore is unlikely to pursue repossession.

The creditor is using the threat of repossession as leverage to force you to pay off that creditor's debt first, even though it is in your overall best interest to pay off other debts instead. Sometimes creditors also make these threats to build up their reputation as being tough on defaulters.

Several factors help tip you off that a threat to seize your goods is false. A threat to seize household goods is false if the debt does not fall within any of the four categories of allowable seizures listed at the beginning of this chapter.

Even if one of these four situations apply, the threat is still usually false. This is particularly the case where the creditor is threatening to execute on household goods under a court judgment, since state laws usually protect most common household goods from execution.

Beyond that, evaluating a threat will often depend on the value of the collateral, the difficulty of seizing it, and the nature and reputation of the creditor. For example, a consumer electronics store is more likely to seize $2000 worth of its own stereo and video equipment it sold you a few months ago than a loan company is to seize the family photo album or the 15 year old kitchen refrigerator.

If the threat is false, obviously you should not worry about it. Moreover, false threats are illegal, and you may be able to recover as much as $1000 plus your attorney fees even if you are not injured. See Chapter Five.

As outlined below, even if the threat is not false, you have a series of strategies to protect the goods or make it very expensive for the creditor to seize them. In protecting your household goods, you have the upper hand in dealing with the creditor; do not be frightened into doing something stupid.

2. Can the Creditor Take the Household Goods as Collateral?

Federal law prohibits creditors from taking "non-purchase money security interests" in most household goods. This rule is particularly important in dealing with finance companies, but usually not helpful in dealing with furniture or appliance dealers that are seeking to seize the goods you purchased from them.

A creditor *can* take household goods as collateral if you use the loan *to purchase those particular goods*, although it may not choose to do so. The only way to tell is to check your credit agreement to see if it is taking a security interest in the goods purchased.

Under federal law, a creditor *cannot* take the following household goods as collateral for a loan which is *not* used to purchase the goods: clothing, furniture, appliances, one radio, one television, linens, china, crockery, kitchenware, and other personal effects such as wedding rings and photographs. The federal law probably allows the following types of loan collateral, even if the loan is not used to purchase these items: art, lawn equipment, tools, audio systems, a second television or radio, cameras, boats, sporting goods, typewriters, firearms, bicycles, musical instruments or jewelry (other than wedding rings).

No creditor can take a security interest in all of a consumer's household goods or all items located at a particular residence, because this will include many types of prohibited collateral. In addition, creditors cannot take as collateral goods which you do not yet own at the time of the loan, but will own in the future. As a consequence, a creditor, for example, cannot take a security interest in all tools or audio systems you will ever own. Creditors are limited to identified items you own at the time of the loan.

Sears, Montgomery Ward, and other merchants sometimes try to take a security interest in all goods you purchase in their store with their credit card. (This applies to the Sears card, but not to the Discover card that is also offered by Sears.) They may or may not be successful in taking purchased items as collateral, depending on how they comply with various technical requirements as to signatures and the like. You will have to ask an attorney whether the security interest is valid.

3. Do Not Consent to the Creditor Coming Into Your Home. This strategy pertains *only* if the person coming to your home works for the creditor. See the next item if a sheriff or other government official comes to your home. If people who work for the creditor are doing the seizure, you can easily stop them simply by refusing to allow them into your home.

Politely but firmly refuse to consent to the creditor entering your dwelling. Repeat the objections each time a repossession threat or effort is made, and instruct landlords, spouses, children, and/or roommates not to consent to repossessors entering your residence. People hired by the creditor are not permitted to force their way into your home or even to enter when you are not there.

You can stop a creditor's self-help
repossession simply by refusing to
allow the repossessor to enter your
home. The creditor has no right
to enter unless invited by you.

Do not physically resist the entry, just politely and firmly object to the entry. Repossessors can only legally enter your house if they are invited inside. Walking uninvited through an open door makes the repossession illegal. If repossessors still force themselves in, the first concern should be for the safety of individuals in the house. After the repossession, contact the police and an attorney, because the repossessor's action was an illegal breach of the peace. Witnesses, of course, are helpful.

4. *Do* Cooperate with the Sheriff. In rare cases, it will not be the creditor who is seizing the goods, but a government official, the sheriff or constable. This situation is unusual because the creditor would have had first to obtain a court order to arrange for the sheriff to come. Obtaining a court order is likely to cost more than the goods are worth. If it is the sheriff (and not the creditor claiming to be the sheriff), ask for identification and then comply with any order the sheriff makes.

5. Claim that the Household Goods Are Exempt. When a sheriff is seizing the goods, it is important to determine which creditor has asked for the seizure, a creditor who has taken the property to be seized as collateral or some other creditor. Furniture and appliance stores are the most likely creditors to obtain a court order sending a sheriff to seize collateral.

If the creditor had *not* previously taken the goods as collateral, but is merely attempting to seize them after obtaining a court judgment, you have important rights under state law. States almost uniformly protect certain household goods from seizure to satisfy a court judgment.

The state laws offering this protection are usually called exemption statutes. They may provide blanket protection for all household goods, for household goods under a certain dollar figure, or for certain types of household goods. It is important to know the exemption law for your state. Ask a legal services office or other attorney, or a credit counseling agency. Often the information is available in pamphlet form.

In addition, property in your residence owned by someone else should not be seized to satisfy a judgment against you. This may even apply to property owned by other family members.

If property is exempt or owned by someone else, this should be pointed out to the sheriff, or, even better, to the court before the sheriff comes. Usually, there is a form which will be sent to you before the seizure. It should be returned as soon as possible, and definitely *before* the scheduled date for the seizure.

If the sheriff still takes the goods, *quickly* go to court after the sheriff takes the goods to explain that the household goods are exempt under state law or belong to someone else. The court clerk's office or sheriff's office may have a form to fill out to help you with your claim.

6. Challenge the Replevin Procedure. Some sheriff seizures are not to enforce a judgment on a debt, but a creditor's right to recover its collateral. If you gave a creditor a security interest in certain goods, the creditor can go to court (sometimes without even telling you) and claim that you are behind on your payments and that the sheriff should seize the collateral. (Depending on what state you are in, this proceeding may be called "replevin," "sequestration," "detinue," "claim and delivery," or "bail." State law generally does *not* exempt any of your property from seizure by a creditor if you have given it as collateral to that creditor.)

Sometimes you will be given notice and the opportunity to contest this seizure before it happens, and sometimes you can only do so after it happens. (If your hearing is not until after the seizure, the creditor will not obtain permanent custody of the property until *after* your hearing.) In either case, just as in other types of lawsuits, the creditor is not expecting you to contest the matter or to be represented by an attorney. Raising a serious defense may be enough for the creditor to drop the suit, allowing you to retain or recover your property.

7. RTO Repossessions. Rent-to-own (RTO) contracts give you ownership of rented goods after you make all the payments. If you stop making payments, the RTO company has the right to take the rented property back. But most states prohibit the RTO company from repossessing over your objection or entering your home without permission. This result is not changed even if you gave permission in the small print of the sales agreement to the repossession or entry into your home. Be careful of the "switch out" technique whereby the RTO company claims it is taking a item in for repair, maintenance, or upgrading, when it is actually repossessing it.

RTO companies may also threaten criminal action under a state's lease larceny statute if you do not return rented goods. But these statutes may not apply to RTO sales, failure to let RTO personnel into your home is not enough to trigger criminal conduct on your part, and the RTO company usually has no intent to pursue a criminal action.

Nevertheless, unless you have made a lot of payments on a rent-to-own contract, it is usually a good idea just to return the goods and stop paying. There will be no liability except for back due payments. And, typically, the rent is fantastically overpriced and you will have paid for the goods many times over before you own them.

8. File for Bankruptcy. The cost and other complications of filing bankruptcy may not make sense just to protect certain household goods. But a bankruptcy filing also offers you benefits in adjusting your other debts, and bankruptcy may make sense for you to deal with all of your debt problems. It is thus important to know how bankruptcy can protect your household goods.

Filing for bankruptcy provides immediate relief by automatically stopping *any* threatened seizure of the household goods. This applies to seizures of collateral and even to rented items.

Bankruptcy can usually protect your household goods in the long run as well, unless you give them as collateral for a loan to purchase these items. If the household goods are exempt under applicable law, then bankruptcy permanently prevents their seizure to satisfy a court judgment.

Moreover, many non-purchase money security interests in household goods can also be canceled in bankruptcy if the goods are exempt under the bankruptcy law. Even if the creditor had a purchase money security interest, that interest may be voided in certain situations if the creditor has since refinanced the original loan used to purchase the goods.

Even if a security interest in certain household goods cannot be cancelled in bankruptcy, you may be able to keep the property after a bankruptcy filing by paying the creditor only what the property is worth. This is called "redemption." Used household goods may be worth far less than the outstanding debt.

In an RTO transaction, if you want to keep the goods after filing bankruptcy, you can pay any delinquent payments over time and keep current on future rent payments. In certain states you can categorize the RTO transaction as a sale, and this will give you additional strategies in bankruptcy, including the possibility of redemption for the goods' real value. For more on bankruptcy, see Chapter Eighteen.

17

Student Loan and Federal Income Tax Collections

• *How to Postpone Your Student Loan Payments When You Are In Financial Trouble*
• *Coping With Collection on Seriously Overdue Student Loans*
• *Your Rights If the School Ripped You Off*
• *What to Do If You Owe the IRS*

STUDENT LOANS

Why You Should Pay Special Attention to Your Student Loans. Your past due student loans require special attention. The government has special powers to collect on these loans not available to most other creditors — including seizure of your tax refunds, denying you new student loans and grants, seizing up to 10% of your wages without a court order, and charging you up to 43% in collection fees.

On the other hand, the government provides a number of excellent options when you cannot afford to pay your student loan. Unfortunately, you cannot sit back and wait for the government to offer these choices to you. *You must know about and request these options on your own.* Requesting one of these options may allow you to skip payments for a while, reduce your payments, stop collection efforts against you, and, in certain cases involving a school closure or school misconduct, even cancel out the loan and receive a refund!

Identify What Kind of Loans You Have and To Whom You Owe Them. There are three major types of student loans, and a number of different lenders to whom you might owe repayment. Your rights and best strategies will vary depending on what type of loan you have and to whom it is owed.

From about 1980 to 1995, the most common type of student loan was a Stafford Loan, also known as a Guaranteed Student Loan (GSL). Stafford Loans come in two types: subsidized (where the government pays part of the interest costs) and unsubsidized. Stafford loans are very confusing, and it often hard to figure out who to talk to about payment problems.

Although the school might have helped you fill out the loan papers, the loan was actually from a bank to you. That bank may have sold the loan to another lender, such as the Student Loan Marketing Association (Sallie Mae). Whoever is holding the loan might hire another company to "service" the loan — receive your payments and correspond with you. If you stopped making payments on that loan, the loan was then turned over to a guaranty agency. For certain older loans, it was eventually passed on to the U.S. Department of Education.

Related to GSLs are Supplemental Loans for Students (SLSs) and PLUS loans taken out by students' parents. Generally, the rules concerning GSL loans also apply to SLS and PLUS loans. GSL, SLS and PLUS loans today are all called Federal Family Education Loans, or FFELs.

Starting in about 1994, certain schools started offering a new type of loan called a Federal Direct Student Loan, often called an FDSL or a Direct Loan. The school arranges for a loan between the United States Department of Education and the student. Payments are made directly to the United States Department of Education.

A third type of loan is a Perkins Loan, formerly called a National Direct Student Loan or NDSL. This loan is made directly from the school you attended, and you repay the amount to the school. If you stop paying the school, the loan is eventually turned over to the U.S. Department of Education.

Try to figure out what type of loan you have because your options are somewhat different for different types of loans. The first place to look is the loan application and promissory note. You can also ask the lender or collector with whom you are dealing.

What to Do If Your Loan Is Not Yet Seriously Delinquent. If you are not yet too far behind in your loan payments, you can often obtain effective relief for several years, but you must apply for this help, and you must do so quickly. The best option is to obtain a loan deferment from the creditor to whom you make your loan payments.

A loan deferment means that you can delay repaying your loan, usually for a year. The deferment may then be renewed for one or two additional years. If the loan is a subsidized loan, the government makes interest payments for you during the deferment period, but eventually you will have to pay the full loan principal.

You have a legal right to a loan deferment under specified conditions: if you have gone back to school, have lost your job, or are experiencing certain other specified financial hardships. The exact grounds for deferment vary with the type of loan involved and when you took out the loan. For example, deferment rules for GSLs vary dramatically depending on whether you took out the loan before or after July 1, 1993. If you are having financial difficulties, ask your lender whether you can qualify for a deferment.

If you get too far behind on your payments, you will no longer qualify for a deferment. So it is essential to apply for a deferment as early as possible, certainly before you are six months delinquent, and preferably much earlier.

You can delay loan repayment if you are
having financial problems, but only if you
take the initiative to ask for assistance.

If you cannot qualify for a deferment, an alternative is to request loan "forbearance." Forbearance means that you do not have to pay for a while, and no adverse action will be taken against you during the forbearance period. (If you want, you can arrange to make small payments during the forbearance period.) But, unlike a deferment on a subsidized Stafford loan, the government does not pay interest for you. You will eventually have to repay the full loan amount and all accrued interest.

Lenders have wide discretion to grant forbearance. In addition, you have a legal right to forbearance if a GSL payment exceeds 20% of your income, even if you are many months delinquent, as long as a guaranty agency has not yet taken over the loan.

Another option is to consolidate, that is exchange, the type of student loans you have with one new loan. You can choose either a Direct Loan with "income contingent repayment" or an FFEL loan with "income sensitive repayment." Such loans have low payments when your income is low and higher payments when your income is higher. Income contingent Direct Loans may even allow you to pay nothing when your income is very low. Loan consolidation is detailed later in this chapter.

The common feature of all of these approaches — deferments, forbearance, or loan consolidation — is that you must apply for them. If you just sit back and wait, your situation can get much worse.

What to Expect If You Have Not Paid Your Student Loan For Several Years. The main method the government uses to collect on defaulted student loans is to seize your federal income tax refunds. This includes any earned income tax credit you are owed. The only safe way to avoid this collection method is not to have a tax refund due by decreasing your withholding or lowering any estimated tax payments you make. Other strategies to deal with tax intercepts are detailed later in this chapter.

If you are seriously behind on your student loan, you also can expect the following:

- you will be denied new federally-backed student loans and grants;
- your default will stay on your credit record for seven years;
- The guaranty agency or the Department of Education may order your employer to pay up to 10% of your wages to them;
- A large portion of anything you pay to a collection agency on the loan will go to collection agency fees and not to pay off your loan.

On the other hand, the odds of your being sued are relatively low, so that you need not worry about losing personal property or your home because of a defaulted student loan.

What to Do If You Have Not Paid Your Student Loan For Several Years. If you have not paid on your student loan for a number of years, you will be in default on the loan, and your loan will have been turned over to a guaranty agency or the United States. You will then generally not be eligible for forbearance or deferment. You will be subjected to the various collection tactics described above.

It may be that you do not have sufficient income to be garnished, no tax refunds to intercept, no special concern for your credit rating, and no interest in applying for new student loans and grants. In that case, you may decide to do nothing, and instead use what income you have to pay your rent, mortgage, utility payments or other priority debts.

But if you are concerned with the above described collection tactics, and you cannot afford to pay all your debts, there are a number of good strategies to pursue. One approach is to contact the party collecting on the loan, and state that you want to renew your eligibility for a new loan and want a reasonable and affordable repayment plan. Then you have a legal right to a schedule of low monthly payments, in some cases as low as $5 a month. Generally, it is best to pay at least as much as your monthly accrued interest, if possible. But federal law states that you should not be required to pay more than you can afford.

Make sure you say words similar to "I want a reasonable and affordable payment plan so that I can renew my eligibility for new loans." Collectors often are very difficult if you do not say the magic words — they may even demand that you pay the whole amount you are behind in one payment. If you use the magic words, they are legally required to give you a plan you can afford. If you get on such a plan, it is important that you stay on it and make all payments on time. If you do not, you will not get another chance at such a low payment plan.

If you get on such a plan, you should expect no debt collection harassment, no tax intercepts, and no wage garnishment. If you make six consecutive monthly payments, you will also re-establish your eligibility for new student loans and grants. Your credit rating will still list the loan in default, a portion of what you pay may be going toward collection costs rather than to reduce your debt, interest charges will continue to mount, and you must continue to make monthly payments in order to remain eligible for new student loans and grants.

After twelve monthly payments, you may, but need not, request "loan rehabilitation," which means that the loan holder attempts to sell your defaulted loan to a lender. If your loan is purchased, you are no longer in default, the default is removed from your credit record, and a ten year repayment schedule is established. Usually, the schedule will require you to make larger payments than you were paying under the reasonable and affordable payment plan.

Another alternative is to "consolidate" your loans into either a new Direct Loan with "income contingent repayments" or a new FFEL loan with "income sensitive repayments." You can do this even if you are in default, even if you only have one loan, and even if that loan is very small. The advantage of this option is it requires only that you pay an amount that is related to your income. You are no longer in default. You will not be dunned in any way if you keep the new loan current. You will be eligible for new loans and grants, you will have a credit record showing a past delinquency but no current default, and what you owe for collection fees will be reduced. Perhaps most importantly, you can then apply for a deferment based on your returning to school, unemployment or economic hardship.

After losing her job, Jane Doe
stopped paying on her Stafford Loan,
and faced all kinds of collection efforts.
Her loan amount kept going up with
interest charges and collection fees.
She solved her problem by converting
her loan to a Direct Consolidation Loan.
Because her income was low, her monthly
payments were *zero*! Then she received
an unemployment deferment, so that
no interest charges were added to
her loan for up to three years.

If you are in default on your old loan, you can obtain a Direct Consolidation Loan immediately and a FFEL Consolidation Loan after making three payments that the guaranty agency specifies as reasonable and affordable. The form to request a Direct Consolidation Loan application is reproduced on the right. Make sure you fill in all the requested information, even if it must be an estimate. (Information on existing loans can be obtained from your existing lender.) The government will not process a request for an application if it is incomplete. Since this is only a request for an application, and not the application itself, the more exact information can be supplied later.

If You Feel the School Ripped You Off. If you feel that the school you attended (particularly a for-profit trade or vocational school) ripped you off, you may have certain rights. If you received a school loan after January 1, 1986, you can cancel your loan, get all of your payments back, and clean up your credit record if the school closed while you were still enrolled or within 90 days of your leaving the school. Ask whomever is holding your loan for an application for a closed school discharge.

You can also apply for loan cancellation if you were "falsely certified as eligible," which is defined in the regulations as any one of three types of fraud:

1. At the time of enrollment, you were ineligible under state law to obtain the employment for which you were being trained (for example, the school enrolled you in a truck driving school even though you had a physical handicap that prevents you from obtaining a truck-driving license).
2. If you did not have a high school diploma when you went to the school, the school had the responsibility to make sure you could benefit from the educational program, usually by giving you an exam. You can receive a loan discharge if your exam score was falsified, for example, if a school employee took the test for you.
3. The school forged your name on the loan papers or check endorsements, and you never went to school for the times covered by the forgery.

If you were victimized by one of these types of fraud, you should seek a loan cancellation by requesting a false certification discharge application from whomever is holding your loan. Be prepared to meet resistance and delay. You will have to insist on your rights.

In addition, the fact that the school defrauded you may be a defense to

To obtain a Direct Consolidation application

1. Fill out this form by
   - ■ completing the Borrower information
   - ■ listing all your educational loans (including your spouse's loans if you wish to consolidate them as well)
   - ■ indicating which loans you want to consolidate
2. Return this form by mail to U.S. Department of Education, Consolidations Department, Direct Loan Servicing Center, PO Box 4640, Utica, NY 13504-4640 or FAX to 1-800-848-0984
3. We'll do the calculations and send you an estimate of your payments under each repayment plan.

Borrower Information

Name: _____

Address: _____

_____

City: _____ State: _____ Zip: _____

Soc. Sec. #: _____

Yearly Income*: _____

Family Size*: _____

Daytime Phone Number: _____

*This information is required to estimate your Income Contingent Repayment amount.

Current Student Loan Information							
Loan #	Student Loan**		Current Balance	Interest Rate	Monthly Payment	Consolidate This Loan	
	Yes	No				Yes	No
1							
2							
3							
4							
5							
6							
7							
8							
9							
10							

**If you have a PLUS (parent) loan, check "No."

loan repayment. Stafford (GSL) loans after January 1, 1994 state that you can raise this defense where the for-profit trade school referred you to the lender. You can also raise the school's fraud as a defense on any Direct loan or Perkins (NDSL) loan. For GSLs before 1994, you will have to consult a lawyer.

Other Ways to Wipe Out a Student Loan. There are few other grounds for canceling a student loan. That the loan is very old is not such a ground. However, the student's death or permanent disability are grounds for canceling the loan permanently.

It is generally difficult to discharge a student loan in bankruptcy. The loan must originally have come due more than seven years ago (this time can be even greater if you had a deferment, consolidation, or forbearance) or you must convince the bankruptcy judge that it will be a significant hardship for the foreseeable future to repay the loan. It is usually better to ask the bankruptcy court to make a substantial hardship determination at the time of the bankruptcy filing, but if you fail to do so, the bankruptcy court or a state court can later make that determination when collection attempts on the student loan are renewed. The type of hardship required usually involves serious economic problems which are likely to persist for reasons beyond your control.

Dealing with Tax Intercepts. Seizure of tax refunds is the number one way the government collects on defaulted student loans. There are several steps you can take to deal with this seizure. If your joint tax refund is seized to pay for your student loan, your spouse can recover some of the amount seized by filling in a simple IRS form.

Before any actual interception, you will also be notified of the pending tax intercept. Check whatever boxes are appropriate on the form (e.g. the school closed, false certification, or the school defrauded you) and return it immediately, asking for a hearing. Send the form back return receipt requested as proof you sent it in. (There are widespread stories of the government failing to process requests for hearings.) You will have to do this every year you get a notice.

You should also be notified after any seizure. You should complain to the Department of Education if you did not have a chance to raise your defenses before your refund was seized.

Responding to a Wage Garnishment. Student loan collectors often threaten wage garnishment, but less frequently actually send you a notice of an impending garnishment and your right to contest the seizure of your wages. There are four ways you can stop such a wage garnishment to repay your student loan:

1. You can ask for a repayment agreement instead of the garnishment.
2. You can stop a wage seizure if you lost your old job against your wishes and you have not been continuously employed in your new job for a full year.
3. You can stop seizure of your first $127.50 a week in take-home pay. (This number is 30 times the curent minimum wage of $4.25. If the minimum wage increases, for example, to $5, $150 a week will be protected instead.)
4. You should receive a notice about how your right to a hearing. Request a hearing and explain any reason why you think you need not repay the loan.

FEDERAL INCOME TAXES

When your debt burden is overwhelming, you may find yourself behind on your taxes. Most people have a variety of tax obligations, the most common three being property taxes and federal and state income taxes. Some advice on property taxes is found at Chapter Two. This section concentrates on back due federal income taxes.

Always file your tax return even if you
do not send in your tax payment — the
penalties will be *much* smaller.

You must give special consideration to your federal income tax obligations for two reasons. First, the IRS has special powers to collect back taxes that make it more important for you to pay these taxes than many other types of debt. Second, the IRS sets out specific procedures and protections that you should know about if you are behind on your tax obligation.

File the Return on Time Even If You Do Not Pay the Taxes Owed.

One of the worst things you can do if you cannot afford to pay your taxes is not to file your tax return. If you fail to file your tax return, you may be (although usually you will not be) prosecuted for a misdemeanor crime. More likely, the government will assess a fine of 5.5% per month, up to a maximum of 50% of the amount owed, plus interest.

If you do file your return without paying the taxes owed, you have not committed a crime, but are merely behind on a debt. The penalty for late payment is only a fraction of the larger penalty for not filing a return — it is only .5% per month up to a maximum of 25%, plus interest.

Negotiating with the IRS.

When you file a return, but cannot afford to pay the taxes due, one option is to ask the IRS to put the tax obligation on your credit card (if you still have a card that works). The credit card interest will generally be less than IRS interest and penalties, and you need only pay the minimum required by the card company.

You should only put amounts on your credit card you believe you can repay. But, if your circumstances change, and you cannot repay the debt as soon as you are required, you may prefer to deal with the credit card company rather than the IRS.

Another option is to ask the IRS to let you pay the amount due in installments over time. The IRS will generally allow this. Sometimes you can even get the IRS to drop penalties. (The IRS will only drop interest if the IRS made an error that resulted in the tax liability.)

Be sure to document the severe financial hardship you are undergoing, and why this was caused by factors outside your control. Also make sure that any installment payment plan or reduction in the amount owed is in writing.

It is very important to either pay your taxes or set up a payment schedule with the IRS. If not, the IRS will quickly take steps to seize your property, steps that most other creditors cannot take.

Steps the IRS Can Take to Force Payment.

If you do not set up a payment plan, the IRS will force payment. If you have not filed a return admitting a certain amount as due, the IRS will send you a series of several letters asking for payment of a certain amount. The last letter gives you 90 days to file a petition with the tax court disputing the amount owed. This is the last opportunity you have to protest the tax without paying it first.

If you still do not respond, or if you have already filed a return admitting the amount owed, the IRS will send an assessment notice saying that it is placing a tax lien on all your property. This will give the IRS the authority to seize any of your property, with the exception of certain exempt types of income and property. In practice, the IRS will wait awhile and then go after bank accounts, paychecks, and even homes.

Exempt from IRS seizure is about $100 a week in wages (depending on your personal exemption and standard deduction), unemployment and workers' compensation, public assistance, job training benefits, income needed to pay court-ordered child support, and certain federal retirement and disability benefits. Other exempt property will be certain amounts of clothing, furniture, personal effects and job-related tools. A state homestead exemption will *not* protect your home from an IRS tax lien or seizure.

Unless most of your assets and all of your income are exempt from seizure, it makes sense to negotiate a payment schedule with the IRS to avoid seizure of personal property and income. Make sure any agreement is in writing.

Bankruptcy. Bankruptcy is not as effective a remedy when dealing with taxes as with other debts. In general, the only taxes (including interest and penalties) that you can discharge in a chapter 7 straight bankruptcy are taxes over three years delinquent where you properly filed the tax return for the year in question. Any tax liens on your property will remain in force even after the bankruptcy. In a chapter 13 reorganization, the taxes owed can be paid out over the life of the plan, that is paid in installments over a three to five year period.

Bankruptcy

- *Ten Factors in Deciding Whether to File Bankruptcy*
- *What Bankruptcy Can and Cannot Do for You*
- *How to Choose What Type of Bankruptcy, Whether You Should File With Your Spouse, and When to File*
- *The Basic Steps Involved in Chapter 7 and 13 Bankruptcies*
- *How To Get Help With Your Bankruptcy Filing*

IS BANKRUPTCY THE RIGHT CHOICE FOR YOU? 10 IMPORTANT CONSIDERATIONS

1. Bankruptcy May Be the Easiest and Fastest Way to Deal with All Types of Debt Problems. Bankruptcy is a process under federal law designed to help people and businesses get protection from their creditors. Bankruptcy can be the right choice if you have no better way to deal with your debts. Although you may want to try other options first, you should not wait until the last minute to think about bankruptcy because some important bankruptcy rights may be lost by delay.

2. Most Bankruptcy Cases Are Complicated. You should consider getting professional help. Bankruptcy is a legal proceeding with complicated rules and paperwork. You may want to get professional legal help, especially if you hope to use bankruptcy to prevent foreclosure or repossession. Most bankruptcy professionals will provide a free consultation to help you decide whether bankruptcy is the right choice.

3. Bankruptcy Temporarily Stops Almost All Creditors from Taking Any Steps Against You Except Through the Bankruptcy Process.

This benefit is provided by the "automatic stay" which is created by filing the necessary paperwork at the beginning of a bankruptcy case. Foreclosures, repossessions, utility shut-offs, lawsuits, and other creditor actions will be immediately, but perhaps only temporarily stopped.

4. Bankruptcy Can Permanently Wipe Out Your Legal Obligation to Pay Back Many of Your Debts.

This benefit arises because of the bankruptcy "discharge" which you get for successfully completing a bankruptcy case. Certain debts may not be discharged, such as certain student loans, liens associated with many secured debts, alimony, child support, and debts you incurred after the bankruptcy case was started. After bankruptcy, you will continue to owe those debts. In the long term, for those debts, you may have to fall back on strategies which are discussed in other parts of this book.

5. Where Bankruptcy Does Not Wipe Out a Debt, a Chapter 13 Bankruptcy (a Debt Reorganization) Gives You Time to Catch Up on that Debt.

For example, bankruptcy will not allow you to discharge home mortgages or car loans without repayment. If you want to deal with debts of that type in the bankruptcy process, you will need to propose a chapter 13 repayment plan. That requires affordable payments from your income over a period of three to five years.

6. In Most Cases You Will *Not* Lose Property by Filing for Bankruptcy.

However, if you have certain types of very valuable property, the bankruptcy law may not allow you to keep it unless you pay its value to your creditors over a number of years in a chapter 13 plan.

7. The Initial Fee for Bankruptcy is Presently $160 Dollars Under Chapter 13 and $175 Under Chapter 7. That Fee Is Likely to Go Up in the Future.

The fee is not usually waivable, but it can be paid in installments over a period up to 120 days (and 180 days with court permission). In addition to the initial fee, a variety of papers concerning your financial situation must be provided to the court.

8. If You File Bankruptcy, You Usually Do *Not* Need to Go to Court. You will have to attend one meeting with the bankruptcy trustee (not with a judge). Creditors are invited to that meeting, but rarely attend. You will not usually have to go to court for your bankruptcy case unless something out of the ordinary occurs. If you do receive a notice to go to court, it is important that you go.

9. Bankruptcy Will Usually Not Make Your Credit Record Any Worse. Most people filing bankruptcy already are behind on their bills and thus already have a tarnished credit record. It is unlikely that bankruptcy will make a bad credit record worse. Some creditors may be more wiling to lend you money than if you have a number of debts remaining in default. However, the fact that you filed bankruptcy can remain on your credit record for 10 years, while your default on other bills may stay on your record for only seven years.

10. Watch Out for Bankruptcy Related Scams. There are many people and companies which advertise bankruptcy related services in order to take advantage of vulnerable, financially distressed consumers. Some of these enterprises charge enormous fees. Others make promises which they cannot possibly keep. Do not pay money for debt counseling or bankruptcy without being sure you are dealing with a reputable business.

GENERAL INFORMATION ABOUT BANKRUPTCY

The right to file bankruptcy is an important tool which society provides for people with debt problems. In the short term, bankruptcy prevents continued efforts by creditors to collect debts. In the long term, bankruptcy can completely eliminate repayment obligations so that you can get a fresh financial start.

It is often stated that bankruptcy should be considered as a "last resort" for financially troubled consumers. This advice is oversimplified. It should be remembered that in some cases a loss of legal rights can result from delay. You should be especially careful to get early advice about bankruptcy if you are hoping to use the bankruptcy process to help save your home or your car. (For example, bankruptcy cannot help you keep a home after a foreclosure sale has already occurred.)

This chapter will provide you with an overview about bankruptcy. It is not a complete bankruptcy guide. If you are interested in filing bankruptcy, you should seek the services of a professional specializing in bankruptcy.

If you want a more detailed discussion of bankruptcy, several published books focus on bankruptcy exclusively. The National Consumer Law Center publishes *Consumer Bankruptcy Law and Practice* (4th ed. 1992) which is a very detailed analysis of bankruptcy for lawyers and others specializing in bankruptcy.

This chapter may answer some of your basic questions. It explains:

- how a bankruptcy filing can help with your financial problems and the two types of bankruptcy filings most commonly utilized by consumers;
- the advantages and possible disadvantages of a bankruptcy filing and when bankruptcy may be the wrong solution;
- choosing which type of bankruptcy to file, when to file, and whether you and your spouse should file together;
- the basic steps of a chapter 7 straight bankruptcy and a chapter 13 reorganization; and
- how to hire a bankruptcy attorney, how to prepare to meet with the bankruptcy attorney, and whether to use a for-profit debt counselor or document preparation service.

WHAT BANKRUPTCY CAN
AND CANNOT DO FOR YOU

Bankruptcy may make it possible for you to:

- Eliminate legal responsibility for many of your debts and get a fresh start. This is called a "discharge." When a debt is discharged at the close of a successful bankruptcy case, you will have no further legal obligation to pay that debt.
- Stop foreclosure on your house or mobile home and allow you an opportunity to catch up on missed payments.
- Prevent repossession of your car or other property, or force the creditor to return property even after it has been repossessed.

- Stop wage garnishment, debt collection harassment, and other similar collection activities and give you some breathing room.
- Prevent termination of utility service or restore service if it has already been terminated.
- Lower the monthly payments on some debts, including some secured debts such as car loans.
- Allow you an opportunity to challenge the claims of certain creditors who have committed fraud or who are otherwise seeking to collect more than they are legally entitled to.

Bankruptcy, however, cannot cure every financial problem, nor is it an appropriate step for every individual. In bankruptcy, it is usually *not* possible to:

- Eliminate certain rights of "secured" creditors. A "secured" creditor has taken an interest in your property as collateral for the loan. Common examples are car loans and home mortgages. Although you can force secured creditors to take payments over time in the bankruptcy process, you generally cannot keep the collateral unless you continue to pay the debt.
- Discharge types of debts singled out by the federal bankruptcy law for special treatment, such as child support, alimony, some student loans, court restitution orders, criminal fines, and some taxes.
- Protect all cosigners on their debts. When a relative or friend has cosigned a loan, and you discharge the loan in bankruptcy, the cosigner may still have an obligation to repay all or part of the loan.
- Discharge debts that are incurred after bankruptcy has been filed.

POSSIBLE ADVANTAGES
OF BANKRUPTCY

The Automatic Stay of Foreclosures, Evictions, Repossessions, Utility Shutoffs, and Other Creditor Actions. Your bankruptcy filing will automatically, without any further legal proceedings, stop most creditor actions against you and your property.

Your request for bankruptcy protection creates an "automatic stay" which will prevent commencement or continuation of repossessions, garnishments, attachments, utility shut-offs, foreclosures, evictions and debt collection harassment. The automatic stay will offer you a breathing spell, providing time to sort things out and to solve your financial problems.

If you file bankruptcy, a creditor cannot take any further action against you or your property unless the creditor obtains permission from the bankruptcy court. Sometimes creditors will seek such permission immediately, and sometimes they will never seek permission.

Filing bankruptcy will automatically, without further action, stop almost all creditor activities to collect from you.

Permission to continue collection activity is rarely, if ever, granted to unsecured creditors. It is common for secured creditors to get relief from the stay in a *chapter 7* case to continue foreclosure or repossession of their collateral. (As described below, a chapter 7 bankruptcy has minimal impact on a secured creditor's collateral.) On the other hand, an automatic stay will almost always continue in effect to protect you in a *chapter 13* bankruptcy case as long as payments are being made on the secured debt.

If the creditor takes action against you despite the automatic stay, the creditor can be held in violation of the stay and may have to pay you money damages and attorney's fees. If necessary, the creditor's actions against you can also be reversed. For example, a foreclosure sale which is held in violation of the stay can be set aside.

Discharge of Most Debts. The principal goal of most bankruptcies is quite simple. It is to achieve a discharge, which eliminates your obligation to repay many unsecured debts. Bankruptcy is thus a relatively easy way, though not the only way, to permanently end creditor harassment, and the hardship, anxiety and stress associated with debt overload. (See Chapter Five for other strategies to stop debt harassment).

On the other hand, a creditor's collateral is not affected by your bankruptcy filing unless you pay off those debts being secured by the collateral. A bankruptcy discharge does offer some protection for these secured debts. After you obtain a discharge, a secured creditor has no right to seek a deficiency judgment or to collect money from you in any way other than by selling the collateral.

This means that after bankruptcy, the creditor can seize its collateral if you don't pay, but cannot otherwise try to collect the debt. For example, if you do not pay a car loan, the creditor can seize your car and sell it. But it cannot sue you for the deficiency between what you owe and the amount for which the car was sold.

Protection Against Wage Garnishment and Enforcement of Judgment Liens. After you file a bankruptcy petition, creditors are prohibited from garnishing your wages or other income. This not only protects your income, but is also important if your employer frowns upon wage garnishments. Bankruptcy even stops government agencies from recouping Social Security or other public benefit overpayments, so long as your receipt of the overpayment was not deliberate.

Bankruptcy is also an effective tool to deal with some types of legal judgments against you. If a creditor's judgment for money against you does not create a lien against any of your property, that creditor is unsecured and the debt can be discharged in bankruptcy as if no judgment ever existed. Even if the judgment does create a lien on your property, you may request the bankruptcy court that the lien be lifted if it affects otherwise exempt property.

Which items of your property are exempt, and thus protected from a court judgment, is discussed in more detail in Chapter Seven. Bankruptcy offers two extra protections for this exempt property. First, bankruptcy can wipe out a lien entirely, while state exemption laws only prevent the creditor from seizing certain property — the lien still exists. Without a bankruptcy filing, if your assets increase in the future, a lien may then allow the creditor to seize some of your property. A second extra protection offered by bankruptcy is that in some states you may use federal exemptions if those provide better protections for you than those offered by your state law.

Added Flexibility in Dealing with Secured Creditors. Bankruptcy can be advantageous in dealing with secured creditors, that is lenders who have taken items of your property as collateral for their loans. Common examples are home mortgages and car loans. With certain exceptions, you still have to make payments on your secured debts if you want to keep the collateral. But bankruptcy does provide added flexibility in dealing with these secured creditors.

First, in some situations, bankruptcy can even eliminate certain secured creditors' right to seize collateral by "avoiding" (meaning removing or eliminating) the creditor's lien. This makes the debt unsecured.

For example, when you file bankruptcy, you can avoid liens on household goods taken where the loan is not used to purchase those goods. To the extent that household goods are exempt — and most families' household goods will be completely exempt — in bankruptcy you can request the court to forever eliminate the creditor's ability to seize that collateral.

Second, bankruptcy allows you to keep collateral by redeeming it, that is essentially paying the creditor not the amount of the loan, but the value of the collateral. For example, if a car is only worth $1000, even though the car loan is $3000, you can keep the car by paying the creditor only the $1000.

The greatest flexibility in dealing with secured creditors is available when a chapter 13 bankruptcy is filed. For example, if you are six months delinquent on a mortgage, filing a chapter 13 bankruptcy will stop the threatened foreclosure and allow you to gradually catch up on the back payments, perhaps over as long a period as several years. In some cases a chapter 13 filing may also allow you to revise a loan schedule by extending the repayment period or lowering the interest rate to make lower monthly payments.

Utility Terminations. A bankruptcy filing will not only stop a threatened utility termination, but will automatically and immediately restore terminated utility service, at least for twenty days. To keep utility service beyond twenty days after the bankruptcy filing, you must provide a security deposit or other security for future payments, and keep current on the new utility charges. To keep service, you need not pay bills incurred *before* the bankruptcy was filed.

Driver Licenses. A driver's license can be critical to keeping a job or in finding a new job. In some states a driver's license is subject to revocation because you have not paid a court judgment arising from an automobile accident. In that situation, bankruptcy is sometimes the only possible way for you to keep or regain the license. Normally, bankruptcy can be used to discharge the obligation to pay the court judgment, and you then have a right to regain or retain the driver's license.

OTHER BANKRUPTCY CONSIDERATIONS, INCLUDING POSSIBLE DISADVANTAGES

In Most Cases You Will Lose Little or None of Your Property. Some people believe that a bankruptcy filing results in the loss of all or most of their property. This belief is wrong. Everyone who files bankruptcy gets to keep some of their possessions. Most people get to keep all of them.

> You will get to keep some of your
> property in bankruptcy, and most bankruptcy
> filers get to keep all of their property.

Whether you get to keep *all* your possessions depends on a number of factors. These factors include whether you file a chapter 7 or a chapter 13 bankruptcy, whether certain debts are secured or unsecured, and how much of your property is exempt.

Generally, you will keep all or virtually all your property in a bankruptcy, except property which is very valuable or which is subject to a lien which you cannot avoid or afford to pay. In most circumstances, bankruptcy should be seen as a method of preventing loss of property rather than causing the loss of property.

In a chapter 7 bankruptcy, all of your *equity* in property is divided into two categories — exempt and nonexempt. State law or in some cases the federal bankruptcy law will specify which property is exempt. Usually, at least a certain amount of equity in your home, car, clothes, jewelry, appliances and furniture will be exempt.

In valuing property for the purposes of bankruptcy, the question is not the property's original cost, but rather what the property could be sold for at the time of filing. It is often useful to imagine a hypothetical yard sale to try to estimate what particular items would bring. Remember also that exemption laws vary widely from state to state. It is important to check what exemptions are available in the state where you live.

It is also important to understand how the concept of equity relates to exemption laws. If an exemption law protects a $5000 motor vehicle, this relates to $5000 of your equity in the car, not to the total value of the car. If you have a $12,000 car with a $7000 car loan balance, you have only $5,000 in equity. You can thus fully protect the $12,000 car with the $5000 exemption. You will only have to repay the car loan.

If you have significant *non*-exempt assets, a chapter 13 bankruptcy may be a viable alternative through which you can retain all of your possessions. In a chapter 13 bankruptcy, you keep your possessions (unless you choose to sell them) and instead pay their non-exempt value over time from future income under a plan approved by the bankruptcy court.

The Effect of Bankruptcy on Your Credit Record. A bankruptcy can remain part of your credit history for ten years. The effect of a bankruptcy on your credit record is unpredictable, but of understandable concern.

For most people, this concern alone should not be considered a disadvantage of bankruptcy. If you are seriously delinquent on a number of debts, this information will already appear on your credit record. A bankruptcy is unlikely to make your credit worse. In fact, there is some evidence that the bankruptcy will make it *easier* to obtain future credit, because new creditors will see that old obligations have been discharged, and that the new creditor will therefore be first in line for payment from your income. Also, once a discharge is received, many new creditors recognize that you cannot then receive a new chapter 7 discharge for the next six years.

If you do not yet have problem credit, the impact of a bankruptcy on your ability to obtain credit is more difficult to answer. Research on the effects of bankruptcy on future credit is inconclusive. It seems fair to say that most credit decisions depend upon the judgement of individual lenders. Most lenders seem to look at a potential customer's income and income stability more than anything else.

After bankruptcy, some lenders may demand collateral as security, ask for a cosigner, or want to know why bankruptcy was filed. Other creditors, such as some local retailers, do not check credit reports or inquire about bankruptcy on credit applications at all.

You should remember that you always have the option after bankruptcy of voluntarily paying certain creditors, such as preferred doctors or hospitals, with whom you wish to maintain good relationships. You can make voluntary partial payments without legally obligating yourself to pay the entire debt.

The Effect of Bankruptcy on Your Reputation in the Community.

Creditors might continue to extend credit despite a prior bankruptcy, but what about friends, neighbors, and coworkers? What happens to an individual's reputation? Most people find their reputations suffer no perceptible harm.

Bankruptcies are not generally announced in newspapers, although they are a matter of public record. It is unlikely that your friends and neighbors will know that you filed bankruptcy unless you choose to tell them.

However, in a small town, where debts are owed to local people, some difficulties connected with filing bankruptcy may still be present. Embarrassment and damage to reputation must be personally evaluated and weighed against bankruptcy's potential advantages. If you believe that this is a problem, you may choose to pay selected debts after bankruptcy. Voluntary payment of discharged debts is specifically allowed by the bankruptcy law, but you cannot leave certain creditors out of the bankruptcy process entirely.

> You should not feel embarrassed
> about filing bankruptcy if it is the best
> solution to your financial problems.

Feelings of Moral Obligation.

For some people, a feeling of moral obligation creates a hesitation about filing bankruptcy. Most people do want to pay their debts and they should make every effort to do so if payment is possible. However, if bankruptcy is the right solution for your financial problems, you should balance your feelings of moral obligation with other considerations. Remember that bankruptcy is your right under the United States Constitution, intended to provide a fresh start for individuals in precisely your situation. Big corporations like TWA, A.H. Robbins, Johns Manville, Macy's and Penn Central, and famous people like Jerry Lewis, John Connally, Tammy Wynette and Mickey Rooney, have chosen to file bankruptcy.

You may find comfort in the fact that the Bible mentions the need for a process which is like bankruptcy. The book of Deuteronomy states:

> At the end of every seven years thou shalt make a release. And this is the manner of the release: every creditor shall release that which he has lent unto his neighbor and his brother; because the Lord's release hath been proclaimed. (Deut. 15:1-2.)

Creditors know that a small portion of the people to whom they extend credit will be forced to go bankrupt; therefore they protect themselves by charging enough interest and overhead to cover these losses. The "embarrassment of bankruptcy" is largely a concept created by creditors who have a self-interest to make bankruptcy appear unattractive.

Most importantly, whatever its negative connotations, bankruptcy should be considered in relation to the hardships it can avoid. During hard times, bankruptcy may be the only way to provide your family with food, clothing, and shelter. This book does explore alternatives to bankruptcy, and these should be considered carefully. But it may be that bankruptcy is your best or only realistic alternative.

Potential Discrimination After Bankruptcy. The bankruptcy law offers you some protection against later discrimination by creditors and others. Government agencies, such as housing authorities and licensing departments, cannot deny you benefits because of a previous bankruptcy discharge of your debts to those agencies.

Similarly, utilities cannot deny service because of a bankruptcy, although a utility company can require a deposit to cover charges incurred after the bankruptcy is filed. Private employers cannot discriminate against employees or terminate employment on the basis of bankruptcy.

You are fully protected by law from any such discrimination and can enforce these rights in court, if necessary. However, the bankruptcy law does not prevent discrimination by others, including private creditors deciding whether to grant new loans.

Cost of Filing a Bankruptcy Petition. There are several expenses related to filing bankruptcy. First, there may be costs associated with hiring an attorney to handle the bankruptcy. Hiring an attorney and the advisability of alternatives are discussed later in this chapter.

In addition to an attorney's fee, a bankruptcy petition presently requires a $160 filing fee under chapter 13 and a $175 filing fee for chapter 7. In most parts of the country, this filing fee cannot be waived. In all places, however, the fee can be paid in installments.

In a chapter 13 reorganization case, the trustee is usually entitled to a commission of about ten percent of the payments made through the plan. These payments must be included with the amount that you pay the trustee under a plan.

In addition, utility companies may be entitled to collect a security deposit following a bankruptcy (usually equal to approximately twice the average monthly bill) just as if you were a new customer. Some, but not all utility companies take advantage of this right. In most localities, you can request up to 60 days to make this payment.

Ability to File Another Bankruptcy If You Have More Financial Problems. One consideration about filing bankruptcy is whether you will have the opportunity to file again if a new financial problem arises. The answer depends on what type of bankruptcy you file both times.

The different types of bankruptcy are discussed immediately below. For simplicity, you can think of a chapter 7 as an immediate discharge of many of your debts with the liquidation of any of your assets that are not exempt. A chapter 13 is a reorganization of your debt where you pay your creditors some or all of what they are owed over a period of years, but where you generally lose none of your property.

You can receive only one discharge under chapter 7 every six years. That means that if you choose to file bankruptcy under chapter 7 now, you may not be able to do so again for a period of time. For this reason it is usually best to wait until other options have been explored before filing a chapter 7 case.

However, if you have filed under chapter 7, you may still be able to file again under chapter 13 (or another chapter), before six years have expired. Similarly, you can file more than one case under chapter 13 in a six year period as long as you meet the requirements under that chapter when you file.

Other issues can arise if your case is unsuccessful for some reason. (It is rare to have an unsuccessful chapter 7 case, but chapter 13 cases frequently fail because the consumer cannot afford the necessary payments.) If your case is dismissed, that dismissal will sometimes bar a new case from being filed for 180 days.

WHEN BANKRUPTCY MAY
BE THE WRONG SOLUTION

For some individuals bankruptcy is the wrong solution. There are five situations in which bankruptcy may be a bad option:

1. You have only a few debts and strong defenses for each. Instead of filing for bankruptcy, you can raise these defenses vigorously. Usually the disputes can be settled out of court in an acceptable way. If they are not settled, you can use bankruptcy later. (You can also raise claims and defenses in the bankruptcy court if they have not been decided in other courts.)

2. The debts at issue are secured by your property — such as home mortgages or car loans — and you do not have sufficient income to keep up payments and also catch up on past due amounts, even with the help bankruptcy provides. That is, bankruptcy may not be able to help you if you want to keep your property, but where the long term expense of doing so exceeds your long term income.

3. You have valuable assets that are not exempt in the bankruptcy process and you do not want to lose these assets. (Note that a chapter 13 filing may still help if you can afford the necessary payments.)

4. Because of a prior bankruptcy, you cannot receive a discharge in a chapter 7 bankruptcy. However, in most cases a chapter 13 petition can still be filed.

5. You can afford to pay all of your current debts without hardship.

There is also a situation in which there is no urgency to the bankruptcy filing. Where state exemption laws are generous, you may be totally "judgment-proof" at the time you are thinking about bankruptcy. If that is the case, creditors can do virtually nothing to harm you. There is no action they can take which will affect your property or your wages.

When there is no urgency for you to file for bankruptcy, it often makes sense not to file immediately. If you wait, additional debts may arise which can also be included and discharged in the bankruptcy case. For a more detailed analysis of the advantages and disadvantages of a bankruptcy filing, see the National Consumer Law Center's *Consumer Bankruptcy Law and Practice* Ch. 6 (4th ed. 1992).

CHOOSING THE TYPE
OF BANKRUPTCY TO FILE

The Two Common Types of Bankruptcy for Consumers. The bankruptcy law generally provides for two types of consumer cases. These are generally known as liquidation and debt adjustment.

Liquidation (Under Chapter 7). A liquidation case usually takes place under chapter 7 of the bankruptcy law. In a liquidation case, your assets are examined by a court appointed trustee to determine if anything is available to be sold for the benefit of creditors. Certain property cannot be sold, and instead you keep it despite the bankruptcy. This property is called "exempt."

The trustee may sell only property which is either not exempt or which has value which exceeds the exemption limits. In most consumer bankruptcies, virtually all, if not all, of the assets are exempt; therefore, little or none of the consumer's property is taken away and sold. If property is partly exempt and partly non-exempt, the trustee may sell it and pay you the value of your exemption in cash. Or, if you have the money, you may pay the trustee the amount of the non-exempt value and keep the property.

Exemption laws vary from state to state and may be fairly complicated. You cannot make a final choice about bankruptcy without understanding the exemption laws for your particular state.

The best way to do this is to ask for a listing from a neighborhood legal services office, a private attorney, or pro bono bar organization. Another approach is to see if there is an accurate and up-to-date listing in a legal publication for your state. See Chapter Seven for more detail on state exemption laws.

In deciding what can be sold, the trustee will only look to your *equity* in property. For example, if you owe money on a mortgage or other lien on a home, that mortgage or lien reduces your equity in the home. The trustee will not sell property if your equity in the property is fully exempt.

For example, if the applicable state exemption for your home is $50,000, the home's value is $150,000, and you have a $100,000 mortgage, all of your $50,000 equity in the home is exempt. The trustee will *not* sell the home in a chapter 7 liquidation. (The trustee also is unlikely to sell your home if there is a small amount of non-exempt equity. That is because the equity would not cover the costs of sale including realtor's fees and taxes. In the above example, the trustee is unlikely to sell the home even if it could be sold for $160,000.)

Even in a straight bankruptcy liquidation, you get to keep all of your exempt assets, which usually include your home and your car.

At the end of a liquidation case, you obtain a discharge of most unsecured debts. This means that you will no longer have a legal obligation to pay those debts. Generally the discharge will include credit card debts, medical bills, utility arrearages, and other similar debts for which the creditor does not have collateral.

Some unsecured debts, such as student loans which are less than 7 years old, debts based on fraud or malicious conduct, drunk driving debts, some tax debts, government fines, alimony, and child support, may not be discharged, depending on the circumstances. Whether such debts can be discharged is sometimes a complicated question that is resolved by detailed bankruptcy rules.

It is important to stress that chapter 7 bankruptcies rarely help with large secured debts, such as home mortgages, because the creditor retains its rights in the collateral. While bankruptcy discharges most personal debts, it does not prevent secured creditors from recovering their collateral if a debt is not repaid. This means that a chapter 7 case will not affect, except temporarily, the rights of a bank to foreclose on a home or repossess a car that is loan collateral.

A liquidation bankruptcy can delay a foreclosure or repossession, but it cannot provide long term relief. (There is one significant exception—after a chapter 7 discharge, the creditor loses the right to sue you for any deficiency if the creditor sells the collateral for less than the outstanding debt.)

Debt Adjustment/Reorganization (Under Chapter 13). Debt Adjustment (also called "reorganization") cases work very differently from liquidations. In a debt adjustment case, you put forward a plan (meeting the rules set out in the bankruptcy law) to repay your creditors over time, usually from future income. Most consumer reorganization cases take place under chapter 13 of the bankruptcy law. However, some debtors with large amounts of debt may be required (or prefer) to proceed under chapter 11. Family farmers can also proceed under chapter 12.

In certain circumstances, there are advantages to filing a reorganization case rather than a liquidation. Most importantly, in a reorganization case, you are allowed to get caught up on mortgages or car loans over a period of time.

For example, most mortgages and car loans allow the bank to call the whole loan due when you miss a payment or two. Although the bank may let you work out an agreement to catch up over time on back payments (and you should call to find out if this is possible), the bank usually is not legally required to let you catch up. Where the bank or any creditor is uncooperative, a bankruptcy reorganization may be the only way to force it to let you keep the property while you make back payments over a period of time.

Reorganizations also allow you to keep both exempt property (which would be protected in a liquidation) and non-exempt property (which would be sold in a liquidation). You can keep the non-exempt property by paying its value to creditors under a court approved plan, usually over a period from three to five years.

The heart of any reorganization is your bankruptcy plan. This is a simple document outlining how you propose to make payments to various creditors while the plan is in effect.

The law places certain limits on what you may do under a plan. Nevertheless, there are substantial opportunities for reorganizing your debt payments and protecting your property from creditors, including mortgage and other lien holders, as long as appropriate payments are made. The reorganization option is thus particularly useful if you have fallen behind on a mortgage or car loan due to temporary financial hardship and you are now able to begin making payments again.

A chapter 13 bankruptcy plan normally requires monthly payments to the bankruptcy trustee over a period of three years. However, plans can go for as long as five years with court approval. In most jurisdictions, bankruptcy courts will routinely approve requests to have the monthly payments to the trustee paid automatically by wage deduction.

In a chapter 13 bankruptcy, you may have as long as five years to catch up with overdue payments on secured debts, and you may be able to keep all of your property.

Once your payments are completed under the plan, you are entitled to a discharge just as in a chapter 7 bankruptcy. The discharge available in chapter 13 is broader than a discharge under chapter 7 and may cover more debts. If you have caught up on any mortgage or other secured loan, the loan will be reinstated and the law requires the creditor to treat you as if you never fell behind.

Reorganization cases can be quite complicated. Working out the most advantageous possible bankruptcy plan is frequently difficult. If you are considering a reorganization in bankruptcy, consult with an attorney specializing in bankruptcy as quickly as possible. Your delay may allow a foreclosure or repossession to proceed to the point where bankruptcy can no longer help.

Advantages of a Chapter 7 Bankruptcy. If a chapter 7 bankruptcy will accomplish your goals, it is generally the best choice because it is simpler and quicker than a chapter 13 bankruptcy. Once the papers are filed, unless unusual issues are raised, you will receive a discharge within six months. A chapter 7 bankruptcy will generally meet your goals if it will discharge most of your debts and not result in the loss of any of your property.

Generally, chapter 7 is the best option when three factors are present:

- All or nearly all of your property is exempt;
- The debts which are causing problems for you are unsecured; and

- The debts which are causing problems for you are dischargeable under chapter 7.

Even if some of your property is not exempt, a chapter 7 bankruptcy
may be the right choice for you where you can exchange that non-exempt
property for exempt property. This is called exemption planning and is
legitimate in most cases, just as tax planning is an appropriate course for
wealthier families.

Some view chapter 7 as appropriate only where a consumer's debts are all
unsecured, with chapter 13 being the appropriate choice if there are secured
debts. But, even where there are secured debts, a chapter 13 filing may not
be necessary.

This is particularly true if you are current on your mortgage, car loan and
other secured debt payments. If you can keep current on secured debt payments, you can keep your home or other collateral, if it is exempt, even
while going through a chapter 7 bankruptcy. (A chapter 13 filing is generally preferable if you are delinquent on a secured debt and want to cure this
default over time.)

Some Considerations Favoring Chapter 13 Bankruptcies.
Probably the most common reason for filing a chapter 13 petition is that
one or more secured creditors cannot be dealt with satisfactorily in any
other way. Few legal procedures create opportunities to deal with foreclosures and repossessions as quickly and effectively as a chapter 13 petition
and plan. The plan can lower monthly payments and even reduce the balance due on your car loan or mortgage.

Another reason to file a chapter 13 bankruptcy is to protect non-exempt
assets, which would be sold in a chapter 7 case. However, the current value
of the non-exempt property usually has to be paid over the course of the
plan.

Other important reasons favoring a chapter 13 filing include:

- Debts that are not dischargeable in chapter 7 can be discharged in chapter 13, including some taxes, debts incurred
  through false financial statements, false pretenses or fraud,
  willful and malicious torts, and breach of fiduciary duties, as
  well as debts for which a previous bankruptcy discharge was
  denied or waived. Even for nondischargeable, priority debts

such as taxes, a chapter 13 plan allows you to stretch out payments over a longer period than would otherwise be possible.

- A chapter 13 case helps consumers who want to pay their debts, but who need the protection of the bankruptcy court and who can profit from the discipline of a chapter 13 plan.
- Chapter 13 usually eliminates any further finance charges and late charges for debts that have no collateral.
- Some experts consider a chapter 13 filing, compared to a chapter 7 filing, to be less harmful to the consumer's credit rating and reputation.
- For people who have obtained a chapter 7 discharge within the previous six years, a chapter 7 filing is not available, leaving only the option of a chapter 13 filing.

Whichever type of bankruptcy you choose is not irrevocable. It is easy to convert at least once from chapter 7 to chapter 13 or vice versa.

Should Both Spouses File? If you and your spouse are living together, it is usually preferable for you to file bankruptcy jointly. The filing fee is the same whether you file jointly or alone. If you file together, you will both get the advantages of a bankruptcy discharge. If you file alone, your spouse will remain responsible for your joint debts.

Most couples are jointly responsible for their debts; therefore a spouse who does not file remains liable as a codebtor, and may be pursued by creditors. (However if one spouse files under chapter 13, the other spouse obtains some protection at least to the extent that the plan provides for joint debts).

There is, of course, no requirement that you file together with your spouse. Therefore, if you want to file and your spouse does not (or vice versa), or if you and your spouse are estranged, there is nothing to prevent a married individual from filing alone. However, the consequences of not filing jointly should be considered carefully.

THE TIMING OF
YOUR BANKRUPTCY FILING

The Emergency Bankruptcy. You may have no choice other than to file immediately to prevent a foreclosure, repossession, eviction, execution sale, or utility shut-off. Bankruptcies in an emergency can be filed with as little as ten minutes preparation. A good discussion of how to do this is set out in the National Consumer Law Center's *Consumer Bankruptcy Law and Practice* § 7.2.2 (4th ed. 1992), "The Emergency Bankruptcy Case, or How to Prepare a Bankruptcy Case in Under Ten Minutes."

Delaying Bankruptcy in Anticipation of Further Debt. If you are not facing immediate loss of property and anticipate further unavoidable debts, such as new medical, utility or unpaid rent bills, a bankruptcy filing should be delayed until after these debts occur. That way you will gain the maximum benefit from the discharge.

Debts incurred after the bankruptcy filing are *not* discharged in that bankruptcy case — you will still be obligated to repay them. As a general rule, bankruptcy should not be filed until your debts have peaked.

Once a chapter 7 bankruptcy case has been filed, you will have to wait another six years before filing another chapter 7 bankruptcy and obtaining another chapter 7 discharge for debts incurred after the first bankruptcy was filed. You can file a chapter 13 case with no waiting period after the chapter 7 discharge, as long as bad faith is not involved.

If you decide to wait to file bankruptcy, you must avoid the temptation to obtain goods or services on credit for which you do not intend to pay. In a chapter 7 bankruptcy, debts incurred in this way can be declared nondischargeable. Debts for prebankruptcy vacation trips and credit card shopping-sprees have frequently been found non-dischargeable. Expenses for medical bills and other essentials are rarely challenged.

Exemption Planning. You can legally take a number of steps to improve your legal position prior to filing bankruptcy. These steps are generally called exemption planning. Basically, exemption planning means arranging one's affairs so that a maximum amount of property can be claimed under exemption provisions, and a minimum amount is lost to creditors.

It is similar to making arrangements to take maximum advantage of tax laws, and, if done reasonably, is perfectly legal. Excessive transfer of property to create exempt assets, however, can sometimes be found to be in bad faith.

Also, you cannot simply give away nonexempt property or sell it at nominal cost. Any transfer of property within a year of filing must be disclosed. Improper transfers of property to third parties can be recovered and may be grounds for denying a discharge.

CHAPTER 7 BANKRUPTCY: THE BASIC STEPS

Chapter 7 consumer bankruptcy cases are usually straightforward. Occasionally, complications arise if creditors take aggressive action, if the trustee thinks you are hiding assets, or if you wish to challenge creditors' claims. Those potential complications are not covered in detail here. This section explains only what happens in a typical chapter 7 bankruptcy case.

In a chapter 7 case, all of your nonexempt assets are distributed to creditors, and you receive a bankruptcy discharge at the end of the proceedings. From the beginning of the case until its conclusion, each step in the process is directed toward one or both of these goals. For more detail on the basic steps involved in filing a chapter 7 case, see the National Consumer Law Center's *Consumer Bankruptcy Law and Practice* Ch. 3 (4th ed. 1992).

1. Who Can File? Any individual who lives in the United States or has property or a business in the United States can file a chapter 7 bankruptcy. There are no preconditions to a bankruptcy filing, such as insolvency, although a judge can dismiss your chapter 7 case if you are engaged in a substantial abuse of the bankruptcy system. (This is very rare.) If you received a bankruptcy discharge within the past six years (with some exceptions for chapter 13 cases), you are disqualified from receiving another discharge.

2. Initial Forms. The first step in a chapter 7 bankruptcy is completion of certain basic forms. The most important is a two page initial "petition." The fee for filing a petition is currently $175. The fee for a husband and wife filing jointly is the same as for an individual filing alone.

You can request, when you file your petition, that the fee be paid in installments over the next several months. (If you must pay your bankruptcy attorney before filing the case, the rules prevent you from paying the filing fee in installments.) If you do not eventually pay the fee in full or if you do not file all the required forms, your bankruptcy case will be dismissed.

A number of other forms must also be filed either at the same time as the petition or shortly thereafter. These include your statement of financial affairs, statement of intentions with respect to certain debts, and a set of schedules — listing all your debts, property, income and expenses. If your schedules are not filed with the petition, you will need to file a list of creditors at the outset of the case.

At the beginning of the case you will also need to file a mailing list including all of your creditors. All of these forms must meet certain specifications required by the court. You should check with a bankruptcy specialist or your local bankruptcy court for a full list of necessary papers.

3.First Steps After Filing. Filing the petition triggers the automatic stay. With few exceptions, this stay stops anyone from taking collection action or pursuing a court case against you, or seizing your property based on debts that arose before you filed your bankruptcy petition. Your attorney or the court clerk will notify your creditors that a bankruptcy has been filed. If you are worried about a creditor action like a foreclosure or repossession, you should make a special effort to notify that creditor so that the action is stopped before it occurs.

If a creditor does take action which violates the stay, including collection calls or letters, you should politely inform the creditor about the bankruptcy. You should also tell your attorney about the contact. This may start a process to obtain a remedy for a violation of the stay.

Within a few weeks after filing, the bankruptcy court or the trustee mails a notice of the stay and of the date and place for a "meeting of creditors." This notice will be mailed to all creditors, to you, and to your attorney, if you have one. This notice also contains deadlines for creditors who wish to file claims or complaints raising objections to the discharge or to the dischargeability of a particular debt. If it appears that all of your property is exempt, the court may notify creditors that claims need not be filed unless they are later notified that you possess assets.

4. The Chapter 7 Trustee. For both chapter 7 and chapter 13 bankruptcies, a trustee is appointed to represent the interests of unsecured creditors (creditors who do not have any collateral). In a chapter 7 bankruptcy, the trustee collects any property that can be sold, handles the sale, distributes the property to creditors with valid claims, and makes a final accounting to the court.

5. The Meeting of Creditors. The meeting of creditors is conducted by the trustee, usually at a place outside the courthouse. This proceeding gives the various parties a chance to examine your financial affairs. It is usually the way the chapter 7 trustee learns whatever is necessary for the performance of his or her duties.

Despite the name, creditors rarely appear at the meeting of creditors in a consumer bankruptcy. The meeting consists of a series of routine questions addressed to the consumer by the court-appointed trustee covering most of the information in the statement of affairs and schedules, and lasts from five minutes to half an hour. Usually, the best thing you can do to prepare for this meeting is review the papers you or your attorney have filed with the court.

6. After the Meeting of Creditors. At this point, you take one of several steps to deal with your secured debts. You can surrender collateral to the secured creditor if that is your intention, or you can keep the collateral outright by paying the creditor the value of the collateral. Alternatively, you can deal with the secured debt outside of the bankruptcy, for example by keeping the collateral by remaining current on your payments.

After the meeting of creditors, your other property is also dealt with. Unless there is an objection to your exemptions, you always keep property claimed as exempt. Property that has little nonexempt value is usually abandoned by the trustee, which means that you get to keep it.

If larger assets remain, they are turned over to the trustee at or after the first meeting. The consumer is usually offered the option of paying the nonexempt value of the assets to the trustee in cash instead of turning over those assets. The trustee then collects any other property that is neither exempt nor abandoned, and sells this property, converting it to cash.

The trustee must give notice of intent to sell the property. Any party, including you, can object (within specified time limits) to the proposed sale, which is either private or by public auction.

If the trustee collects any cash by selling property, it is distributed to creditors in order of their priority under the bankruptcy law. Creditors will be paid according to their filed claims unless you, the trustee or some other party objects to those claims.

7. The Discharge. The final step in most chapter 7 bankruptcy cases is the discharge. In most jurisdictions, if no one objects to your discharge, the court enters the discharge without a hearing. You simply get the discharge order in the mail.

If there is an objection or if you do not have an attorney, but you choose to reaffirm your legal obligation on any debt, you may be called to a hearing before the judge. (You should rarely agree to reaffirm a debt. Reaffirmation requires that you agree to remain legally obligated to pay a debt which could be discharged.)

The discharge is effective for all unsecured debts with some exceptions including:

- Certain taxes;
- Debts not listed in the schedules;
- Most debts for alimony and child support and some property settlements;
- Most fines and penalties owed to government agencies;
- Some student loans;
- Debts listed in a prior bankruptcy where discharge was denied or waived;
- Debts incurred by driving while intoxicated;
- Debts incurred to pay certain taxes;
- Most criminal restitution obligations; and
- Debts you have formally agreed to repay despite the bankruptcy (by "reaffirming" your obligation to pay). Reaffirmation is a voluntary process and it is usually not a good idea.

In addition some other debts may be determined to be nondischargeable, but only if the particular creditor seeks determination of nondischargeability within sixty days from the first date set for the meeting of creditors. Debts that the court must first determine are nondischargeable include:

- debts incurred by certain types of fraud;
- debts incurred while acting as a trustee for someone else's property;
- debts for causing willful or malicious injuries; and
- some property settlement debts.

CHAPTER 13 BANKRUPTCY: THE BASIC STEPS

A chapter 13 bankruptcy allows you to reorganize your financial affairs without having to give up your assets. It allows you to choose between making payments on debts out of future income or out of sale of current assets.

You can keep and use all property, whether exempt or not.

Chapter 13 also gives you an opportunity to cure defaults. That is, the chapter 13 filing can allow you to catch up — gradually over time—past due delinquencies. At the completion of this plan, or before, you are given a discharge which is basically similar to the discharge received in a chapter 7 case. For more detail on the basic steps involved in filing a chapter 13 case, see the National Consumer Law Center's *Consumer Bankruptcy Law and Practice* Ch. 4 (4th ed. 1992).

1. Who Can File? Chapter 13 is available to "individuals with regular income" who live in the United States, or have a place of business or property in the United States. An "individual with regular income" includes not only wage earners, but also recipients of government benefits, alimony or support payments, or any other regular type of income.

A chapter 13 discharge can be obtained even by a debtor who has received a chapter 7 discharge within six years before filing, or who would not be granted a discharge because of some other provision in chapter 7.

2. The Initial Forms and First Steps. As with chapter 7, a chapter 13 bankruptcy begins with a two-page petition. A chapter 13 petition must be accompanied by a $160 filing fee, charged both to single individuals and to husbands and wives filing jointly. An application to pay that fee in installments may be filed if you have not already paid an attorney. No waiver of the fee is permitted.

Several other required forms are usually filed at the same time as the petition, including the schedules, the statement of financial affairs, the statement of compensation of your attorney or bankruptcy professional, and the chapter 13 plan, which is your description of when creditors will be paid, how they will be paid, and how much they will be paid.

If you are unable to file the chapter 13 paperwork and plan with the petition, the case can begin by filing the petition, along with the fee (or the application to pay the fee in installments), and a list of your creditors. The other papers must then be filed within fifteen days, unless that time is extended by the court. Local practice may require that certain other papers be filed, either with the petition or shortly thereafter.

As with chapter 7, filing a petition sets the bankruptcy process in motion. A trustee is appointed, and, if applicable, an order for paying the filing fee in installments is entered.

The filing immediately establishes the automatic stay, which prevents any further creditor acts against you or your property. Filing a chapter 13 petition also puts into effect a prohibition that prevents creditors from taking any action against any codebtors (co-signers) who have not filed bankruptcy.

You or your attorney should usually give notice of the stay to creditors likely to take quick action against you. This prevents seizures before the bankruptcy court formally notifies the creditor. Permission of the bankruptcy court is then necessary before creditors can proceed with any of the acts prohibited by the stay. As discussed above, such permission will only be granted in limited situations.

Within a relatively short time after filing, the court will issue a notice of the "meeting of creditors." This form also gives notice to creditors of the automatic stay and of the deadlines for filing their claims with the court.

3. Making Payments Under the Plan. You must begin making plan payments within thirty days after filing the plan, unless the court orders otherwise. These payments are held by the chapter 13 trustee and not paid out to creditors until your chapter 13 plan is approved by the court. (In the interim, the automatic stay protects you from any collection action by these creditors.) If the court does not approve your chapter 13 plan, the payments are returned to you after deduction of administrative costs.

Your payments will be based on the debts you intend to pay, the rules of chapter 13, and your ability to pay based on your budget. This means that after paying for necessary living expenses, you will need to pay the balance of your income to the trustee under your plan while your bankruptcy proceeds. If you so choose, this can occur automatically by wage deduction.

Once your plan is in place, if you fail to make payments, your case is likely to be dismissed. Dismissal will put you back to the situation you were in prior to bankruptcy. In some cases dismissal can be avoided, as noted below, by voluntarily converting a chapter 13 case to a case under chapter 7 or by seeking a "hardship discharge." These options are discussed below under section 7, below, "Failure to Complete the Plan."

4. The Chapter 13 Trustee. The chapter 13 trustee has considerably more to do than the chapter 7 trustee. In addition to the duties of a chapter 7 trustee, the chapter 13 trustee must collect your payments, distribute money to creditors, and attend all hearings dealing with secured claims and approval of your plan. The trustee can also advise you on matters related to the bankruptcy and assist you in performance of the plan.

Depending upon the type of case or the matter involved, and in some cases the trustee's personality, a trustee is either your friend or foe. In either case, the trustee's opinion is not necessarily the last word on any matter. You have the right to raise any appropriate issue with the bankruptcy judge. Trustees are not judges and have no power to rule on disputes between creditors and debtors.

5. The Meeting of Creditors. As with chapter 7 bankruptcy, the primary purpose of the meeting of creditors is to give the trustee an opportunity to ask you questions and discover any grounds for objecting to the plan. The trustee will inquire generally into the information presented in the statement of affairs, schedules and plan, including your ability to make the proposed payments.

Despite the name for the proceedings, creditors rarely appear, and the bankruptcy judge is not permitted to be present. The meeting is likely to last between five minutes and a half hour, and follows the same pattern of routine questioning as chapter 7 cases. Your best preparation for the meeting of creditors is to review any papers you have filed with the court, including your schedules and plan.

6. The Confirmation Hearing. The confirmation hearing occurs either on the same day as the first meeting of creditors, or some time within the next several months, depending upon local practice. The purpose of the confirmation hearing is to provide a basis for the court to decide on whether your plan will be approved, to inquire into whether the requirements of chapter 13 have been met, and to hear any objections to approval of your chapter 13 plan raised by creditors or the trustee.

Prior to the hearing, you or your attorney should review the creditors' "proofs of claims" (the creditor's statement of how much you owe). You can object to those proofs if there is a dispute. The effect of confirmation is to bind you and all of your creditors to the terms of the plan.

In many jurisdictions there is no formal hearing at the time of confirmation unless there is an objection by a creditor or the trustee. Also, in many cases, if the plan is uncontested, you will be advised that you do not need to come to court.

For various reasons, consumers sometimes want to modify their original plan after it has been filed. Before confirmation, a plan can be modified freely, so long as the modified plan meets the chapter 13 requirements. After confirmation, plans can still be modified, but only after giving notice and opportunity for a court hearing. Creditors or the trustee may object.

7. Failure to Complete the Plan. Some people are unable to complete their chapter 13 plans by making payments as proposed, usually because of loss of income. When this occurs, four options are normally available, each having somewhat different consequences:

- *Hardship Discharge.* The federal bankruptcy law provides for a hardship discharge of debts if problems are caused by circumstances for which you are not responsible, such as serious deterioration of your financial circumstances.
- *Modification.* It is possible to modify a plan to address new problems, but creditors have a right to object to the modification, and, if so, the court will decide whether to allow the modification. Plan payments can be reduced or even terminated if the modified plan still complies with the requirements of chapter 13.
- *Conversion.* You have the right to convert to a chapter 7 bankruptcy; in most cases such a conversion provides the same relief as a hardship discharge. After the conversion, nonexempt property is liquidated and you receive a chapter 7 discharge. If you have no nonexempt property, you receive a discharge without further action. Debts arising after the chapter 13 case was commenced, but before conversion, can be included in the chapter 7 discharge.
- *Dismissal.* Occasionally, dismissal is preferable to any of the other options. You have the right to dismiss your chapter 13 case unless the case was previously converted from chapter 7. This option is particularly attractive if it appears that the case may be converted to chapter 7 against your will, and if you have nonexempt property that you do not wish to see liquidated.

8. Discharge. The final step in a successfully completed chapter 13 case, or in a case ended under hardship provisions, is the discharge. In the wording of the law, a discharge must be granted by the court "as soon as practicable" after completion of all payments under a confirmed plan.

The discharge received in a chapter 13 bankruptcy is usually broader than in a chapter 7. It includes all debts provided for by the plan, except for most support and alimony payments and for long term debts with final payments due after the completion of the plan. Other exceptions to discharge in chapter 13 are some student loans, drunk driving debts and criminal restitution debts. Thus, a chapter 13 discharge can eliminate legal responsibility on debts not dischargeable in a chapter 7 case, including debts incurred through fraud or false pretenses, and claims for willful and malicious injuries.

Promptly after the discharge, a notice of discharge is mailed to all creditors and to the trustee. You and your attorney also receive a copy of this notice. Shortly afterwards, the trustee files a final report and the case is officially closed.

HOW TO GET HELP WITH
YOUR BANKRUPTCY FILING

Hiring a Bankruptcy Attorney. Generally, the best course of action if you are considering bankruptcy is to obtain the services of an attorney who is expert in the field of bankruptcy. Hiring an attorney to handle any legal case is a difficult process. This is especially true in hiring a bankruptcy attorney.

As with any area of the law, it is important to carefully select an attorney who will be responsive to your personal situation. The attorney should not be too busy to meet with you individually and to answer your questions. You should take care before hiring an attorney to meet the attorney personally and to be comfortable with the attorney's style.

At all points in the case, your attorney should take time to answer questions either directly or through an office paralegal. If an attorney does not respond to your telephone calls, you should keep trying and demand an answer.

If you file a chapter 13 bankruptcy, make sure the attorney will continue to represent you during the several year life of the bankruptcy. If you have a dispute with your attorney, you can file a complaint with the court or the bar association.

The best way to find a trustworthy bankruptcy attorney is to seek recommendations from family, friends or other members of the community. Retainers and other documents should be read carefully. An attorney retainer is a contract under which you hire the attorney. It governs what the attorney proposes to do for you and the fees for the proposed work. Remember that the lawyer advertising the cheapest rate is not necessarily the best.

Avoid For-Profit Debt Counseling. For-profit bankruptcy counseling is rarely a good idea. Unfortunately, there are many people who offer counseling and credit repair to people with debt problems in order to rip them off. If you are going to pay for debt counseling, you should be careful to avoid scams and offers of high-rate debt consolidation loans as a way out of debt. Most of these deals will only make your situation worse. If a deal seems too good to be true or if a solution to your problems seems too easy, it probably is.

It is very easy to get ripped off by a for-profit debt or bankruptcy counselor or to get into trouble using a bankruptcy document preparation service.

Concerning bankruptcy, there is little that a for-profit debt counselor can offer other than a recommendation about whether bankruptcy is appropriate. When bankruptcy is the right choice, they will simply recommend a lawyer. There is no good reason to pay someone for this service.

A reputable attorney will offer advice on whether bankruptcy is appropriate and prepare the case only if relief is available. This avoids the double charge of having to pay a counselor and then an attorney. If bankruptcy is not appropriate, a good attorney will offer a range of other strategies which you can pursue independently.

In most communities, there are *non*-profit counselors who may be able to help you deal with your debts. However, they are not always easy to find. Try to get a referral, if possible, from local officials, from a friend or neighbor, or from a legal services office. If someone approaches you by mail or telephone because they read a foreclosure notice or announcement of a court proceeding against you, think twice before paying them for assistance.

Problems With Document Preparation Services. Document preparation services have recently generated a large number of consumer complaints. These services involve non-lawyers who offer to prepare the initial bankruptcy forms for a fee.

There are several reasons for consumer dissatisfaction with these services. Non-lawyers cannot legally offer advice on bankruptcy cases. Document preparation services also offer no services after a bankruptcy case is started. This means that if issues arise after your forms are filed, you will have nowhere to turn for help. Often, the actual case will involve complications or even simple problems which you may not be prepared to meet. For these reasons, document preparation services are rarely a good place to get help with bankruptcy.

Preparing to Meet With a Bankruptcy Specialist. You should be prepared when first meeting a bankruptcy specialist to answer the following questions:

- What types of debt are causing you the most trouble?
- What are your significant assets?
- How were the debts incurred and are they secured by your property?
- Has any creditor started a process to collect any debt, or to foreclose or repossess property? You should be prepared to report on the status of any pending lawsuits or foreclosures.

The answers to these general questions will reveal not only whether bankruptcy is likely to help you, but also the dimensions of your financial problems — their cause, scope, and likelihood of recurring. Whenever possible, it is helpful to take written information about these issues to the bankruptcy specialist, particularly copies of your bills. This will help the specialist understand how much is owed and to whom. It will also provide necessary information such as account numbers and addresses of creditors.

Complete information is essential to an effective bankruptcy. If information is not complete, then unexpected rights such as tax refunds might be denied, major debts might turn out to be nondischargeable or unaffected because of security interests, and property might unexpectedly be considered nonexempt.

Additionally, without complete information, a bankruptcy specialist cannot help you make use of the maximum benefits that bankruptcy offers. For example, your right to avoid or modify a lien may be lost if the existence of the lien is not discovered in the fact-gathering stage. Debts not listed in bankruptcy papers sometimes survive a discharge. Even if they are discovered during the pendency of the case and are included later, they can mean additional fees for you and more work for your attorney.

In the fact gathering process, some people accidentally overlook certain types of property and debts. Common types of property you might overlook include:

- long-dormant accounts with banks and credit unions;
- your right to a tax refund or credit;
- a security deposit given to a landlord or utility;
- accrued vacation pay, future commissions from sales positions, salary or pension rights;
- legal claims and claims for money owed to you by others;
- your share in a housing, shopping, or agricultural cooperative;
- entitlements to government grants, such as energy assistance grants; or
- accrued insurance interest.

All of these things should be reported to your bankruptcy specialist to avoid unnecessary loss of property or, in extreme cases, denial of a discharge.

Every possible debt should be unearthed so that the opportunity to discharge your legal liability can be used to its fullest. Debts not listed in the bankruptcy may not be discharged. You may not remember the full extent or nature of your debts, especially if payments have not been recently demanded for those debts. Just as a legal claim can be a form of property, it can also be a debt if you are the one being sued. If you have recently obtained a credit report, a bankruptcy specialist can use that report to remind you about debts you may have forgotten.

— Appendix —

Budget Charts

INCOME BUDGET				
SOURCE OF INCOME	**LAST MONTH ACTUAL (1)**	**THIS MONTH EXPECTED (2)**	**THIS MONTH ACTUAL (3)**	**ADJUSTED MONTHLY (4)**
Employment (5)	$	$	$	$
Overtime				
Child Support/Alimony (7)				
Pension				
Interest				
Public Benefits (8)				
Dividends				
Trust Payments				
Royalties				
Rents Received				
Other (List) (9)				
TOTAL (MONTHLY)	$	$	$	$

NOTES

(1) This should be based on your income records for the past month.

(2) This column should include your best projections of your regular monthly income for coming months.

(3) After making your initial budget, keep careful records for the next month. Then fill in your actual income from each source. This will help you determine if your actual income meets your budget projections.

(4) After keeping records of your actual income for at least a month, go back and fill in this column based on your experience. Although this column will be a projection for the future, it should be more accurate than the projection you made when you started the budgeting process, because it will be based on actual monthly income for one month or more.

(5) Include the income of all household members who will be contributing to the family budget.

(6) You can list either your take home pay or your total employment income. If you use the total, remember to list all of your payroll deductions as expenses in the expense budget. If you use your take home pay, remember to check your pay stub to make sure that there are no unnecessary deductions.

(7) Include only the amounts you are actually expecting to receive, if any.

(8) This should include all money received from public benefits each month including food stamps, welfare, social security, disability, unemployment compensation, worker's compensation etc. If you are receiving more than one type of income, then you may want to use as box labeled "other" at the bottom of the budget.

(9) If you need more space, combine two or more other sources of income on a separate sheet and then list them together as one line in your budget.

EXPENSE BUDGET				
TYPE OF EXPENSE (10)	LAST MONTH ACTUAL (11)	THIS MONTH EXPECTED (12)	THIS MONTH ACTUAL (13)	ADJUSTED MONTH (14)
Payroll Deduction (15)				
Income Tax Withheld				
Social Security				
FICA				
Wage Garnishments (16)				
Credit Union (17)				
Other				
Home Related Expenses (18)				
Mortgage or Rent (19)				
Second Mortgage				
Third Mortgage				
Real Estate Taxes (20)				
Insurance (21)				
Condo Fees &				
Mobile Home Lot Rent				
Home Maintenance/Upkeep				
Utilities (22)				
Gas				
Electric				
Oil				
Water/Sewer				
Telephone				
Other (23)				
Food				
Clothing				
Laundry and Cleaning				
Medical (24)				
Current Needs				
Prescriptions				
Dental				
Other				
SUBTOTAL PAGE 1				

Transportation				
Auto Payments				
Car Insurance				
Gas and Maintenance				
Public Transportation				
Life Insurance				
Alimony or Support Paid				
Student Loan Payments (25)				
Amounts Owed on Debts (26)				
Credit Card (27)				
Credit Card				
Credit Card				
Medical Bill (28)				
Medical Bill				
Other Back Bills (List)(29)				
Cosigned Debts (30)				
Business Debts (List)(31)				
Other Expenses (List)(32)				
Miscellaneous (33)				
TOTAL				

INCOME AND EXPENSE TOTALS				
	LAST MONTH ACTUAL	**THIS MONTH EXPECTED**	**THIS MONTH ACTUAL**	**ADJUSTED EXPECTED**
A. TOTAL PROJECTED MONTHLY INCOME (34)				
B. TOTAL PROJECTED MONTHLY EXPENSES (35)				
EXCESS INCOME OR SHORTFALL (A MINUS B)				

NOTES

(10) Include the total expenses of everyone in your household who shares expenses.

(11) This should be based, as closely as possible, on your experience in the most recent month. Estimate items for which you have not kept complete records.

(12) This column should include your best projections of your monthly expenses for coming months.

(13) After making your initial budget, keep careful records for the next month. Then fill in your actual expenses for each item. This will help you determine if your actual expenses meet the budgeted amount.

(14) After keeping records of your actual expenses for at least a month, go back and fill in this column based on your experience. Although this column will be a projection for the future, it should be more accurate than the projection you made when you started the budgeting process, because it will be based on actual monthly expenses for one month or more.

(15) Do *not* fill this section out if you have used your take home pay in your income budget. However, you should check your pay stub to make sure that there are no unnecessary deductions from your pay. *Do fill this section out if you used your gross employment income budget or if you are self employed.*

(16) Bankruptcy can eliminate many types of wage garnishments. See Chapter 18.

(17) These payments can usually be eliminated during a period of financial hardship.

(18) Ways to keep your home during periods of financial crisis are discussed in Chapters Nine through Twelve if you own, and in Chapter Thirteen if you are a renter.

(19) Include amounts here only for your primary home. If you have a vacation home or a time share, include that separately below under "other expenses". This will help you determine whether you can make ends meet by giving up your second home or time share.

(20) Include your real estate taxes only if these amounts are not included with your escrow payment on your mortgage.

(21) Include your home insurance payments if these amounts are for renter's insurance or if they are not included with your escrow payment on your mortgage.

(22) Many options for reducing these amounts are discussed in Chapter Fourteen.

(23) For example, propane and cable television subscriptions are discussed in Chapter Fourteen.

(24) This should not include your back bills. Back medical bills are unsecured debts which should be handled differently in your budget and listed below under "Amounts Owed on Debts". Generally, they should only be paid in times of financial hardship if you can afford to pay. Strategies for dealing with back medical bills and other unsecured debts are covered in Chapter One.

(25) Many options for dealing with or reducing student loan obligations are discussed in Chapter Seventeen.

(26) List here the monthly payments you plan to make on your unsecured debts like credit cards and medical bills. These are low priority debts as discussed in Chapter One. You may plan to pay little or nothing if you are trying to deal with other more important expenses on a limited income. It does not make sense to make even "minimum" payments on these debts unless you can afford to do so after paying for your necessities and higher priority bills. A variety of choices for dealing with these debts and with collection activities by creditors are discussed in Chapter One and Chapter Five. Dealing with lawsuits on unsecured debts is discussed in Chapter Seven. Using bankruptcy to address unsecured debts is discussed in Chapter Eighteen.

(27) In most cases you should list the minimum required payment unless you can afford to pay more. This can be costly however, since with credit card bills, interest will mount up very quickly if you pay only the minimum. If you cannot afford even the minimum monthly payment, then list zero and look into your other options for dealing with these debts as discussed in the prior note.

(28) List your back bills here. Current anticipated medical expenses should be listed separately above as a higher priority expense. Old bills can generally be dealt with like other low priority unsecured debts.

(29) Some examples might include other debts owed to professionals such as lawyers or accountants, personal loans, bills owed to prior landlords, deficiency claims on prior foreclosures or repossessions and any other debt for which the creditor has no collateral.

(30) You need to treat debts on which you are a cosigner as a high priority debt if you have given your property as collateral for the debt. Cosigned debts are a lower priority if your property does not serve as collateral. See Chapter One.

(31) Your obligations on business related debts can be complicated and depends on the type of business. You may want to get special legal assistance on whether payment on these debts should be included in your budget as a high priority.

(32) Everyone has a different situation. You should think about any other source of regular household expenses and list them here. Some frequently overlooked items include cigarettes, diapers, pet related expenses, children's allowances, lay-away payments, rent-to-own, etc. Some of these item,s can be quite costly and will throw your budget out of whack if they are not accounted for.

(33) You may want to include a small sum here for the miscellaneous small expenses or for emergencies which are unaccounted for elsewhere.

(34) Take this amount from your income budget above.

(35) Take this amount from your expense budget above.

(36) If you have excess income — congratulations. However, make sure that your budget actually works by trying it out for a few months. You may want to use your excess income to pay down any back debts which are carrying interest — particularly credit cards. If you have a shortfall, you should consider limiting or ending any discretionary items in your budget, terminating payment on your credit cards in order to maintain your necessities and reading the rest of this book for strategies to use to help you survive your debt while you are getting back on your feet.

Bibliography

*All National Consumer Law Publications
can be ordered from Publications,
National Consumer Law Center,
18 Tremont Street, Boston, MA 02108
617-523-8089.*

BOOKS

Center on Budget and Policy Priorities, *EITC Community Outreach Kit* is a particularly helpful resource on the Earned Income Tax Credit. It is updated yearly and designed for organizations and counselors to help them inform low-income families about their potential eligibility for tax refunds. The kit contains a fact sheet, eligibility guidelines, campaign posters, flyers printed in English and Spanish, and a summary of effective outreach strategies. To receive the kit, write to the EITC Campaign, Center on Budget and Policy Priorities, 777 N. Capitol St., Suite 705, Washington D.C. 20002, 202-408-1080.

Elias, Leonard, & Renauer, *How to File for Bankruptcy*, is an excellent guide for those attempting to file bankruptcy on their own. Available from the Nolo Press, 950 Parker Street, Berkeley, California 94710, 1-800-992-6656.

Federal Home Mortgage Association, *Sellers' and Servicers' Guide* contains the guidelines all Freddie Mac lenders must utilize in foreclosing on a home and negotiating repayment schedules. The cost is $275, which includes a one year update service. Available from Freddie Mac, Attn: Subscription Services, 8200 Jones Branch Drive, McLean VA 22102.

Federal National Mortgage Association, *Servicing Guide* contains the guidelines all Fannie Mae lenders must utilize in foreclosing on a home and negotiating repayment schedules. The cost is $300, which includes a continual upkeep service. Available from Fannie Mae, 510 Walnut St., 16th Floor, Philadelphia, Pennsylvania 19106 and from other Fannie Mae regional offices.

Food Research Action Center, *Guide to the Food Stamp Program* (9th ed. 1995) is an excellent resource on the federal food stamp program and is available for $20 directly from the Food Research Action Center, 1875 Connecticut Ave. NW, Suite 540, Washington. D.C. 20009-5728, 202-986-2200.

Leonard, Robin, *Money Troubles: Legal Strategies to Cope With Your Debts* (ed ed.) is a good consumer self-help manual for certain types of less serious consumer debt problems, such as straightening out a credit report or dealing with billing errors. Available from the Nolo Press, 950 Parker Street, Berkeley, California 94710, 1-800-992-6656.

National Consumer Law Center, *Consumer Bankruptcy Law and Practice* (4th ed. 1992 and Supplement). The best resource available on all aspects of consumer bankruptcy filings, including hundreds of model forms.

———— , *Fair Debt Collection* (3d ed. 1996), the definitive treatise on consumer remedies to fight debt collection harassment, including extensive treatment of the federal Fair Debt Collection Practices Act.

———— , *Repossessions and Foreclosures* (3d ed. 1995) covers all aspects of consumer repossession and foreclosure law, including seizure of homes, automobiles, mobile homes, and household goods.

———— , *Fair Credit Reporting Act* (3d ed. 1994 and Supplement) explains a consumer's rights in dealing with credit reporting agencies, including extensive treatment of the federal Fair Credit Reporting Act.

—— , *Unfair and Deceptive Acts and Practices* (3d ed. 1991 and Supplement) is a unique resource covering all types of unfair and deceptive conduct in the marketplace, including special sections on student loans, the federal racketeering statute, other consumer remedies, and insurance issues.

—— , *Truth in Lending* (3d ed. 1995) is the essential guide for anyone handling a Truth in Lending case, either to obtain statutory damages or to cancel a loan. Also included is a detailed analysis of the federal Consumer Leasing Act.

—— , *Access to Utility Service* (1996) covers all aspects of utility service issues — termination protections, terminations relating to service in landlord's name, concerns of mobile home park tenants, erroneous billing, impact of bankruptcy, federal energy assistance benefits, weatherization programs, and more.

—— , *Sales of Goods and Services* (2d ed. 1989 and Supplement) is a detailed manual on all aspects of consumer warranty law and the rights of consumer purchasers of goods and services.

—— , *Credit Discrimination* (1993 and Supplement) covers consumers' rights when they are denied credit, including a thorough analysis of the federal Equal Credit Opportunity Act.

—— , *The Cost of Credit* (1995 and Supplement) is a unique legal resource, covering federal and state law regulating interest rates and other credit terms for consumer loans and credit sales.

—— , *Odometer Law* (3d ed. 1992 and Supplement) explains consumers' special remedies when they purchase a used car with a tampered odometer. The best treatment available of the federal Odometer Act and state laws.

—— , *The Regulation of Rural Electric Cooperatives* (1993) provides a number of innovative strategies that REC customers can utilize to combat utility termination and bill collection.

——— , *Consumer Class Actions: A Practical Litigation Guide* (3d ed. 1995) explains how even a small law firm can mount a consumer class action, thus obtaining widespread relief for victims of a consumer scam.

——— , *Consumer Law Pleadings with Disk, Numbers One and Two* (1994, 1995) presents sample pleadings for use in consumer law cases — sample complaints, interrogatories, other discovery, motions, settlements, and more.

National Health Law Program, *Advocates' Guide to the Medicaid Program* (1993) is the best source for information on Medicaid benefits. It is available for $50 from NHELP, 2639 S. La Cienega Blvd., Los Angeles, California 90034, 310-204-6010.

National Housing Law Project, *FmHA Housing Programs: Tenants' and Purchasers' Rights* (2d ed. 1995) is an excellent resource for any FmHA housing issue. The volume is $98 from the National Housing Law Project, 2201 Broadway Street, Suite 815, Oakland, California 94612, 510-251-9400.

PERIODICALS

Clearinghouse Review (National Clearinghouse for Legal Services) is an invaluable monthly magazine covering recent developments in all areas of poverty law, including government assistance, rights of consumer debtors, housing issues, health law, and special issues relating to the elderly, migrant workers, immigrants, and veterans. Annual subscription is available from the National Clearinghouse for Legal Services, 205 W. Monroe Street, Second Floor, Chicago, Illinois 60606, 312-263-3830.

The Health Advocate (National Health Law Program) is a quarterly publication concentrating on Medicaid benefits and other low income health law issues. It is available from NHELP, 2639 S. La Cienega Blvd., Los Angeles, California 90034, 310-204-6010.

Welfare News and Welfare Bulletin (Center on Social Welfare Policy and Law) is for those who want to keep up to date on current developments concerning welfare law. To subscribe, send $40 to the Center on Social Welfare Policy and Law at 275 Seventh Ave., Suite 1205, New York, New York 100001-6708, 212-633-6967.

NCLC Energy & Utility Update (National Consumer Law Center), a bi-monthly newsletter that keeps readers current on low income utility issues, such as utility terminations, low income payment plans, the federal fuel assistance program, low income weatherization, and telephone and water issues.

NCLC Reports (National Consumer Law Center) covers the latest developments in all major areas of low income consumer law. Twenty-four issues a year are divided into four different editions each published bi-monthly: Bankruptcy & Foreclosures Edition; Debt Collection & Repossessions Edition; Consumer Credit & Usury Edition; and Deceptive Practices & Warranties Edition.

Glossary

Words in italics are separately defined in this glossary

Acceleration. When a *creditor* claims the total balance of a loan as due immediately. This cannot usually occur unless you have fallen behind on payments. In the case of a home mortgage, receipt of a letter stating that a loan has been "accelerated" is normally an important warning sign of foreclosure. See Chapter 9.

Amount Financed. The amount of money you are getting in a loan, as expressed under rules required by federal law. This is the amount of money you are borrowing after deduction of certain loan charges which the *Truth in Lending Act* defines as *finance charges*. You should think of the amount financed as the real amount you are borrowing. You will find the amount financed for a loan on the *disclosure statement* which is given to you when the loan papers are signed. See Chapter 4.

Annual Percentage Rate. The interest rate on a loan expressed under rules required by federal law. It is more accurate to look at the annual percentage rate (as opposed to the stated interest rate) to determine the true cost of a loan, because it tells you the full cost of the loan including many of the lender's fees. You will find the annual percentage rate for a loan on the *disclosure statement* which is given to you when the loan papers are signed. See Chapter 4.

Answer. In a lawsuit, this is a legal document which the *defendant* must file to respond to the claims being raised. There are often short time deadlines to file an answer. Failure to file an answer can result in a *default judgment*. See Chapter 7.

Arrears. The total amount you are behind on a debt; usually the amount of all back payments plus any collection costs.

Attachment. A legal process which allows a creditor to "attach" a *lien* to property which you own. Depending on state law, almost any kind of property may be subject to attachment, including your home, automobile, bank accounts and wages. Once a *lien* is attached to the property, you may face further collection action on that property, including *execution, garnishment* or *foreclosure.* See Chapters 7 and 16.

Automatic Stay. A *bankruptcy* case automatically prevents continuation of creditor collection activity. Filing bankruptcy is the only way to get this protection. See Chapter 18.

Bankruptcy. A legal process available in all states which allows you to address your debt problems according to a set of special rules, while getting protection from continued collection activity. See Chapter 18.

Bond. Amounts required by a court order to protect a party to a lawsuit while the case proceeds. A bond may be required in some circumstances to pursue an appeal. See Chapter 7.

Collateral. Property put up to secure a loan. If you have given a creditor collateral, that creditor can normally take and sell the collateral if you are not able to repay the loan. A creditor with collateral is normally known as a *"secured creditor."* See Chapter 1.

Complaint. A document commencing a lawsuit. A complaint normally includes a statement of all of the claims being raised by the person bringing the lawsuit. See chapter 7.

Cosign. Agreeing to be responsible for someone else's debt. A "cosigner" is normally responsible to pay back a debt just as if he or she had received the money.

Counterclaim. A response to a lawsuit in which the person being sued raises legal claims against the person (or business) which started the case. For example, if you are sued by an automobile seller who claims you did not pay for a car, you might counterclaim that the car was a "lemon." See Chapter 8.

Credit Bureau, also called consumer reporting agency or credit reporting agency. This is a company that receives information about a consumer's credit history and keeps records which are available to those seeking data about that consumer. See Chapter 6.

Credit Record, also called a consumer report or a credit report, is the information about a consumer that a credit bureau has on file that it can report to others. See Chapter 6.

Creditor. Any person or business to whom you owe money.

Cure a Default. If you have defaulted on a debt, this is a process for correcting the *default*. Most often, a "cure" refers to getting caught up on missed payments (paying the *arrears*). A cure may also be called *reinstatement*.

Debtor. Any person who owes money to another. In *bankruptcy*, the term "debtor" refers to the person who begins a bankruptcy case.

Debtor's Examination, also known as "post-judgment process," "asset examination" and "supplementary process." This is normally a court ordered proceeding in which a debtor must appear in court or in an attorney's office to answer questions about current income and assets from which a *judgment* may be collected. In many states, failure to appear at a debtor's examination can result in an arrest warrant. See Chapter 7.

Deed in Lieu. This is an agreement to turn real estate over to a lender as an alternative to *foreclosure*. See Chapter 10.

Deed of Trust. In some states, this is the term used for a pledge of real estate as *collateral*. It is similar to a *mortgage*.

Default. Failing to meet the requirements of an agreement. Most defaults involve failure to make required payments. However, other types of defaults are possible, including failure to maintain necessary insurance and failure to keep *collateral* in proper condition.

Default Judgment. A *judgment* in a lawsuit against a party who did not meet legal requirements in connection with the case. The most common reason for a default judgment is failing to file an *answer* or other necessary papers before deadlines specified by law. See Chapter 7.

Defendant. In a lawsuit, this is the person or business that is being sued. See chapter 7.

Defense. A legal reason why a court should not award any or all of what is requested in a lawsuit. For example, a statement that the money is not owed is a defense to a collection lawsuit. See Chapter 7.

Deficiency. The amount a debtor owes a *creditor* on a debt after the creditor seizes and sells the *collateral.* A deficiency arises when the collateral is sold for less than the amount of the debt. Normally a creditor must bring a lawsuit to collect a deficiency. See Chapters 7, 9, and 15.

Discharge. A document which ends a *debtor's* legally enforceable obligation to pay a debt. It is common to get a discharge of a *mortgage* debt after the mortgage is fully paid off. In addition, most *bankruptcies* result in a discharge at the end of the case which applies to many debts. See Chapters 9 and 18.

Disclosure Statement. This term is commonly used to refer to the document which explains loan terms according to the *Truth in Lending Act.* This Act requires most lenders to provide a disclosure statement in connection with any loan to a consumer. The consumer may have a *defense* to repaying a loan where the loan disclosures were not properly made. See Chapters 8 and 12.

Discovery. This term covers a variety of legal processes by which the parties to a lawsuit obtain information from each other about facts and documents related to the case.

Escrow. Amounts set aside for a particular purpose. A formal escrow usually requires a legal agreement which covers permissible usage of the escrow and how and where the money is to be kept. One type of escrow is money you pay to your *mortgage* company to cover taxes and insurance. Another use of escrow is in circumstances in which you have a dispute with a *creditor*. You may choose to set up an escrow to pay the debt in the event you lose the dispute.

Eviction. A legal process terminating the right to occupy a home, apartment or business property. State law eviction proceedings are a prerequisite to putting someone out. See Chapter 13.

Execution. The process of enforcing a court *judgment* by taking property from the *defendant*. Execution of a judgment of eviction, for example, involves the sheriff or a public official putting the tenants out. Execution of a *judgment lien* involves seizing and selling the property subject to the lien. See Chapter 7.

Exempt Property. This is property which the law allows you to keep when you are being faced with collection on an *unsecured debt*. In *bankruptcy*, exempt property is protected from sale to satisfy the claims of creditors. See chapters 7, 16 and 18.

Exemptions. These are laws which give you the right to maintain your *exempt property*.

Fair Credit Reporting Act. A federal (national) law which governs the conduct of *credit bureaus* and which regulates use of credit reports. See Chapter 6.

Fair Debt Collection Practices Act. A federal (national) law which governs the conduct of debt collectors and which prevents many abusive collection tactics. See Chapter 5.

Finance Charge. The amount of money a loan will cost you expressed as a dollar figure. The finance charge includes the interest together with certain other loan charges specified by the *Truth in Lending Act.* You will find the loan's finance charge on the *disclosure statement* given to you when you sign the loan papers. See Chapters 4 and 12.

Foreclosure. This is a legal process to terminate your ownership of real estate which is *collateral* for a debt, based on a *mortgage* or *deed of trust.* In some states, foreclosure involves a court proceeding ("judicial foreclosure"), while in others foreclosure occurs by creditor action alone ("non-judicial foreclosure"). See Chapters 9 - 12.

Fraudulent Transfer. Giving away property to keep it out of the hands of creditors. The law allows *creditors* to sue to get the property back. See Chapter 3.

Garnishment. A *creditor's* seizure, to satisfy a debt, of property belonging to the *debtor* that is in the possession of a third party. Usually a court has to authorize the seizure in advance. An example would be seizure of money in your bank account to repay a court judgment. Wages owed to you can also be garnished in many states. See Chapter 7.

Guarantor. A person who agrees to pay another person's debt in the event that he or she does not pay. The term guarantor is often used interchangeably with *cosigner,* even though there are some minor legal distinctions in the collection process.

Homestead Exemption. The right, available in most states and in the *bankruptcy* process, to treat your residence as *exempt property* which cannot be sold to satisfy the claims of *unsecured creditors.* In most states, the homestead exemption covers a certain dollar amount of your equity in your residence. A home cannot normally be sold to pay claims of your creditors unless your equity in the home exceeds the amount of the exemption. A homestead exemption will not normally protect you from *foreclosure* when you have voluntarily pledged your home as *collateral.* See Chapters 7 and 12.

Insolvent. A person or business which does not have sufficient assets to pay its debts.

Judgment. A determination by a court as to the outcome of a lawsuit, including any amounts owed.

Judgment Lien. A lien which attaches to property as the result of a *judgment*. For example, if you lose a collection lawsuit, the creditor normally has the right to an *attachment* on any real estate which you own. Once a judgment lien is placed on the property, the creditor may be entitled to *execution* by a forced sale of the property. Judgment liens can attach to property other than real estate.

Judgment-Proof. This term is applied to people or businesses with property of minimal value, which can be entirely protected by *exemptions*. If you are judgment-proof, it is difficult or impossible for any *creditor* to force you to pay a debt. See Chapter 1.

Lemon Law. This is a state law which gives you protection if you purchase an automobile which does not work properly and cannot easily be fixed. Most lemon laws only apply to new cars, but some also apply to used cars. See Chapters 8 and 15.

Levy. A process, in some states, for *attachment* of a *judgment lien* and/or *execution* of that *lien.*

Lien, also called a "security interest," is a legal interest taken by creditors in your property to secure repayment of a debt. A lien can be created voluntarily in connection with a loan, such as when you pledge real estate by giving a creditor a *mortgage* or *deed of trust.* A lien can also be created without your consent by *attachment* based on a court order. A creditor with a lien is called a *secured creditor.*

Liquidation. Sale of property to pay creditors. The term is also used as a shorthand name for the chapter 7 *bankruptcy* process, even though property is not always sold in that bankruptcy process. See Chapter 18.

Mortgage. An agreement in which a property owner grants a *creditor* the right to satisfy a debt by selling the property in the event of a *default.* See Chapters 8-12.

Mortgage Servicer. A bank, mortgage company, or a similar business which communicates with property owners concerning their *mortgage* loans. The servicer usually works for another company which owns the mortgage. It may accept and record payments, negotiate *workouts*, and supervise the *foreclosure* process in the event of a *default*. See Chapters 9 and 10.

Non-Purchase Money Security Interest. A *lien* on property which is unrelated to a loan taken to purchase that property. See chapter 16.

Note. This term is commonly used as a name for a contract involving the loan of money.

Notice of Right to Cancel. This document explains your right to cancel a loan in some circumstances. You should receive such a notice in connection with most door-to-door sales and for *mortgage* loans which are not used to buy your residence. Cancellation rights are discussed in Chapters 4 and 12.

Notice to Quit. In most states, this is a notice given by an owner of property (usually a landlord) demanding that a tenant leave within a specified period of time or face eviction proceedings. See Chapter 13.

Personal Property. Property other than real estate.

Plaintiff. This is a person or business which begins a lawsuit.

Pre-Sale. Sale of property in anticipation of *foreclosure* or *repossession*, usually with the lender's consent. A pre-sale is likely to lead to a higher sale price than foreclosure or repossession. See Chapters 10 and 15.

Pro Se (also called "pro per"). Representing yourself (without an attorney) in a legal case or bankruptcy proceeding.

Reaffirmation. An agreement in the *bankruptcy* process to pay back a debt which would otherwise be *discharged* in bankruptcy. Most reaffirmation agreements are a bad idea. See Chapter 18.

Redeem. Recovering *collateral* from a *creditor* by paying the entire amount you owe (whether past due or not). In *bankruptcy*, property can be redeemed in some situations by paying the collateral's value even if that amount is less than the entire amount owed.

Refinancing. The process of paying back old debts by borrowing new money either from an existing *creditor* or a new creditor. Many of the pitfalls to refinancing an existing debt when you are having financial problems are discussed in Chapter 4.

Reinstatement. The process of remedying a *default* so that the lender will treat you as if you had never fallen behind. See definition of *curing a default*.

Rent to Own. A process in which you rent property until you have paid enough to qualify for ownership. Most rent to own deals are very expensive and a bad idea for the consumer. See Chapter 3.

Reorganization (Chapter 13 Bankruptcy). This is a *bankruptcy* process to get relief from debts by making court-supervised payments over a period of time. The alternative is usually *liquidation* under chapter 7. See chapter 18.

Replevin. The legal process in which a *creditor* seeks to recover *personal property* on which it claims a *lien*. Replevin is often threatened, but rarely occurs. See Chapter 16.

Repossession (often called "self-help repossession"). Seizure by the creditor of *collateral* after the debtor's *default*, usually without court supervision or permission. Repossession is most common in connection with car loans. See Chapters 15 and 16.

Retaliatory Eviction. An *eviction* where a landlord seeks to punish a tenant for exercising his or her legal rights (such as complaining to the building inspector or forming a tenant's organization). While retaliatory evictions are generally illegal, they may be hard to prove. See Chapter 13.

Reverse Mortgage. A *refinancing* option usually available only to older homeowners who have built up substantial equity in their property. In a reverse mortgage, money is drawn based on the value of the property without an immediate repayment obligation, because the lender expects repayment by sale of the property at some point in the future. See Chapter 4.

Satisfaction. This is a legal document which states that a debt has been fully paid or that partial payment has been accepted as payment in full. A satisfaction is a type of *discharge*.

Secured Credit Cards. A credit card for which the card issuer requires that the card holder place a certain amount of money in a bank account with the card issuer. If the debtor does not repay the credit card, the card issuer can seize the money in the bank account. See Chapter 6.

Secured Creditor. Any *creditor* which has *collateral* for a debt.

Secured Debt. A debt for which the *creditor* has *collateral* in the form of a *mortgage, lien,* or *security interest* in certain items of property. The creditor can seize the property (collateral) if the *debtor defaults* in repayment of the debt.

Security Interest. See "*Lien,*" above.

Servicer. See "*Mortgage Servicer,*" above.

Short Sale. A type of *pre-sale* in which the *creditor* agrees to let you sell property (usually real estate) for less than the full amount owed and to accept the proceeds of the sale as full *satisfaction* of the debt. See Chapter 10.

Subpoena. A document which normally is issued by a court in connection with a lawsuit, and which directs your attendance in a court or law office at a particular time. A subpoena may require production of documents related to the case.

Summons (also called "original notice" or "notice of suit"). This is a document which is provided at the beginning of the lawsuit to tell the *defendant* what is being requested and what must be done to respond to the *complaint.* The term summons is also sometimes used interchangeably with *subpoena* for other legal papers which direct a person to be at a particular place at a particular time.

Tax Refund Anticipation Loan. A loan to the *debtor* to be repaid out of the debtor's tax refund. The refund is often then sent directly to the lender. These loans can be very expensive. See Chapter 3.

Truth in Lending Act. A federal (national) law which requires that most lenders, when they make a loan, provide standard form disclosures of the cost and payment terms of the loan. Always review and retain these disclosures whenever they are provided to you. See Chapters 4 and 12.

Unsecured Creditor. A *creditor* which has no *collateral* for the debt owed. See Chapter 1.

Unsecured Debt. A debt which does not involve *collateral.*

Variable Rate Mortgage. This is a *mortgage* loan on which the interest rate can change over time. The changes can affect the amount of your monthly payments. See Chapter 4.

Wage Assignment. An agreement to have wages paid to a person other than yourself. For example, some people assign a portion of their wages to be paid directly to cover a credit union bill. When experiencing financial problems, you should reevaluate any voluntary wage assignments you have made. See Chapter 1.

Wage Garnishment. *Garnishment* of the *debtor*'s wages from the debtor's employer. See chapter 7.

Warranty. Goods or services you purchase contain explicit and/or implicit promises (called warranties) that the goods or services sold will meet certain standards. Sellers may try to disavow these warranties, but failure to live up to warranties often can be a defense to repayment of the debt created by the sale contract. See Chapter 8.

Workout. This term covers a variety of negotiated agreements you might arrange with *creditors* to address a debt you are having trouble paying. Most commonly, the term is used with respect to agreements with a *mortgage* lender to restructure a loan to avoid *foreclosure*. See Chapter 10.

Index

TO ORDER

To order *Surviving Debt,* contact your local bookstore, or order directly from National Consumer Law Center by sending $15 (shipping and handling included) for each copy. Please call (617) 523-8089 for bulk discount orders of five or more. MasterCard and Visa are accepted. Please include card number, expiration date, and signature. Send your check or card information to:

National Consumer Law Center
18 Tremont Street, Suite 400
Boston, MA 02108
(617) 523-8089
Fax (617)-523-7398

For more information on NCLC's other legal publications, write or fax at the above address.